Park and Recreation Maintenance Management

Robert E. Sternloff & Roger Warren

North Carolina State University
Raleigh

HOLBROOK PRESS, INC.

BOSTON

Library of Congress Cataloging in Publication Data

Sternloff, Robert E.   1923–
    Park & recreation maintenance management.

    Includes bibliographies and index.
    1. Parks—Maintenance—Management.   2. Recreation
areas—Maintenance—Management.   3. Parks—United States.
4. Recreation areas—United States.   I. Warren, Roger,
1932–   joint author.   II. Title.
SB482.A4S87   350'.863'0973   76-26556
ISBN 0-205-05601-6

To our Parents
and our Wives

Contents

Figures

Tables

Photo Credits

Raleigh Parks and Recreation Department, Raleigh, N. C.; pp. 8 (top), 285.

Oglebay Park, Wheeling, W. Va.; pp. 8 (bottom), 244.

Durham Recreation Department, Durham, N. C.; p. 21.

National Park Concessions, Inc., photo by W. Ray Scott; p. 23 (top).

Jerry Hagler, p. 226.

Marlin Warren, p. 258.

Metropolitan Board of Parks and Recreation, Nashville, Tenn.; p. 284.

Steve Emery, p. 301.

National Park Service, Blue Ridge Parkway, photo by C. E. Westveer; p. 315

Preface

Park and recreation maintenance management is a multi-disciplined field that has developed during an era when park and recreation facilities have increased tremendously, both in number and variety. The knowledge needed to solve park and recreation maintenance problems is not unique; rather, knowledge from a wide variety of disciplines is needed if competent park and recreation administrators and maintenance superintendents are going to manage the areas and facilities under their jurisdiction intelligently and effectively. Maintenance management presupposes knowledge of many fields including landscape architecture; horticulture; turf management; civil, electrical, mechanical, and chemical engineering; forestry; ecology; plant pathology; and hydrology; as well as business and personnel management. The maintenance manager does not have to be an expert in all of these fields; but, he must have some knowledge of each. He must know when to seek the advice of an expert, and he must be able to discuss pertinent problems intelligently with such specialists.

This book was written with the hope of filling a void in professional park and recreation literature. We have attempted to bring together information from a variety of disciplines that are directly related to maintenance/management problems. At present, there is no comprehensive literature in the field of park and recreation maintenance management attempting such a synthesis.

We have chosen to approach the subject of park and recreation maintenance from a standpoint of management. We have not attempted to describe how to do a job or use a material, but instead, we have dealt with such questions in general terms evaluating the techniques and materials and other alternatives. For example, this book does not deal with the various methods of constructing check dams to control gully erosion, ways of maintaining a variety of specific floor coverings that might be used in a community center, or lists of plant materials that can be used for landscaping. Such detailed information is available from other sources when and if the maintenance manager has a need for it. The subject of maintenance management is approached much more

broadly, attempting to look at the total maintenance program that
must be developed in a variety of park and recreation settings if
the program is to be successfully planned and operated.

This book does not deal with maintenance of specific park
and recreation facilities; rather it deals with principles that are
broadly applicable to a variety of types of areas and facilities. To
approach the subject of maintenance management from the
standpoint of how to maintain each of the tremendous variety of
specific facilities the park and recreation professional must maintain
would be extremely repetitive, requiring many volumes. The park
and recreation professional should have little difficulty applying
the principles of building maintenance discussed in this book to a
community center, a resort lodge, a swimming pool bathhouse, or a
family campground restroom. The principles discussed in the
chapter on general outdoor maintenance can easily be applied to
park and recreation facilities ranging from a neighborhood park to
a picnic area in a national forest.

One approach that has been used throughout the book is the
use of evaluative criteria for making judgments that are necessary
for the maintenance manager to operate an effective maintenance
program. We believe that the park and recreation administrator
who purchases maintenance equipment on the basis of a set of
criteria established to help him make a realistic value judgment
will make a better choice than the individual who bases his
purchase solely on the arguments of a persuasive salesman. We do
not suggest or believe that the criteria and factors to be considered
for a variety of purposes in this book are the last word. They should
be refined in the future if the field of maintenance management is
to advance. We do believe that the technique of using evaluative
criteria is a valuable one and that the maintenance manager who
uses this concept when making the value judgments that confront
him in the day-to-day operation of his department will do a better
job. We encourage the maintenance manager to constantly ask the
question, Why? He should always have a substantive basis for
performing a particular maintenance function in a certain way or
selecting a particular material, supply, or piece of equipment to do
a job.

We hope this book will be a valuable resource for a variety of
people involved in the park and recreation field. It is intended for
park and recreation students in both two- and four-year colleges

and universities. This book is designed to give the student the basic understanding necessary to function either in a supervisory or management position in a maintenance department or as a general park and recreation supervisor or administrator who must deal intelligently with the maintenance function as he seeks to coordinate the efforts of the entire park and recreation agency. We also hope the book will be of value to the professional in the fields of college and university physical plant maintenance, private institutions and parks, school districts, and military bases. The professional working directly in the field of maintenance or the administrator with the responsibility to see that the maintenance function is adequately carried out in his agency can use the book as a standard to measure the quality of his agency's maintenance operation. The book attempts to take a comprehensive look at the problems of maintaining park and recreation areas and facilities, and it should be valuable for individuals who have varying responsibilities for the maintenance function.

R.E.S.
R.W.

Chapter 1

Maintenance Principles

Introduction

In the United States, we tend to think that the organized park and recreation movement is quite young. Viewing it historically, the development of park and recreation facilities is actually quite old. Descriptions of the early Babylonian, Assyrian, Persian, and Indian gardens antedate the birth of Christ by many centuries. Historical records indicate that many of these early parks and gardens must have been quite elaborate, with floral displays and fountains. Many provided sanctuaries for wild animals and were established as private hunting grounds for the nobility.

During the Greco-Roman era, gardens, parks, and recreation facility development became considerably more elaborate. In and around Rome, villas were developed with elaborate gardens, courts for ball games, and baths. Most of these were privately owned and used; however, some were opened for public use at a later date.

Subsequently, large parks and gardens such as Tuileries, Luxembourg, and Versailles in Paris; Kensington, Victoria, and Hyde Park in London; Friedrickshain in Berlin; and Central Park in New York were developed. With few exceptions, early parks and gardens were developed for aesthetic reasons. Roads, trails, and benches provided access to these areas so people could stroll leisurely, ride, or sit quietly, enjoying the beauty. The development of facilities in parks for intensive recreation use is, for the most part, a recent phenomenon.

Historical records reveal little insight into the maintenance practices carried out in these early parks and gardens. There are

3

occasional references to "groundsmen" and "gardeners", and it must be assumed that maintenance was performed by people who we would term horticultural and urban forestry specialists. At any rate, the tools and equipment used by park maintenance personnel must have been primitive. It is safe to assume that much hand labor was employed in maintaining the grass, trees, shrubs, and flowers grown in these parks and gardens. When we compare the maintenance tasks needed to maintain early gardens and parks used for recreation with maintenance requirements for modern park and recreation facilities, the differences are astounding.

Today's park and recreation maintenance manager must be concerned with maintaining indoor recreation facilities—gymnasiums, bowling alleys, community centers, museums, art galleries, auditoriums, theatres, dance pavillions, arenas, and so on. Outdoor recreation facilities, such as tennis courts, athletic fields, picnic areas, family campgrounds, ice skating rinks, multiple-use game courts, swimming pools, public beaches, archery ranges, shooting ranges, stadia, toboggan slides, ski slopes, golf courses, zoos, amphitheatres, and marinas, must also be maintained. When one considers the tremendous variety of facilities to be maintained, with the inherent peculiar maintenance problems associated with each of the facilities, the maintenance manager's job becomes seemingly impossible. Indeed, park and recreation maintenance-management is a complex job, and as new types of facilities and new equipment are developed, the job becomes more complex.

This book proposes to examine the principles of park and recreation maintenance-management. The problem of maintenance of a particular type of facility, a family campground for example, will be dealt with only in very general terms. When the principles related to establishing maintenance objectives and standards, planning and organization, supervision of personnel, general outdoor maintenance, grounds maintenance, maintenance of vehicles and equipment, building maintenance, and public relations are understood, application of these principles to specific park and recreation facilities can be made by the recreation professional.

The Role of Park and Recreation Service

Any park and recreation maintenance department which does not have a sound, basic understanding of the purpose, aims, and objectives of the total park and recreation agency cannot operate at peak efficiency. Maintenance is a service function and must be geared to help meet agency goals. The maintenance department that functions in a vacuum, as a separate, and independent entity, unresponsive to agency needs, is not performing its assigned function within the agency. Traditionally, many maintenance units have assumed this independent role, creating havoc as the maintenance and program functions tug in opposite directions. For this reason, it is important to consider, simply and briefly, the role of park and recreation services today.

To understand the role of park and recreation service, it is important to first examine some of the many factors influencing leisure in American society. Such an examination gives some indication of the trends expected in the park and recreation movement in the near and distant future.

The single, most important factor affecting recreation service in the United States is the increase in population. The total population has increased from 76 million in 1900, to 132 million in 1940, to 213 million in 1975. Current projections are for a population of about 300 million by the year 2000. If population controls are effectively implemented, it is estimated that the population of the United States will level off at about 320 million.[1]

The United States is becoming an increasingly more urbanized nation. According to 1970 U.S. Census figures, 73.5 percent of our population lives in urban areas, as compared with 40 percent in 1900. Population densities have risen from an average of 30 people per square mile in 1920, to 57.5 in 1970. A majority of the states east of the Mississippi have population densities of more than 100 people per square mile.[2]

Our large cities are a serious problem and they must be dealt with during the coming decade. Most cities, large and small, have not met (or are just beginning to meet) the open space challenge. Park and recreation facilities remain far behind the demands and needs of the people. The pressures of urban living present problems that are just now being recognized and studied by sociologists and psychologists.

Affluence is another factor that directly affects the recreation movement. Americans own 96 million cars, and 82 percent of all families own at least one automobile. Ninety-six percent of all American families own TV sets. Spending for leisure pursuits has been estimated to be between 100–150 billion dollars per year in the early 1970s. Sales of camping vehicles ($1.8 billion per year), vacation homes ($2.0 billion per year), and recreation-sports equipment ($18 billion per year) reflect our willingness to spend a large portion of our discretionary income for leisure services and equipment.[3]

Inflation and the energy crisis can have an effect on leisure use patterns. However, present indications are that Americans place a high priority on recreation spending. Despite great affluence in America, millions still live at poverty or near poverty levels, causing a difficult dilemma for agencies seeking to provide recreation service for *all* people.

Social change is another factor with major implications for park and recreation agencies. Increased crime and delinquency, women's liberation movements, changing sexual mores, changing family patterns, and the loss of primary group contacts are all factors that must be considered by any agency seeking to provide recreation service.

The changing nature of work, both in qualitative and quantitative terms, is a vital issue. With the advent of industrialization, automation, and cybernation, millions of men and women have been forced into dull, monotonous jobs which provide little challenge and even less satisfaction. More holidays, longer vacation periods, early retirement, and the four-day work week are changes that greatly modify people's use of leisure.

Changes in education have the potential to produce profound changes in leisure use patterns. The very real need to educate for leisure-centered living is just now being realized and translated into programs at all educational levels. The 12-month school has become a reality in some sections of the country, and it will most certainly move to others. If this phenomenon becomes a widespread reality, the implications for change in leisure patterns are enormous and self-evident.

The late 1960s and early 1970s have seen a revolution in environmental reform and awareness. This movement will surely continue and gather momentum. As the public generally begins to develop a land ethic, park and recreation agencies as primary land holding agents of the people will be expected to exhibit responsible stewardship for lands under their jurisdiction. The movement will demand more and better outdoor recreation opportunities for ever-increasing numbers of people. Hopefully, the movement will also educate people as to the more intelligent and responsible use of our natural resources.

The changes discussed thus far all indicate the tremendous increase of leisure available to masses of people and the need to use this leisure wisely. We have many indications that increased leisure for masses is not a myth. The increased spending for leisure is one strong indicator. The increased use of a great variety of recreation facilities is in itself proof that increased leisure is indeed a reality. Leisure itself is neither good nor bad. The individual who fails to use his or her leisure intelligently will discover the curse of leisure. Unwisely used, leisure is dehumanizing and leads to further human misery. Conversely, the individual who learns to use leisure in a wholesome manner can add a new dimension to life. Wise use of leisure can provide an exciting, dynamic quality to life that can transform the human mind and spirit.

The challenge to the recreation profession is to provide an opportunity for an individual to experience the positive rather than the negative side of leisure. Although the recreation professional cannot ensure a positive leisure experience (the individual's freedom of choice predicates this assumption), he or she has the responsibility of leading the public to these experiences by providing facilities and programs where such experiences may occur. The recreation specialist has a further responsibility of making the facility and program opportunities as attractive and appealing as possible.

The reader may think this is a strange introduction to a book dealing with maintenance management, but, in reality, it is the very essence of the subject. Recreation is defined as an experience that takes place during leisure (discretionary time) and is self-gratifying to the individual who participates. A great many of an individual's recreation experiences occur at a facility especially provided for that purpose—a golf course, a gymnasium, a community center, a hiking trail, a ski slope—an endless variety of areas and facilities appropriate for a given experience or activity. Unless the facility is constructed, maintained, and operated in the best possible manner, the individual's chances of experiencing self-gratification are minimal. The desire to provide the highest quality experience for each individual who participates in park and recreation programs should be the basic, underlying goal of every park and recreation agency. Good maintenance is a vital ingredient if the agency is to reach this goal. Without it, all other efforts will surely fail.

High quality maintenance will enhance visitor enjoyment of park and recreation facilities.

Maintenance and Operation Defined

For purposes of this book, park and recreation maintenance is defined as keeping park and recreation areas and facilities in their original state or as nearly so as possible. In this definition maintenance includes routine, recurring work, repair work (both major and minor), and minor construction work. Areas and facilities where maintenance is performed include properties owned or under the jurisdiction of a park and recreation agency.

Park and recreation operation deals with park and recreation programs and with the organization and/or regulation which allows optimum public use of areas and facilities. The park and recreation agency basically deals with two types of program opportunities for people. The first are directed programs where the park and recreation agency plans and organizes the program and probably provides direct leadership. Examples of directed recreation programs include day camps, playground programs, little league baseball, and arts and crafts instruction. The second type of program opportunities are self-directed—an area or facility is provided by the park and recreation agency and use is unplanned and unorganized. Custodial leadership may be provided, but the participant need not have any direct contact with an agency employee. Examples of self-directed recreation programs include picnicking, hiking, free play in a gymnasium or game room, and golf.

Park and recreation agencies need to provide opportunities for both directed and self-directed recreation. However, if the agency is to provide for the mass recreation needs of the community, state, or nation, efforts must be aimed more and more toward self-direction. For example, swimming instruction classes are offered so the individual who participates can enjoy swimming at a pool or beach on his own.

More is involved in operating a self-directed recreation facility than just constructing the facility and opening it to public use. The agency must follow a minimum of these basic steps: (1) establish operating policies—for example, determine who may use the facility, hours of operation, and under what conditions; (2) provide supervision to ensure that the established policies are carried out; and (3) maintain the facility according to well established maintenance standards.

Fortunately, the era of "keep off the grass" signs in our public parks is over. Parks should be aesthetically pleasing, but they are also provided for people to use. The maxim, parks are for people, accurately reflects the thinking of today's park and recreation professional. Maintenance and operating policies must be geared to provide optimum use, and the recreation professional should be concerned both with the quantity and quality of the recreation experience. Quantity of use is assured by providing an adequate number of areas and facilities for public use. Quality is provided through good management—by operating and maintaining areas and facilities according to the highest possible standards.

The recreation professional has a dual responsibility: (1) to provide an opportunity for the finest possible recreation experience for people, and (2) to protect the resource, natural or man-made. Both of these obligations are vitally important, and to some they seem diametrically opposed. This, however, is not the case; they go hand in hand. Unless both goals are achieved, the recreation professional has not done a good job.

Principles of Maintenance—Management

In establishing an effective maintenance operation it must be realized that each agency has problems and needs unique to that agency. The maintenance operation of no two agencies will be exactly alike because of differences in geography, facilities to be maintained, recreation programs provided, and public being served. Despite these differences, there are certain principles or fundamental truths that are basic to any effective maintenance operation. The following thirteen principles are suggested to provide general guidelines for establishing a maintenance program. These principles can also be used as standards to measure the effectiveness of an existing maintenance program. These principles also provide a basis upon which the entire maintenance operation of a department should be developed. A breach of any one principle can cause a serious disruption in providing high quality recreation service by the park and recreation agency.

Maintenance Objectives and Standards
The first step in establishing a maintenance program should be to establish general objectives. General objectives are statements of the purposes and goals of a park and recreation maintenance department. Although maintenance standards may vary from one department to another, the general objectives of park and recrea-

tion maintenance will vary little. The general objectives of park and recreation maintenance may be stated as:

1. Park and recreation areas and facilities should have a clean, orderly appearance at all times.
2. Areas and facilities that are aesthetically pleasing should be developed and maintained.
3. Areas and facilities should be maintained to create a healthful environment.
4. Areas and facilities should be maintained to create a safe environment.
5. Maintenance should promote good public relations by providing areas and facilities where people have an opportunity for an enjoyable leisure experience.

Maintenance standards are the stepping stones used to accomplish the general maintenance objectives. Obviously, these standards can be established only after the general objectives for the department have been formulated.

Factors that affect how maintenance standards are achieved include; intensity of use, weather, topography, quality and quantity of supervision, types of programs being carried out, and vandalism.

Although objectives are general in nature, maintenance standards must be established for specific areas and facilities contingent upon the criteria previously listed. Maintenance standards describe the conditions that will exist when maintenance tasks have been successfully completed. Maintenance standards provide a means to compare conditions as they are found by inspection or observation and the accepted standards for the particular area or facility. Maintenance standards should be established for all areas and facilities including grounds, signs, fences, buildings and other structures, roads, parking lots, trails, utilities, and specific facilities such as picnic areas, campgrounds, ballfields, etc. The quality of the maintenance program is established as standards are determined. A maintenance standard is established for guidance in developing and carrying out a maintenance plan for the park and recreation department. Examples of maintenance standards are given in the Appendix to Chapter 4.

Economy of time. All maintenance tasks should be done as quickly as possible. Every effort should be made to accomplish

Maintenance and Economy

Recreation areas that are pleasing to use require high quality maintenance.

requested maintenance work as soon as possible after a legitimate request has been made. Month old requests for repairs and service are irksome to the staff member making such requests, and they lead to conflicts between maintenance and program personnel. It is also important that maintenance work not interfere with the program function. For example, grass cutting or building maintenance at a facility where a day camp program is being carried out should be performed when the camp program is not in session. That is, the maintenance on such a facility should be performed early in the morning before the campers arrive or late in the afternoon when they have departed for the day.

Economy of personnel. The optimum number of workers should be assigned to perform various maintenance functions. Each maintenance task, whether it be mowing a golf green, winterizing a swimming pool filter system, or maintaining a baseball diamond, can best be performed by one, two, three, or a dozen men determined by experience in doing the job. A conscious effort should be made to determine the optimum number of workers required to perform the task. Economy of personnel also implies using workers trained to do a particular job. Assigning workers to a job they cannot efficiently perform because of lack of skill or training is wasteful.

Economy of equipment. It is important to have the proper equipment necessary to do the job. In attempting to do the maintenance job in the most economical manner possible, the use of mechanized equipment plays a vital role. Historically, many maintenance tasks have been performed with hand tools and back-breaking labor. Considering its high cost, hand labor should be reduced to a minimum. Switching from hand labor to power equipment is not the total solution to the problem. Modern maintenance operation implies having the right power equipment to do the job.

Economy of materials. Along with adequate equipment to do a job, proper materials are also necessary. Workmen must be provided with appropriate cleaning materials and chemicals to accomplish their tasks. Economy of materials is particularly applicable to all types of repair work. Communication, about the job to be done, between the person requesting the work be done and the maintenance department supervisor assigning the task to a work crew is essential. If proper assessment of the job is made initially, the work crew can take all tools and materials needed to accomplish the task rather than having to return to the shop or storeroom for additional supplies once they see what has to be done.

Maintenance costs keep rising each year as the cost of personnel, equipment, and materials increases. One way the maintenance department can combat these rising costs is to do the job more economically and more efficiently.

Maintenance Plan   Every maintenance department should have a detailed, comprehensive maintenance plan in the form of a maintenance manual. The values of a maintenance plan are: (1) to provide a systematic approach to accomplish the work of the department, (2) to provide a sound method of justifying budget requests, and (3) to serve as a communication device for persons higher or lower in the organization.

The maintenance plan should never be the work of one individual (although one individual can best coordinate the actual writing of the plan). It should be a cooperative, coordinated effort encompassing the entire maintenance staff. The plan must be dynamic, that is, subject to constant revision as conditions change and/or better ways of accomplishing certain tasks are found. Above all, the maintenance plan should allow no substitute for quality. If compromises must be made because of a lack of personnel or equipment, these should be made after the plan has been completed and not incorporated into the plan. A detailed discussion of how the maintenance plan is formulated is presented in Chapter 2.

Operating Expenses   Park and recreation agencies must provide adequate fiscal resources to support the maintenance program. Although there is great variation among park and recreation agencies, maintenance costs are a major expenditure for all. In a National Recreation and Park Association survey based on 1970 expenditures, it was disclosed that municipal park and recreation agencies surveyed spent $954 million in operating expenses. Fifty-five percent ($366 million) was spent on facilities and maintenance. Thirty-three percent was spent on program and 12 percent on administration.[4] These figures clearly indicate the scope and importance of maintenance management to the park and recreation administrator. If ways can be found to do the maintenance job more efficiently and more economically, more fiscal resources can be made available for new programs and facilities. Unfortunately, too often the maintenance section of the park and recreation budget has become the "whipping boy" for uninformed boards, city councils, and administrators, so inadequate fiscal resources are provided to accomplish the needed maintenance. One of the prime responsibilities of the head of any maintenance program must be to sell budget needs to superiors. This can best be accomplished by well-documented evidence of previous years' expenditures and projected needs for the coming year(s).

One of the most important and most often neglected aspects of the maintenance budget is equipment replacement. A separate, adequate fund, which can be drawn upon as needed, should be established for this purpose. The merit of this system is that equipment can be replaced at the optimum time rather than being replaced because money has been budgeted for that fiscal year, or waiting two years beyond optimum replacement because funds for replacement were not available. In order for an agency to have the equipment needed to get the job done, some workable system of equipment replacement is essential. A more complete discussion of this topic is found in Chapter 7.

One essential policy for all recreation agencies should be: "If you can't maintain it, don't build it." Too often funds for capital improvements are secured and facilities constructed with no regard for the funds needed to operate and maintain them. Operating facilities with inadequate program, supervisory staff, and funds for maintaining the facilities may seem to be beneficial when considering only short-term needs, but ultimately it is costly and poor management practice.

Maintenance should be a primary consideration in the design and construction of park and recreation facilities.

Design and Construction

There is no truer maxim for the park and recreation professional than: "Build it right from the start." In these days of high construction costs, it is easy to rationalize cutting corners to make a construction project economically feasible. Compromising the principle of good design and construction from the beginning is, in the end, more costly than doing it right from the beginning.

One of the most important factors in good construction is the use of appropriate building materials. Materials used in park and recreation facility construction should be (1) durable, (2) easy to maintain, (3) easy to repair, and (4) easy to replace. Good planning and choice of materials can ease the task of replacement when necessary. These factors are critical from the standpoint of maintenance and should be carefully considered along with other considerations such as aesthetics, safety, cost, and function.

The concept of using rustic materials in parks, materials which blend with rather than protrude from the environment, is not incompatible with high quality, easy to maintain materials. Careful design and selection can accomplish both objectives.

The importance of maintenance input into the planning process should not be overlooked. The time to prevent mistakes that will be costly in terms of maintenance time and effort is during the planning process. When maintenance department employees have an opportunity to review plans for new buildings and facilities, potential problems can be averted by adopting alternatives that are acceptable to the designer, program staff, and maintenance staff. One way to assure maintenance input is to have a maintenance engineer on the planning staff. In addition, there should be consultation with the operational maintenance staff when planning new facilities, particularly those with which the maintenance staff has had some experience. Designing facilities that are functional as well as aesthetically pleasing should be the goal of every park and recreation agency.

There is no such thing as a maintenance-free facility; but, there are facilities which are easier to maintain than others. Attention to minor details of the plan can ease the maintenance burden. For example, adequate numbers and placement of electrical outlets and water faucets can avoid the need for long extension cords and hoses when maintaining the facility.

The use of temporary structures should be discouraged and avoided whenever possible. Temporary structures have a way of becoming permanent, and they usually represent high overhead maintenance headaches.

Personnel   Park and recreation agencies must provide adequate personnel to carry out the maintenance function. Because of low wages, park and recreation agencies have traditionally hired the dregs of the labor force for maintenance work. When park and recreation maintenance was largely a matter of manual, back-breaking labor, there

may have been some rationalization in this approach. Today, however, the conditions have changed. Personnel used in maintenance
work should be skilled technicians rather than laborers. This
change has come about primarily because of the use of sophisticated mechanical equipment.

When maintenance labor is approached positively with the
idea of providing work that is important, meaningful, and essential
to the success of the park and recreation agency, a successful maintenance operation is likely to result. When maintenance labor is
viewed as demeaning work which must be accomplished despite its
unpleasantness, failure will be the probable result.

The positive approach to maintenance labor is predicated
upon, (1) hiring quality personnel [the implication here for adequate wages is obvious], (2) a good orientation program to sell the
individual on the importance of his or her job and the overall
importance of what the agency is seeking to accomplish, (3) adequate initial and in-service training to do the job for which the
employee has been hired, (4) good supervision that is responsive to
the needs of the employee, and (5) good communications at the
upper administrative levels to articulate the importance of the job
the maintenance staff is doing.

Preventive Maintenance

All maintenance departments should stress preventive maintenance.
Preventive maintenance is defined as continuous attention and care
to prevent damaging wear and costly repairs. The purpose of a
program of preventive maintenance is to get optimum life from
facilities and equipment used by the park and recreation agency. It
is easy for a maintenance department to get into the rut of constantly trying to catch up with needed maintenance and repair,
while little attention is given to preventive maintenance. Careful
planning and scheduling is necessary to prevent such a situation.

Preventive maintenance is an important consideration in all
aspects of maintenance work. In relation to all types of equipment,
it means daily, weekly, and seasonal attention to lubrication,
changing oil, and replacing worn parts before they fail rather than
when the machine breaks down. In relation to buildings, the con-
cerns must be for care of mechanical systems, care of floor coverings, and a painting schedule. Preventive maintenance applies to
maintaining all recreation surfaces in top notch condition, for
example, tennis court resurfacing or maintaining adequate ground

cover in a picnic area to prevent costly and unsightly erosion. It may involve a spray program to prevent insect and disease damage to turf or shrubbery. In short, preventive maintenance is good maintenance management to prevent damage before it occurs. The advantage of such a system is being able to schedule maintenance at your convenience rather than responding to breakdowns in the system which are likely to occur at times when the maintenance department is understaffed or extremely busy.

Public Safety   The maintenance department has a primary responsibility for public safety. The responsibility for public safety must, of course, be shared by the entire park and recreation agency. The responsibility for the conduct of participants in the recreation program is largely a matter for the program staff; however, the responsibility for providing areas and facilities that are safe for recreation use must be borne largely by the maintenance department.

Public safety is a relative matter. It is not possible or desirable to restrict the public's activities to the point of making an area or facility totally safe. A totally safe recreation facility or activity probably would be boring and uninteresting. When children and adults play, accidents will happen, and some will get hurt. Realizing the inherent dangers associated with many types of recreation activities, the recreation professional must also recognize the responsibility to make park and recreation areas and facilities as safe as possible so that the equipment and facilities provided are not the cause of accidents.

A program designed to reduce accidents must begin with accurate accident records and periodic review of these records. Accident records may be required by law or by the agency's insurance company. But, lacking either of these imperatives, the agency should keep good records for internal use.

When accidents occur and agency facilities or equipment are at fault, action should be taken immediately to prevent additional accidents. This may involve immediate repair of the equipment or facilities at fault or it may mean closing an area or facility until repairs can be made. An analysis of accident reports on a periodic basis will reveal accident-causing areas, and action can be taken to prevent future occurrences.

The maintenance staff should provide a valuable service to the agency by helping to keep areas and facilities as safe as possible. Safety consciousness on the part of the maintenance staff comes only through a concerted staff training effort. The maintenance staff should be trained to routinely observe and report any conditions that they feel may endanger public safety. Many times an individual performing a maintenance function may be the only staff person to come into contact with expansive parkland facilities over a long period of time. In addition to routine observation by staff, periodic inspection tours should be conducted by a safety engineer trained to look for hazardous conditions.

Public safety should be carefully considered during the planning and construction stages. Errors made with regard to public safety at this juncture are difficult, and often impossible, to correct.

The maintenance program must have a high regard for employee safety. The National Safety Council reports an alarming accident rate among park and recreation maintenance employees. In 1973, the number of disabling injuries in park and recreation areas was three times higher than that of all industry in the United States.[5] Other hazardous occupations have successfully controlled accidents through active accident prevention and safety programs. There is a need for park and recreation agencies, and maintenance departments in particular, to embark on the same kind of effort.

Employee Safety

One of the most constructive steps in the direction of improving employee safety was taken with the passage of the Williams-Steiger Occupational Safety and Health Act of 1970 (OSHA). As a result of this act employee safety standards have been established for many maintenance activities directly related to park and recreation work. In addition, states have established employee safety standards for governmental employees. The OSHA program has had, and will continue to have, far-reaching positive effects in improving employee safety.

That the administrative and supervisory personnel in the agency recognize the problem and desire to rectify it is a basic requisite for a workable safety program. Putting up a few posters is not enough; the department must be dedicated to preventing accidents.

Expert help, essential for establishing a worthwhile safety program, is available in most communities through a variety of sources, including insurance company safety engineers, industrial safety engineers, local safety councils, National Safety Council, or Occupational Safety and Health Administration. It is irresponsible not to take advantage of these sources of assistance. The details of how to establish an employee safety program are discussed in Chapter 3.

Schedules   Maintenance work schedules must be based on sound policies and priorities. When assigning work priorities, value judgments are constantly being made by administrative and supervisory maintenance personnel. Someone must make the decision to fix the leak in a golf course irrigation system or at the drinking fountain in a picnic area. While the elimination of these value judgments might at times seem desirable, pragmatically it is impossible to eliminate this responsibility. Part of a maintenance supervisor's job is to make these decisions. Although these value judgments cannot be eliminated, guidelines can be established which will be helpful in the decision-making process. Every maintenance department should carefully consider the criteria upon which maintenance scheduling decisions are to be made. Once criteria have been established, work scheduling gains consistence and judgments made can be evaluated in terms of their conformity to the criteria. For a more complete discussion of this topic see Chapter 2.

Environmental Protection   The maintenance program must be designed to protect the natural environment. The park and recreation professional must accept the responsibility as a steward of the natural environment for the public. Park and recreation agencies, particularly in urban communities, often have under their jurisdiction a high percentage of the open space and natural areas remaining in a community. Stewardship of this land must be viewed as a serious responsibility. If we expect the general public to take seriously the environmental crisis confronting our nation and the world, the recreation profession must accept a leadership position through good environmental management of the lands under their jurisdiction. This is particularly applicable to the way in which we develop and maintain land under our jurisdiction for recreation use. The impact upon the environment should be carefully considered in all aspects of park and recreation management.

Good stewardship means preserving natural beauty.

There are a number of rather specific ways in which the park and recreation professional should act to protect the natural environment. First, he or she must act in the role of a preserver. The administrator must preserve all park resources from encroachments and seek to add open space to insure parkland for the future. He or she must act as a preserver of natural beauty in those areas now controlled and acquire land to preserve areas, which are perceived as beautiful, for present and future generations. The aesthetic values of park and recreation areas cannot be minimized. Developing areas where people observe beauty in a spirit of contemplation may indeed be one of the highest forms of recreation. Beauty is inherent in an environment where people can breathe clean air, swim, or fish in clean lakes and streams. Beauty is also inherent where urban populations can enjoy greenery and open space. Implicit is the necessity of making this beauty available and accessible to people as long as access does not destroy the natural resource. Management techniques must be developed to realize these goals more fully.

The administrator must ensure protection of the natural resource when areas for intensive recreation use are developed. Picnic areas, campgrounds, athletic fields, and any other facilities, which because of poor design and/or construction destroy the environment, are a disgrace to the profession. Facilities must be planned and constructed to blend with rather than intrude upon the natural landscape.

When the park and recreation agency develops and adheres to high standards of maintenance, it has taken a big step toward preservation of the natural environment. The preserver's role extends to providing litter-free picnic areas, well-maintained restrooms, and vandal resistant facilities. A well maintained facility is essential if individuals are to achieve the full potential from their recreation experience.

The second major contribution of the park and recreation professional should come in helping to create environmental beauty where none now exists. Unfortunately, in many urban areas very little, if any, natural beauty remains. Formal gardens, attractively kept parkland, well landscaped and maintained roads and streets, and aesthetically designed play areas provide an opportunity to increase the quality of life for everyone. Opportunities must also be provided for the urban dweller to experience the natural environment.

Well-designed parkways provide vistas of scenic beauty for many Americans.

This picnic shelter was designed to blend with its environment.

The park and recreation professional cannot be expected to solve all environmental problems; however, there are many opportunities where he or she can and should make a positive contribution.

Organization

The maintenance department must be well organized. The purpose of departmental organization is to see that the maintenance function is carried out in the most efficient manner possible. Basically good organization involves making the most efficient and effective use of personnel, equipment, materials, and time. There are no easy solutions to the problem of effective organization. Organizational structure must be tailored to the needs and particular requirements of each park and recreation agency. The problems of organizational structure are discussed in detail in Chapter 2.

Public Relations

Every maintenance employee has a responsibility for the public image of the park and recreation agency. Many park and recreation professionals do not think that maintenance employees have a responsibility for public relations for the department; however, the maintenance staff can be a fine public relations emissary. As the public uses park and recreation facilities, quite commonly the only contact they will have with an agency staff person will be with a maintenance employee; for example, a building janitor, a crew picking up trash in a picnic area or campground, or an individual raking a sand trap on a golf course. When this happens it is important that the image presented to the public be a positive one.

Good public relations begins simply by the maintenance department doing a good job in their routine work. Clean, well kept facilities create a good public image. Public relations extends to a clean, neat personal appearance of all employees, including maintenance workers. Uniforms, although perhaps not essential, are very helpful in conveying the desired impression.

Good public relations on the part of maintenance employees does not just happen because it appears in the individual's job description. It comes through a concerted effort on the part of the department. It begins with an orientation program designed to instill pride in working with the agency and is continued with in-service training opportunities designed to help the employee meet people while on the job. Employees should be able to answer questions, even foolish ones, commonly asked by the public; and, when they do not know the answers they should make the proper referral.

Conscious efforts by program staff can and should be made to involve some of the maintenance staff with the public when appropriate. For example, a gardener with a knowledge of plant propagation and care would make a welcome addition to a garden club tour. Not only would the gardener be a valuable asset to the group by virtue of the information he or she could provide, but also the experience would provide an invaluable boost to the individual's morale by letting him or her know first-hand that the job is worthwhile.

Review Questions

1. Define maintenance and operation.
2. Differentiate between maintenance objectives and standards.
3. What is a maintenance principle?
4. Why is good maintenance important to the park and recreation agency?
5. Discuss some of the ways good or bad design and construction can effect maintenance.
6. What is preventive maintenance?
7. Discuss the park and recreation professional's responsibility with regard to the natural environment.
8. Describe the maintenance employee's role with regard to public relations.

Notes to Chapter 1

1. *World Almanac and Book of Facts, 1976,* see "Population."

2. U. S. Bureau of the Census, *Statistical Abstracts of the United States: 1973,* see "Population."

3. U. S. Bureau of the Census, *Statistical Abstracts of the United States: 1973,* see "Recreation."

4. "Local Parks and Recreation," *Parks and Recreation* August 1971, pp. 17–31.

5. *Public Employee Safety Guide—Parks and Recreation* (Chicago: National Safety Council, 1974), pp. 4–5.

Bibliography

"Local Parks and Recreation." *Parks and Recreation* VI; no. 8 (1971): 17–31.

National Safety Council. *Public Employee Safety Guide—Parks and Recreation.* Chicago: National Safety Council, 1974.

U. S. Bureau of the Census. *Statistical Abstracts of the United States: 1973* (94th edition). See "Population" and "Recreation."

Wilson, Ralph C. "Maintenance and Operating Objectives and Policy." A monograph prepared for the Park and Recreation Maintenance-Management School, North Carolina State University, Raleigh, 1973.

World Almanac and Book of Facts. 1976. See "Population."

Chapter 2

Planning and Organizing

the Maintenance Program

Introduction

If we were asked to accurately locate and describe the place of maintenance in the total park and recreation administrative hierarchy, a rather negative picture would probably result.

Too many ribbon-cutting ceremonies are conducted for new public recreation facilities with inadequate maintenance backup funds being provided by the proud, facility-dedicating public officials. More than a few frustrated park and recreation managers are discouraging the construction and development of new facilities without a guarantee of adequate maintenance funds.

Not only is there competition among the various public service agencies for the tax dollar, but there is also competition based upon public demand among the divisions within the park and recreation service organization. It is common to hear of public demands for new and expanded activity programs, new recreation areas and facilities, but rarely do we hear of public demands for improved maintenance practices beyond the routine complaints for more frequent garbage pickup in campgrounds and picnic areas.

Deterioration of recreation areas and facilities due to lack of adequate maintenance usually occurs in a gradual, methodical manner which is not noticed by the occasional visitor until the condition becomes quite intolerable or dangerous to the user. At this point, corrective maintenance has assumed the proportion of an expensive, major repair project.

The dilemma, then, of the park and recreation manager is continually insisting that maintenance be regarded and supported on an equal footing with all other areas of his or her total responsibilities.

The maintenance of recreation areas and facilities, with their accelerating public use, cannot tolerate a situation where emergencies and crisis maintenance are a regular and continuing condition. Rather, the maintenance program must function on a planned, systematic basis according to maintenance standards—a plan that anticipates deterioration and breakdown rather than reacting to it. To be effective, such a planned maintenance program may not remain static. Instead, it must be evaluated continually and modified according to changing visitor use. It must be evaluated not only in terms of changes in the frequency of maintenance service, but also as a change applies to improved program management: the selection of better materials; improved utilization of personnel, in the selection of tools, equipment, and in the planning of new facilities.

As we would refuse to cross a busy thoroughfare blindfolded, so should we refuse to attempt to conduct a park and recreation maintenance program without a systematic plan which is designed to anticipate problems and promptly respond to emergencies.

The development of an acceptable, realistic maintenance plan should include the following:

1. Inventory of park and recreation facilities and equipment to be maintained.
2. Identification and listing of specific routine maintenance jobs to be done for each facility.
3. The development of positive written maintenance instructions for each area, facility, and piece of equipment.
4. Providing a means of accomplishing nonroutine, nonrecurring jobs. (Repair work and preparation for special events are examples of such work. Thus a work order system must be established.)
5. Assigning responsibility for each maintenance job. This includes designating an individual, crew, or contractor to do the job, and supervisory staff to see that job is done properly.
6. Establishing a system for job planning, workload control, and a well defined time schedule for daily, weekly, and seasonal maintenance work. In the name of economy, the most efficient way of doing a maintenance job must be determined. This

involves time, personnel, tools, equipment, and material estimates. It is also essential that records be kept which will assist
in comparing workload with available manpower.

Facility and Equipment Inventory

If the areas and facilities of a park and recreation system are to be
routinely maintained according to general objectives and established standards, a definite plan for accomplishing this must be
developed and followed. Such a plan must include a detailed inventory of existing areas, facilities, and equipment indicating the
extent and time of their use by days, weekends, holidays and seasons. The detailed inventory must also denote: the types, sizes,
special features and condition of each area and facility which in
turn allows decisions to be made as to the scheduling of work, the
need for specialist personnel, proper maintenance equipment, and
supplies.

Maintenance Task Identification

A maintenance job list must then be prepared for each area and
facility based upon the detailed inventory. The job list for each
facility must include such items as cleaning, lubricating, adjusting,
painting, planting, fertilizing, watering, mowing, and all other jobs
necessary to maintain that particular area or facility. Standards of
maintenance must then be applied to each area and facility with
the full realization that the amount or intensity of use that a given
area is to sustain will determine the amount of maintenance necessary to minimize deterioration and support a particular desired
level of maintenance that is acceptable.

Written Maintenance Job Instructions

Following the identification of routine maintenance jobs for the
various areas and facilities, a written maintenance plan should be
developed and included as a part of the maintenance manual. A
most important consideration in developing a written maintenance
plan for the system is to recognize from the outset that the plan

must be easily and clearly interpreted by field personnel who will be supervising and those who will actually do the prescribed maintenance work. A type of written maintenance plan that has been widely used and found to be a most effective means of interpreting routine maintenance responsibilities to field personnel is developed in the form of an illustrated and written instruction manual. Each sheet in the manual refers to a specific developed area which is presented graphically on one side of the sheet, with corresponding written maintenance work instructions appearing on the opposite page. The written maintenance instructions that correspond to the graphic area illustration should describe procedures and frequency of maintenance for: lawns, meadows, trees, shrubs, structures, trails, roads, bridges, parking areas, drainage systems, picnic grounds, beaches, pools, marinas, the general policing of grounds, building housekeeping techniques, and maintenance methods for other special structures. Written maintenance instructions should include information for soil and turf improvement; fertilizer and seed quantities; plus general instructions regarding the care of lawns, trees, shrubs, and methods of pruning. In addition, instructions should be provided for the care and maintenance of indoor and outdoor recreation surfaces, floors, walls, windows, roofs, including appropriate cleaning supplies and equipment to be used. Effective maintenance plans are the result of continuous evaluation and regular modification based upon these evaluation findings.

Maintenance plans should also be established for specialized equipment and mechanical systems including heating, ventilating, and air conditioning. Maintenance plans are also necessary for utilities such as water systems, sewer systems, irrigation systems, liquid fuel systems, electrical distribution systems, radio systems, fire alarm systems, street and area lighting systems. For small recreation/park organizations, much of the maintenance for the systems mentioned will, because of its highly specialized nature, be delegated to others outside the park and recreation organization on a contractual basis. Nevertheless, these systems are an integral part of the total maintenance operation and should be included, at least in general terms, in the overall written maintenance plan so as to avoid the possibility of overlooking them. Normally, the major portions of maintenance data included in the written maintenance plan regarding specialized equipment are quite general in nature, with the admonition that those responsible for such maintenance consult detailed information and instructions provided by the manufacturer or other sources of specific maintenance information.

Thus, it becomes apparent that the written maintenance plan should be simplified and condensed for easy reference and use while, at the same time, it must cover detailed, specific maintenance requirements by reference to other sources of specialized information.

Accomplishing Nonroutine, Nonrecurring Maintenance

Nonroutine, nonrecurring maintenance work includes such repairs as replacement of broken insect screen wire, replacement of a broken door closer, hinge or lock, or possibly the replacement of a cracked section of pipe in the golf course irrigation system. Nonroutine, nonrecurring maintenance work also includes such nonroutine tasks as the set up and removal of audience chairs for a band concert, the temporary mounting of artificial lighting fixtures for a special event, or the installation of a temporary public address system for a Fourth of July celebration.

The Work Order System

An effective maintenance program depends to a great extent on a work order system that receives all work requests, initiates action, and follows the project through to completion.

Work Control Desk A large park/recreation organization should establish a work control center to effectively coordinate their work order system. In a small system, work control might be assigned to a clerk or to the maintenance manager. It is important to designate a person and place for receipt of work requests and complaints. All operating personnel should be aware of a telephone number for reporting maintenance problems.

Work Order Request Form Work requests come from a variety of sources: building occupants, operational personnel, security officers, tradesmen, and preventive maintenance mechanics. In a well managed maintenance division most requests should come from department employees trained to identify and report problems during normal work rounds. Such training helps the division keep on top of maintenance problems and frees program personnel and their administrators to concentrate on recreational functions.

Work request forms should, however, be distributed to all major operational and program offices to facilitate maintenance requesting. A properly designed work request form such as the one shown in Figure 2-1 aids individual requesting service to provide complete and accurate information, data essential for analyzing the request and issuing a work order. Work request forms also serve as a reminder that the maintenance division carries responsibility for handling maintenance problems.

Some recreation systems attempt to combine the work order request form with the work order form in hope of reducing paperwork. This procedure results in improperly described work, and fails in the effort to deal with complex work requiring several trade crews and compound work orders.

When work requests come to the work control desk via telephone, the work order clerk can, with well-designed forms, elicit from the caller all necessary information to translate the layman's work description into the language of the foremen and tradesmen on the work order form.

Work requests must be analyzed to determine which will not need to become work orders. Where the request is a familiar one and the job elements are simple tasks with clearly established time standards, the clerk can quickly estimate time, assign work order numbers, and work them into the maintenance schedule. If questions remain about the nature and extent of a job, a foreman must investigate and make an analysis to decide whether the request should be rejected or accepted. This final decision should be noted in the bottom section of the work request form entitled "Disposition."

Work Order Form   When a request is accepted as a legitimate job order, the clerk or foreman assigns a number and completes a work order form. The number is, of course, one of the key elements in the whole system. It follows the job through scheduling, completion, and final recording.

The work order analyzes and estimates the work in detail, services as a means for coordinating various work elements within

WORK ORDER
REQUEST

METROPOLITAN RECREATION DISTRICT
Maintenance Division
Repair & Control Section

Dept. No. _____

Control No. _____

Date _____

The following work is requested for _____
(Area where work is to be done)

Requested by: _____
(Name)

Division: _____ Phone: _____

Description of Desired Work: _____

_____

_____

_____

Draw sketches if needed on reverse side of this form.

Special Instructions: _____

_____

Received by: _____ Date _____ Time _____

DISPOSITION: Action 1, 2, or 3

For Maint. Div. Repair & Control Section Only	
ADDITIONAL WORK ORDER	
Trade	W.O.

1. Work Order # _____ written.

2. Assigned to Prevent. Maint. _____
(Date)

3. Returned to Requesting
Division with explanation _____
(Date)

Original — Maintenance Division
Duplicate — Requesting Office

Figure 2-1 A Work Request Form

the maintenance division, collects cost estimates for labor and material, and, finally, authorizes the work to be done. Figure 2-2 illustrates an acceptable work order form.

There should be at least three copies of the work order; the first and second copy go with the workman assigned the task. On this form he notes the hours spent and records or attaches receipts for the materials, parts, and supplies used. Upon completion, the tradesman returns the first copy to the work control clerk.

The third copy remains with the clerk until the workman's copy returns. From the work copy, the clerk compiles all the costs involved—labor, materials and overhead. The clerk then compares the actual totals with the estimates on his form, notes any significant discrepancy, clips the two forms together, and files them in the file for the facility involved. In some situations, periodic reports of work accomplished are required by supervisors.

The historical cost file is one advantage of the work order system. From these records, planners can project maintenance costs for the next year and maintenance unit costs for similar facilities in the planning stage.

Assigning Responsibility for Maintenance Work

Criteria for Determining Maintenance Organization

Organization of the maintenance operation will depend upon many individual local factors such as visitor or participant use of each of the units or facilities within the system broken down by time (weekend, weekday and holiday), the size of the area to be maintained, and the types of facilities and equipment within the units to be maintained.

Only after considering each of these factors can a maintenance work responsibility be assigned and a workable maintenance organization be developed. The maintenance organization must be designed specifically to meet the requirements for each individual park and recreation system because no two are alike. Considerable variation is to be found in terms of areas, buildings, other structures, program offerings, and number of visitors.

METROPOLITAN RECREATION DISTRICT
Maintenance Division
Repair & Control Section

WORK ORDER

W.O. No. _____
Date _____

TO: _____ Department
(person to whom work is assigned)

You are to do the following described work at _____
(location of job)

Description of Work to be Done

_____
_____
_____
_____
_____
_____

Priority: Emergency ☐   Routine ☐   Standing ☐

Job is scheduled for starting on _____ , _____ , _____ M
(day)   (date)   (time)

Work is to be completed by _____ , _____ , _____ M
(day)   (date)   (time)

COST RECORD

LABOR						MATERIALS		
NAME	Date	Hrs.	Rate	Cost	Quan.	ITEM		Cost
TOTALS		xxx				TOTALS		

Use other side for remarks, sketches, etc. ON RECEIPT OF THIS FORM FROM WORK CONTROL CENTER, ENTER ON LOG BOOK AND ASSIGN WORK PARTY, AUTHORIZE MATERIAL DRAW, OR ORDER MATERIALS, ALL IN TIME TO PERMIT WORK TO BE STARTED AND COMPLETED IN TIME.

First two copies to Department performing work. Third copy is retained in Control Center. Original copy is returned to Control Center after completion of work.

DATE COMPLETED: _____ VERIFICATION _____
(signature − requesting dept.)

Figure 2-2 A Work Order Form

Unit Maintenance In utilizing this method, each unit within the park and recreation system would perform its own maintenance. A neighborhood park would, for example, have its own maintenance crew responsible for all of the maintenance tasks necessary to completely maintain the facilities found in that unit, including building maintenance, lawn and shrubbery care, maintenance of ball fields, etc. The advantages to be found in organizing on the basis of unit maintenance are:

1. Maintenance personnel become very familiar with the facility.
2. It is relatively easy to determine responsibility when maintenance service is not properly performed.
3. The director of the unit controls both the maintenance and program staff, resulting in potentially better coordinated effort.
4. Maintenance personnel tend to develop a loyalty to their particular unit and often take more pride in their work.

The disadvantages of the unit method of maintenance organization include the following:

1. Unit maintenance personnel must learn to perform a variety of jobs and use a variety of equipment in a satisfactory manner.
2. The supervisor must also be familiar with the various jobs and equipment necessary to perform these jobs.
3. Unit maintenance does not make the most efficient use of expensive equipment.

The application of the unit method of maintenance work functions best where there is enough work to justify the assignment of maintenance personnel to a unit on a full-time, year-round or on a full-time seasonal basis. The unit method of maintenance is appropriate where the equipment needed to do the job is relatively simple to operate and not too expensive.

Specialized Maintenance Crews In utilizing the specialized-crew method of maintenance, each crew is trained to do a job, such as grass cutting, shrubbery care, floor care, window cleaning, lighting fixture cleaning or replacement, and other specialized work. The specialized crew is scheduled to move from one unit to another to perform their specialized work. The advantages of the specialized crew are as follows:

1. The crew becomes extremely proficient in their specialized type of work.
2. The specialized-crew method provides the best use of expensive equipment which should be used on a regular basis to make the cost of the equipment justifiable.

The major disadvantages of the specialized crew method of maintenance are:

1. The repetition of the job tends to make it monotonous for the crew.
2. There is loss of travel time from area to area.

The most appropriate application of the specialized-crew method of maintenance results when the required skill involved is difficult to learn, where specialized equipment is involved, or where a number of small areas and facilities are involved making the use of full-time unit maintenance personnel impractical.

Maintenance by Contract   The third basic method of maintenance is to arrange for maintenance service by an outside contractor. It is conceivable that the entire maintenance function could be handled by contract through the use of contractors to perform the various maintenance jobs.

The advantages of maintenance by contract are:

1. There is no capital investment in equipment.
2. You hire well-trained specialists for each job.
3. There are no in-house personnel problems.

The disadvantages of maintenance by contract are:

1. Loss of control as to when and how well jobs will be completed.
2. The cost may be higher because the contracting firm must make a profit.

The best application of contractual maintenance is in very remote areas where travel time is excessive, with jobs that require a high degree of specialization of operator and equipment, and when the job is not done routinely, and where the agency has a relatively low demand for the job to be done. Types of maintenance by contract that would be appropriate for many small park and recrea-tion agencies include such tasks as tree trimming and the cleaning and replacement of outdoor lighting fixtures.

Safeguards for the recreation organization to follow when contracting maintenance work should include the following:

1. Choose reputable firms. Recognize that the low bid does not necessarily represent the most competent contractor. If the low bid from an unknown contractor cannot be justified by econ-omy, technique, or method, it would be well to investigate the contractor's previous work and client satisfaction.

2. Develop complete and detailed specifications. Bids may be received on an overall sum basis and/or on time and materials. Accurate detailed specifications will protect the recreation organization in either case. Specifications should be reviewed annually and revised when appropriate. Appendix 2-A is a sample specification for contract exterior painting.

3. Inspection of contractor's work. Usually in-house tradesmen inspect the work of contractors to determine specification compliance before the final contract payment is made. How-ever, it is recommended that the maintenance manager check the work of a new, relatively unknown contractor.

Few park and recreation agencies would exclusively use any one of the three basic methods of organizing the maintenance work. Rather, a combination of each of the three methods of assigning maintenance work is most common.

Figure 2-3 presents a hypothetical organization chart for a park/recreation system of several thousand acres of park land, a number of buildings, and sufficient manpower and equipment to accomplish the maintenance work.

Planning and Scheduling Jobs

Successful annual, seasonal, weekly, and daily maintenance plan-ning and scheduling is dependent upon knowledge of work require-ments coupled with adequate personnel to do the work according to established standards.

Work Requirements   The sources of information necessary to determine maintenance work requirements are—

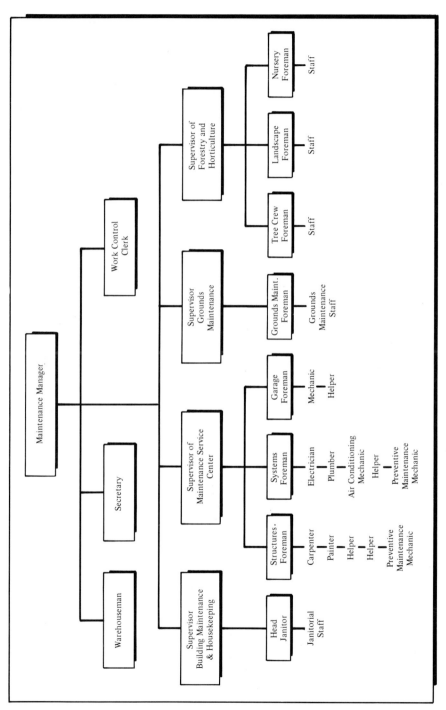

Figure 2-3 A Sample Maintenance Division Organizational Chart

1. a carefully detailed routine maintenance plan for all areas and facilities within the system indicating the frequency of maintenance as dictated by the extent and time of use.

2. the need for repairs, either determined by a systematic inspection procedure dictated by breakdowns which may or may not require immediate emergency repair, depending on their urgency and effect upon over-all operation. (The repairs ought to be communicated by means of a standardized repair-order request and work order system.)

3. a standardized job method which outlines the best way of doing the job, the correct selection of tools, equipment, and materials for the job, and an estimate of work time, thus minimizing the necessity for repeated maintenance job analysis.

Personnel Requirements

For the sake of economy, the optimum number of workers should be hired, trained, and assigned to perform the various maintenance functions. Job standardization will indicate the minimum number and types of competent personnel necessary to accomplish a particular maintenance job. In the absence of job standardization or previous experience doing a particular job, estimates will have to be made as to number and types of competent personnel required with future manpower adjustments made, based upon that experience.

Estimating Time

A major advantage of the work order system is more accurate time estimates for future work orders. An organized approach to estimating requires analyzing each problem according to its basic job elements and assigning a time value for each element. Theoretically, the sum of these values gives the total time estimate. A highly sophisticated approach involves further analyzing the elements into work units and applying internally established work standards for each unit.

Maintenance task time estimating at a small recreation system, however, often begins with informal "guesstimates" by the work order clerk. At this stage, the clerk must rely heavily on the experience and general advice of the maintenance foremen and workmen. To set up the first, rough time standards for work units, the clerk might utilize maintenance manuals developed by the United States Army, Navy, and Air Force.

As historical records accumulate via the work order system, internal work standards can be developed to replace personal intuitions and national standards. With a task time standards list, a capable clerk can quickly and accurately estimate the time requirements for the majority of jobs to be scheduled. The importance of developing internal work standards cannot be overemphasized. National standards are always crude averages that account for wide variations in productivity and working conditions. Although helpful for a start and for comparison with in-house work rates, they should be replaced as soon as a substantial historical file is accumulated.

Each recreation organization should develop maintenance task time standards for those jobs performed most frequently according to their records. For example, a survey of tradesmen task performance for a recreation organization might result in maintenance task personnel and time requirements as indicated in Table 2-1.

Fundamentally, job scheduling requires a comparison of estimated hours of workload with actual man-hours available. The objective is one of maintaining minimum personnel requirements covering skilled craftsmen, shop personnel, roving crews, unit crews, and janitorial personnel in order to accomplish the work according to standards and within acceptable time limits.

A procedure must be established to determine the need to increase or decrease the number of competent personnel assigned to particular maintenance jobs where experience indicates that the work assigned is consistently not accomplished or where manpower exceeds work requirements.

One method for making such a determination is the keeping of detailed, factual records of the work backlog for each maintenance manpower group according to supervisor and area of responsibility.

To keep track of work backlog, the work control clerk should keep a work order log. Such a record is simple to maintain and can serve to reveal unusual delays, identify unproductive crews, and show dollar value of work done during any time period.

The most informal log is one the foreman keeps on his clipboard, listing work order number, date assigned, estimated comple-

Work Order Log

Table 2-1

Time and Labor Estimating Guide for Work Orders

TRADE	Number of Men	Travel Allow (Hrs)	Labor Time (Hrs)	Total (Hrs)
CARPENTRY				
Repair door surface closer	1	½	½	1
Repair concealed door closer	2	½	1	3
Repair door damage at shop	1	1	3	4
Repair and replace screens	1	½	½	1
Replace broken glass	1	½	½	1
Repair and replace ceiling tile	1	½	½	1
Repair small dry-wall damage	1	½	1	1½
Repair and replace sash balance	2	½	1½	4
Change lock on door	1	½	1	1½
Etc.				
PAINT				
Repaint 20' x 15' room, 1 coat	2	1	16	34
Repaint small bathroom, 1 coat	1	½	8	8½
Repaint exterior window	1	½	2	2½
Clean & paint graffiti, sign 30" x 18"	1	Shop	2	2
Etc.				
PLUMBING & STEAMFITTING				
Clear stopped water closet	2	½	1	3
Clear stopped basin	1	½	1	1½
Replace leaking radiator valve	2	½	2	5
Clear external sewer stoppage	2	½	4	9
Install replacement valve, faucet or trap	2	½	3	7
Etc.				
ELECTRICAL				
Replace Fluorescent lamp ballast	1	½	1	2
Reset fire or security alarm				
Replace fractional HP motor	2	1	3	8
Replace blown fuse or reset circuit breaker	1	½	1	1½
Repair exterior light damage	2	½	1	3
Control circuit problems	2	1	2	5
Etc.				

tion date, and projected costs. Several simple yet efficient alternatives are—

1. a general hook file holding all uncompleted work orders.
2. separate hook files for the work orders assigned each trades group or maintenance force whether it be for trails, grounds, buildings, utilities, automotive, equipment, shops, etc.
3. a general list of all work orders assigned, noting date assigned, group responsible and estimated time and cost of completion.
4. separate lists for each trades or maintenance group.

Alternatives *3* and *4* require more paperwork. The clerk must copy pertinent information from each work order form when first assigned and when returned after completion. However, these alternatives do provide a more accurate account of the current backlog and a record of productivity and expense.

The purpose of workload control is to match the work force with the workload. Perfect control would result in no work orders waiting for workmen and no workmen waiting for maintenance problems to develop. Unfortunately this optimum situation rarely occurs because unforeseen maintenance problems and emergencies inevitably arise in random sequence. A backlog of work orders, therefore, should not be regarded negatively but, rather, as a necessary hedge against days when emergencies do not occur and extra work is needed to complete work schedules. A maintenance organization with men consistently sitting around waiting for work orders is, more than likely, overstaffed.

Workload Control

A moderate backlog is ideal but it is difficult to define in the abstract. However, when the rate of new work orders consistently exceeds the rate of job completions, an immoderate backlog exists.

When the backlog accumulates past the maximum time limit allowed for completing all work orders, including low priority tasks, then workload control is breaking down. The next symptom is skipping low priority jobs in the rush to remedy emergency and high priority demands. The final stage of an "out of control" overload takes two forms: either (1) work orders are written only for the most critical problems, or (2) all work orders are given the highest possible priority, unduly delaying many legitimate, high priority tasks.

Recommended remedies include—

1. Hiring temporary help to alleviate the backlog.
2. Hiring a private contractor to handle selected backlogged work orders.
3. Increasing the labor force permanently.

The perfect solution depends upon the conditions causing the backlog. Hiring temporary help or contractors is especially appropriate when a sudden increase in workload can be diagnosed as a passing phenomenon due to a seasonal overload or an unusual number of problems. Increasing the permanent work force is a solution only when it is clear that the backlog would otherwise continue unchecked.

Maintenance Work Schedules

The key to successful maintenance operations is a carefully planned and faithfully followed work schedule. When developing any maintenance work schedule, the following factors should be considered: priority of work items, anticipated visitor use, capabilities of maintenance personnel, man-hours available, season of the year, and availability of materials.

Priority of Work Items Simply stated, those maintenance jobs most critical to ongoing operations should be scheduled first and the least critical last.

Priorities should not be established solely on the basis of critical need and not favoritism. The most effective safeguard against bias and favoritism is a clearly defined priority policy that can be readily understood and easily interpreted by everyone—clerk, complainant, foreman, and tradesman. At least two or, at the most, three priority classes are needed:

1. **Emergency** Problems that create safety hazards or seriously disrupt recreation operations take preference over all other work. Ruptured water mains, backed-up sewers, or electrical outages require immediate repair.
2. **Routine** Problems less serious than emergencies are placed into the work schedule on a first-come, first-served basis. With leaking roofs or malfunctioning air conditioners, it may be practical to delay repair so the regular routine or preventive work can continue as scheduled.

3. **Standing** A miscellaneous category is necessary for (a) shop time work not easily assignable to specific work orders, and (b) seasonally recurring jobs that can be performed to level peaks and valleys in the workload schedule.

Anticipated Visitor Use Priority scheduling should be given to routine maintenance of visitor use areas and facilities during those seasonal periods of greatest use. Major maintenance and new construction generally should be avoided during periods of heavy visitation.

Capabilities of Maintenance Personnel The capabilities of maintenance personnel are determined by skill, experience, and supervision. The productivity and quality levels of performance are influenced greatly by training and motivation. Only when the maintenance manager thoroughly knows the capabilities of his personnel can he organize them into teams or crews and make realistic scheduled assignments.

Man-hours Available The number and types of maintenance personnel together with the methods of organizing and conducting maintenance work varies considerably from system to system because of variations in size, the character of development, and the intensity of visitor use. Therefore, man-hour requirements must be carefully calculated as the basis for staffing so as to allow for efficient personnel scheduling.

Season of the Year Park and recreation maintenance is seasonal. The season of greatest visitor load depends upon the kinds of recreation areas and facilities provided and the section of the country in which these are located. In some areas of the country cold temperatures, extreme heat, and high levels of precipitation during certain seasons of the year limit the kinds of maintenance and construction work that can be performed during those seasons. Under such circumstances, the work schedule must be carefully planned so that work hours are utilized to the fullest, doing those jobs, both indoor and outdoor, that are not adversely influenced by weather.

Availability of Materials A variety of maintenance materials must be provided in order to accomplish the work. Too often, materials are not immediately available and thus create a delay in scheduling work. An adequate materials inventory record system is required to provide information as to the depletion of materials on hand and fixing responsibility for advanced ordering of required stock materials for delivery prior to total depletion.

Daily Maintenance Scheduling

The scheduling of maintenance work involves the sequencing of maintenance jobs according to priority on a *daily planning* and *schedule form.* Each day's schedule should provide for a full day's work for all craft personnel or maintenance groups with another job waiting upon completion of the previous one.

Depending upon the size of the operation, the daily maintenance work schedule may be developed by the park and/or recreation manager, a maintenance manager, or a group of craft foremen. The schedule may include both routine and repair maintenance jobs. Routine maintenance job scheduling should be dictated by a detailed annual maintenance plan, while repair orders indicate repair work that must also be scheduled.

The daily planning and schedule form is usually prepared during the afternoon of the previous day so as to facilitate an immediate start the following work day and also to allow time for review and approval by a superior in the larger organization.

The last job listed on the daily schedule may be underscored or otherwise noted so as to allow for easy identification of additional jobs that are added to the schedule after appraisal. The purpose of such identification is to allow for investigation to determine the reasons for the breakdown in the daily scheduling process.

Effective job planning and scheduling proceeds from the simple to the complex in direct proportion to the growth of the operation. In the small operation, the manager will "wear" many hats and may be required to develop the maintenance plan, inspect areas and facilities for preventive maintenance, handle maintenance emergencies, establish maintenance priorities, schedule maintenance jobs, supervise maintenance work and even participate in actual maintenance work, and rely to a considerable extent upon contractual maintenance service. At the other extreme, in the large highly organized operation, the manager will function through in-house engineers, supervisors, foremen, and crews to accomplish the maintenance function without outside assistance.

Maintenance Cost Analysis and Controls

The maintenance operating budget that is soundly established and properly used will provide valuable information regarding changes in conditions and trends. However, it must be recognized that in the absence of sufficient cost analysis and trend analysis, the operating budget, when used for coordination and comparision, is quite incomplete and may well give misinformation. It is only through sufficient cost analysis and trend analysis, which includes the study of cost variations from the normal, that we can determine the true reasons for variations or deviations from the estimated expenditure for each budget item. Such examination serves the purposes of developing more accurate future budgets and also serves as a basis of action to eliminate or change inefficient or undesirable conditions.

Achievement of Maintenance Cost Controls

Park maintenance costs can be controlled if such activity is carefully programmed or budgeted prior to its beginning, and carefully regulated during the course of its being carried out.

The first step in achieving an adequate maintenance cost control program is the acceptance and application of the following two basic principles:

1. Direct maintenance labor and supervision must be related to definite quantities of measured work.
2. Responsibility for each item of maintenance expense must be assigned to a specific individual.

A program designed to control direct labor and supervisory expense for recreation maintenance requires careful pre-planning so as to assure that the maintenance activity is carried out on a standardized basis. Only then can a "standard cost" be established and thus provide knowledge of what the work should cost. A comparison of the standard cost and the actual cost of a given maintenance operation may then be determined. The variation or difference between the two represents that part of the total expense that can be controlled.

Cost control of maintenance then is really concerned with the amount of money required for the maintenance operation that is in excess of that which would have been spent to get the work done on a standard basis. The underlying concept in this maintenance cost control approach is to first determine what the work should cost, and, knowing this, plan future activities based upon that standard.

Cost Accounting

Considerable effort has been expended to develop methods for determining unit costs of park programs and services. It has been speculated that if adequate cost records are kept, meaningful comparisons between services and facilities can be made on the basis of costs per participant. Unfortunately, cost data relates largely to quantitative aspects of efficiency and not to the qualitative aspects of performance. The most valid application of cost accounting at present is when it is applied to an identical facility, activity, or service. It is only within this realm of rather identical comparisons that cost accounting has validity.

Cost Record System

Separate cost figures for each function carried on by the maintenance division should be recorded, and the cost of each function should be broken down according to an object and a functional classification in the recording of expenditures. If the cost data is to be meaningful and useful, expenditures must be directly related to work accomplished. If this is done, it is necessary to keep separate accounts for each function.

When cost records are kept according to function or separate facilities, the maintenance cost must be recorded for each. It will be necessary to keep an actual record or accurate estimate of the time spent on each maintenance job, the materials and supplies used, so that maintenance costs can be charged against each maintenance function and facility.

When maintenance work is accomplished by contract, or when other governmental departments supply maintenance service, the costs must be charged to each function, if not to each facility.

If figures are to tell a true story of the cost of a particular function or facility, they must include all of the cost items involved. Otherwise, the cost data are incomplete, misleading, and valueless for comparative purposes.

It is true that economies may be affected and unit costs may be decreased through standardization. However, it must be understood that if in affecting economies through standardization the unique values for which the recreation area or facility was initially established are subverted or lost, then the profit or saving means very little. Unfortunately, decisions affecting recreation areas are sometimes made on the basis of a financial measure only with no test of the applicability of the decision as it influences the unique characteristics of the particular park or recreation area. There is no substitute for the careful, considered judgment of the park manager who is dedicated to maximizing the total value of the park to the public.

Unit Costs and Standardization

Review Questions

1. Outline the steps that should be followed in developing a recreation/park maintenance program.

2. Explain the purpose of a work order system.

3. Identify and explain the elements included in an acceptable work order system.

4. Identify three basic personnel organization methods for accomplishing maintenance work.

5. Describe how you would go about estimating maintenance job time.

6. In the overall job of maintenance work scheduling, describe the techniques that might be utilized to keep track of work backlog.

7. Hiring temporary help, hiring a private contractor, or increasing the labor force permanently are possible remedies to alleviate maintenance and repair work backlog. Cite justifications for each of the three remedies.

8. When developing any effective maintenance work schedule, what factors should be considered?

9. What is a standard cost for a given maintenance operation and of what potential use is a standard cost to the maintenance manager?

10. Describe the purpose of cost accounting, and indicate the most valid application of cost accounting at present.

11. What is the greatest potential danger to a particular recreation area or facility when standardization and unit cost comparisons are exclusively relied upon to effect economies?

Bibliography

Dinger, David G. "Maintenance Budgeting and Maintenance Cost Analysis" and "Maintenance Financial Records." Monographs prepared for the Park and Recreation Maintenance Management School, North Carolina State University, Raleigh, 1974.

Kloske, Robert E. "Planning and Organizing the Maintenance Program." A monograph prepared for the Park and Recreation Maintenance Management School, North Carolina State University, Raleigh, 1972.

Owens, Rhodell E. "Planning Your Maintenance Program." Proceedings of the Fifth Annual Southeastern Park and Recreation Planning, Maintenance and Operations Workshop. North Carolina State University, Raleigh, 1960.

Schaefer, Theodore H., Jr. "Maintenance Cost Analysis Budgeting and Maintenance Financial Records." A monograph prepared for the Park and Recreation Maintenance Management School, North Carolina State University, Raleigh, 1975.

Schaefer, Theodore H., Jr. "A Method of Data Collection for Use by Park and Recreation Departments to Analyze Operation and Maintenance Costs." *A Study Report* for the Broome County Department of Parks and Recreation, Binghamton, New York, 1972.

Squires, Cedrick. "Master Planning Your Outdoor Maintenance." Proceedings of the Eighth Annual Southeastern Park and Recreation Training Institute on Planning, Maintenance and Operation. North Carolina State University, Raleigh, 1963.

Wilkinson, C. F., Jr. "Work Program as Related to a Master Personnel Schedule." Proceedings of the Eighth Annual Southeastern Park and Recreation Training Institute on Planning, Maintenance and Operation. North Carolina State University, Raleigh, 1963.

Wilson, Ralph C. "Maintenance and Operating Objectives and Policy." A monograph prepared for the Park and Recreation Maintenance Management School. North Carolina State University. Raleigh, 1972.

Appendix

Sample Specifications
for
Exterior Painting of Various Buildings *

_____ PARK/RECREATION SYSTEM

Maintenance Division   Date _____

Section I—Scope of the Work

The Contractor is to furnish all labor, equipment, materials, etc.,   **1-01**
necessary to accomplish the painting of the exterior trim of various
buildings as listed on the Bid Proposal Form [page 60], and in
strict accordance with these specifications.

Bidders *must* examine the buildings and acquaint themselves with   **1-02**
the exact nature of the work to be done and all the conditions and
obstacles likely to be encountered in their performance and completion of the work.

*Source: *A Basic Manual for Physical Plant Adminsitration* (Washington,
D.C.: The Association, 1974), pp. 123–27. Modified and reproduced with
permission of The Association of Physical Plant Administrators of Universities and Colleges.

1-03   The submission of a bid shall indicate that the Bidder thoroughly understands the specifications and the scope of the work.

1-04   The Park/Recreation System reserves the right to award a contract on any single bid, or combination of bids, whichever is considered to be in the best interest of the Park/Recreation System.

Section II—Material and Workmanship

2-01   Storage facilities for the painting contractor will be provided in the buildings if requested by the Contractor and will be designated by the system representative. Generally, the storage of flammable materials within buildings is not permitted for reasons of fire safety. The rooms to be furnished will be such that they may be locked by the Contractor for the protection of his equipment and materials. The room must be kept clean and orderly. Oily rags, waste, etc., must be removed from the building at the close of each working day. Smoking or the use of matches in paint storage space will not be permitted. Storage of thinners in the paint storage space *WILL NOT BE PERMITTED.*

2-02   All materials must be delivered at the job site in factory sealed containers, clearly marked so as to fully identify the contents. Delivery shall be refused if not so shipped.

2-03   No thinners may be added to any manufactured painting material.

2-04   Each coat of paint shall be tinted a different shade from the final approved color. Each coat of paint shall be inspected and approved before succeeding required coats are applied.

Unless otherwise specified, all surfaces to be painted shall be cleaned free of loose paint, blisters, runs, dirt, grease spots, and all scotch tape is to be removed and spots cleaned with Varsol. All protruding nails and similar items are to be "set" or removed. All holes, cracks or indentations are to be spackled or plaster pointed and sanded smooth. All nail holes and small cracks in the woodwork are to be puttied and sanded smooth.

All materials must be evenly spread and smoothly flowed on with-   **2-05**
out runs or sags; woodwork to be finished with enamel shall be
sanded with fine sandpaper to produce an even, smooth finish.

Section III—Specifications for Painting

In general, all exterior surfaces presently painted shall receive two   **3-01**
coats of paint specified. Those areas previously unpainted are not
to be painted at this time. This applies particularly to unpainted
window guides. These should be given an additional heavy application of linseed oil and painting contractor shall be responsible that
all double-hung windows are operable, i.e., not painted shut.

Extreme care shall be taken to adequately prepare all exterior   **3-02**
wood and metal surfaces on buildings which are to be repainted.
The woodwork and metalwork should be cleaned and sanded
where paint has chipped and blistered. A full-time inspector from
the System will be present on this contract work, and work considered to be unsatisfactory must be repainted by the Contractor at
no additional expense to the Owner.

All loose caulking and putty shall be completely removed and re-   **3-03**
placed with Number M-242 Elastic Glazing Compound as manufactured by the Pecora Paint Company, Inc., Philadelphia,
Pennsylvania, or an approved equal.

All exterior wood surfaces are to receive a good primer or base   **3-04**
undercoat and an oil base finish coat. The paint used shall be
highest quality white exterior house paint as manufactured by
O'Brien, Benjamin Moore, Dutch Boy, or approved equal.

Paint shall be non-chalking of the variety guaranteed by the manu-   **3-05**
facturer not to run down and discolor red brick exterior walls.

A SAMPLE BID PROPOSAL FORM

_____ PARK/RECREATION SYSTEM

_____

(Address)

MAINTENANCE DIVISION _____ Date _____

Gentlemen:

You are invited to submit a proposal for furnishing all labor, equipment, materials, etc., necessary to accomplish the work described in the attached drawings and/or specifications, for the project noted below:

PROJECT NO: _____

PROJECT TITLE: _Exterior Painting of Various Buildings_

LOCATION: _____

ARCHITECT: _____

ENGINEERS: _____

DEPOSIT: _____

<u>BIDS DUE:</u>   Time: _____ Date: _____

Bids will be received and publicly opened at the following address:

Bidders must visit the site prior to the submission of a bid, and are requested to contact the individual(s) noted below to arrange for an appointment and to clear up any questions relative to the drawings and/or specifications. The submission of a bid shall indicate the bidder thoroughly understands the drawings and/or specifications, and the scope of the work.

_____ Phone: _____

Bidders must allow sufficient time for all bids, either mailed or hand carried, to reach this office by the date and time indicated for the bid opening. LATE BIDS, including those postmarked prior to the bid opening date, WILL NOT BE CONSIDERED.

Sincerely,

_____, Manager

Maintenance Division

Enclosures

Exhibit 2-1

A BID PROPOSAL FOR EXTERIOR PAINTING OF VARIOUS BUILDINGS

_____ PARK/RECREATION SYSTEM

_____
(Address)

MAINTENANCE DIVISION _____ Date _____

We propose to furnish all labor, equipment, materials, etc., necessary for EXTERIOR
PAINTING of various buildings of the _____
Park/Recreation System of the _____ of _____
all in accordance with the specifications for the following LUMP SUMS:

BUILDING NUMBER and/or BUILDING NAME	COST	CALENDAR DAYS TO COMPLETE
_____ _____	$_____	_____
_____ _____	$_____	_____
_____ _____	$_____	_____
_____ _____	$_____	_____
_____ _____	$_____	_____
_____ _____	$_____	_____
_____ _____	$_____	_____
_____ _____	$_____	_____
GRAND TOTAL (All Buildings)	$_____	_____

Enclosed with the Proposal is a Bid Bond in the amount of five percent of the total
amount of the above Bid Proposal. It is understood that the Park/Recreation System
reserves the right to award this contract in its entirety, or any portion thereof.

_____
Firm Name

The manufacturers and identifying trade or brand names or numbers of the paints
which we intend to use for the work specified are:

WOODWORK . . . . Base Coat _____
                                                       Finish Coat_____
METAL SURFACES. . . . . ._____

Exhibit 2-2

Page 2 — **BID PROPOSAL FOR EXTERIOR PAINTING OF VARIOUS BUILDINGS**

_____ PARK/RECREATION SYSTEM

Maintenance Division

JOB INSPECTION OF MATERIALS: This requirement is included in order to insure that the Paint Bid shown in this specification is actually used throughout the job. Park system inspectors reserve the right to withdraw one gallon of paint at any time which may be laboratory tested to insure compliance with this requirement of the specification. Contractors found guilty of substitutes of unapproved materials will be required to remove all unapproved material and apply that originally approved and may disqualify themselves in bidding further work for the _____ Park/Recreation System.

Should the Park/Recreation System desire to extend the contract to other work on a "Time and Material" basis, the following proposal shall apply with overhead and profit percentages applied separately to the material and labor costs:

FOR MATERIALS: OVERHEAD AND PROFIT TOTAL..... _____ %

FOR LABOR:	PAINTER FOREMAN	PAINTER
Pay Scale	$ _____ /hr.	$ _____ /hr.
Welfare Benefits	$ _____ /hr.	$ _____ /hr.
Social Security	$ _____ /hr.	$ _____ /hr.
Insurance	$ _____ /hr.	$ _____ /hr.
Overhead & Profit on Labor	$ _____ /hr.	$ _____ /hr.
Other Items (Specify)		
_____	$ _____ /hr.	$ _____ /hr.
_____	$ _____ /hr.	$ _____ /hr.
_____	$ _____ /hr.	$ _____ /hr.

TOTAL LABOR CHARGE PER HOUR $ _____ $ _____

CONTRACTOR'S LICENSE NO.:   Signed: _____

_____   Firm: _____

BID PROPOSAL MUST BE   Address: _____
SUBMITTED IN
TRIPLICATE   Phone: _____

Exhibit 2-2 (Continued)

Chapter 3

Managing

Maintenance Personnel

Introduction

People are the most important consideration in any service operation. This certainly holds true for effective maintenance management. The finest equipment, supplies, and facilities will mean little if competent personnel in sufficient numbers are not available. Not only must personnel be competent and positively motivated to do the jobs that have to be done, but, in addition, they must understand fully and thoroughly the scope of their duties and responsibilities and the general operation of the entire system. Moreover, maintenance personnel must know, without question, to whom they are responsible and who is responsible to them. Capable supervision must be available to provide guidance for those who need direction and to provide training assistance which is designed to make workers more self-sufficient and truly eligible for more responsible, better-paying jobs when these become available.

The Maintenance Personnel Manual

A separate personnel manual or a section of the over-all maintenance manual should be devoted to personnel policies[1] which apply to the maintenance personnel of the organization. Such a document should include an outline of the duties of each staff position, the minimum requirements for appointment to these positions, the rules of employee conduct, and other information that clearly defines what management expects of each employee.

Job Descriptions

Job descriptions should be developed for managers, supervisors, foremen, warehousemen, equipment operators, mechanics, trades-men, manual workers, tree trimmers, heavy equipment operators, storekeepers, and all other maintenance personnel positions in-cluded in the overall organization. Figures 3-1, 3-2, 3-3, and 3-4 are examples of job descriptions written for various kinds of positions in the maintenance field.

Recruiting Maintenance Personnel

Recruiting skilled tradesmen who are reliable is often difficult, especially during times of full employment when recreation systems cannot match salaries offered by the construction industry. The following are suggestions that may be helpful in recruiting capable skilled tradesmen:

1. Promote from within, whenever possible. This tactic insures that the organization and the applicant each know the other's strengths and weaknesses in advance of the promotion, thus minimizing the possibility of negative "surprises."

2. Ask staff personnel for assistance in recruiting candidates. Staff tradesmen are quite likely to be acquainted with, and thus able to recommend, qualified tradesmen in the area. Furthermore, staff members are not likely to recommend men whose perfor-mance would reflect poorly on them.

3. Recruit from the armed services. Armed services tradesmen are usually well trained in one skill area and familiar with several others.

4. Recruit tradesmen from the construction industry. Govern-ment sponsored recreation systems can seldom match private industry salaries paid to tradesmen in areas of rapid growth. However, recreation/park organizations can offer certain com-pensating benefits such as year-round employment, indoor work, and a pleasant environment. Such benefits are often at-tractive to older experienced tradesmen weary of working out-doors during inclement weather and subject to the uncertainty of periods of unemployment.

5. Recruit personnel for grounds maintenance from those with a farming or agricultural background. Farmers usually have learned plant propagation and care techniques. In addition,

METROPOLITAN PARK/RECREATION SYSTEM
JOB DESCRIPTION

POSITION TITLE: RECREATION MAINTENANCE AND REPAIRS FOREMAN

Distinguishing Features of Work

This is skilled and supervisory work in the repair and maintenance of the Recreation and Parks System. Direction and supervision over a group or groups of men performing a variety of tasks is required. Effective planning of work, considerable technical knowledge, and ability to apply independent judgment in carrying out assignments are required.

Illustrative Examples of Work

Supervises and directs subordinates in the performance of their duties.

Maintains time and work records, prepares reports.

Plans, organizes, schedules work crews engaged in various tasks.

Determines need for repair of equipment.

Performs related work as required.

Qualification Requirements

Graduation from an accredited high school or vocational school. Experience in the supervision of recreation and parks facilities, construction, maintenance and repair; or any equivalent combination of training and experience.

Ability to deal efficiently and tactfully with employees and the general public.

Versatility and initiative in dealing constantly with changing assignments.

Ability to supervise and coordinate the activities of a large group of workers engaged in recreation and park repairs and construction activities.

Must have a minimum of one year's experience in a supervisory capacity.

Figure 3-1 A Job Description for a Recreation Maintenance and Repair Foreman

METROPOLITAN PARK/RECREATION SYSTEM
JOB DESCRIPTION

POSITION TITLE: MAINTENANCE MAN I

Distinguishing Features of Work

This is semi-skilled work in the maintenance of park and recreation facilities.

Work involves the performance of semi-skilled manual duties in the maintenance of parks, ball diamonds, indoor facilities, and playground areas. The maintenance man works under the direction of the Maintenance Manager.

Illustrative Examples of Work

General clean-up (pick-up of litter and debris) of playground areas.

Minor repairs to playground apparatus.

Janitorial work in buildings used by the Recreation Department.

General lawn care as may be required.

Minor repairs to buildings such as replacing broken glass.

Assistance in the preparation of equipment and facilities used in the summer recreation program.

Qualification Requirements

Eighteen years of age. High school or vocational school graduate preferred. Experience in maintaining grounds and buildings highly desirable. Ability to follow simple oral and written directions. Skill in operation and care of tools and equipment.

Special Requirement

Must possess a valid state driver's license.

Figure 3–2 A Job Description for a Maintenance Man 1

METROPOLITAN PARK/RECREATION SYSTEM
JOB DESCRIPTION

POSITION TITLE: LIGHT EQUIPMENT OPERATOR

Distinguishing Features of Work

This is semi-skilled and limited skilled work, frequently involving the operation of a truck or related light equipment.

Employees perform a variety of laboring tasks requiring some job acquired skills. Duties are frequently routine, and may be performed with some degree of independence. An employee may be assigned as a truck driver, or operator of similar light equipment, in which case he is responsible for safe and efficient operation of the unit. All work is subject to inspection while in progress and upon completion, although the employee is expected to work with little close supervision on regular phases of the work. Employee may be called upon when necessary to perform laboring type assignments. Employee is under the general supervision of the Section and/or Division Foreman and/or delegated authority.

Illustrative Examples of Work

Operates flat bed, dump, or van-type truck or tractor or fog generator or mobile type power mowers or similar equipment.

Waters and trims lawns, using power mower; trims shrubbery and trees.

Responsible for cleaning and polishing assigned equipment.

Responsible for reporting needed repairs or malfunctioning of equipment.

Ability to perform laboring type work assignments.

Makes necessary oral or written reports as required.

Performs related work as required.

Qualification Requirements

Completion of the eighth school grade. Experience in performing manual and semi-skilled maintenance and construction work; or any equivalent combination of training and experience.

Working knowledge of the tools, methods and materials used in general maintenance work.

Ability to perform semi-skilled tasks without close supervision.

Ability to operate various types of automotive equipment and to learn operation of special types of light equipment.

Skill in the use of common hand tools and equipment to which assigned.

Mechanical aptitude.

Special Requirements

Must have valid chauffeur's license issued by the state.

Minimum age, 21 years.

Figure 3-3 A Job Description for a Light Equipment Operator

METROPOLITAN PARK/RECREATION SYSTEM
JOB DESCRIPTION

POSITION TITLE: SECRETARY-RECEPTIONIST

Distinguishing Features of Work

This is varied office and clerical work including the taking and transcribing of oral dictation.

The main responsibility in this work is for the performance of moderately difficult and varied clerical work; however, the employee must also take and transcribe dictation at a working rate of speed. Employees keep complex clerical records and may perform office management details designated by the Department Director. The nature of this work is such that employees frequently have considerable independence of action in the disposition of routine work matters and in receiving complaints, giving information and other public contact work. The Department Director usually makes only an occasional review of work methods or results and gives general instructions on assignments through conference, although more important or unusual assignments may involve careful instruction and supervisory review.

Illustrative Examples of Work

Takes and transcribes dictation, types letters, memoranda and other materials from rough draft copy, dictation, or other sources; makes and cancels appointments; composes routine correspondence; prepares inter-office forms, requisitions or related papers.

Keeps difficult or complex clerical and accounting records not requiring previous technical training.

Works independently in meeting the public, giving information and answering complaints relating to departmental operations; serves as a representative of the Director as delegated in contacts with vendors, other employees, and the general public in connection with the operation of the department.

Takes and transcribes minutes of official commission meetings, keeps these records properly filed, indexed and up-to-date.

Files office records, determining proper file designation to be used.

Performs related work as required.

Qualification Requirements

Experience in performing progressively responsible clerical and stenographic work; and graduation from a standard high school, including or supplemented by stenographic and general business course work; or any equivalent combination of experience and training which provides the following knowledges, abilities and skills:

Considerable knowledge of business English, spelling and commercial arithmetic.

Working knowledge of modern office equipment, practices and procedures.

Ability to prepare effective correspondence on routine matters and to perform routine office management details without referral to the Director.

Ability to establish and maintain effective working relationships with other employees and the general public.

Skill in the rapid and accurate transcription of oral dictation and in the operation of a typewriter.

Must attain a typing speed of 50 w.p.m.

Figure 3-4 A Job Description for a Secretary/Receptionist

most farmers are acquainted with motorized equipment operation, maintenance, and repair.

6. Secure qualified maintenance personnel through the establishment and operation of your own apprenticeship training programs.

Understanding Personnel

A supervisor gets his work done with and through people, therefore, it is essential that he be concerned with selection, training, placement, motivation, and evaluation of employees. Employee productivity determines supervisory success or failure and therefore guesses and trial-and-error supervisory methods are not good enough. The effective maintenance supervisor succeeds in persuading employees to work toward the goals and objectives of the maintenance division. The effective supervisor recognizes that he must select the best employees from those available and carefully place them in positions where they can function best. The effective supervisor will then train his employees using the best training methods available and motivate his workers to outstanding performance. The effective supervisor must be able to evaluate worker performance and recommend those who will succeed when promoted to the positions of greater responsibility.

In summary, the effective supervisor must get extraordinary performance from ordinary people—a challenging task for the true professional supervisor, not an amateur.

Motivating Employees

Worker performance is regulated by two factors: competence and commitment. Experience, skill, and knowledge applied to the job results in competence. Motivation produces commitment, and committed employees are always in demand because the supervisor can depend upon them to do their best. Workers who are both competent and committed are rare, so we settle for competent workers who can be motivated to outstanding performance.

In attempting to motivate workers, it is well to understand from the outset that there is no such thing as no motivation. Everyone is motivated all of the time, but not always in the direction that the supervisor or management wants. Motivation is not something that a supervisor does to his employees. Rather, motivation is the feeling, attitude, or outlook of the individual about himself and his environment. Every person tries constantly to conduct himself according to his self-perception and how he views and interprets his environment.

Motivation or outlook is most individualistic. If we accept the basic premise that all individuals are different and that each person has his own needs and drives, then we must accept the fact that attempts at group motivation will always come up short of the desired result.

If the supervisor is to be reasonably effective in motivating individual workers to achieve organizational objectives, he must develop an individual approach to motivation, i.e., he must know his workers as individuals. He must understand their drives, needs, and expectations. The supervisor must learn their achievement objectives and their capabilities. In summary, the supervisor must know his people so thoroughly as individuals that he will never have to resort to threats, fear, or rank as devices for motivation or control.

Leadership and Motivation

The Industrial Relations Center of the University of Chicago has identified four classical leadership styles: Bureaucratic, Autocratic, Idiocratic, and Democratic. Each leadership style has its own peculiar motivational effect.

The **Bureaucratic** leader requires each employee to be guided by a book of rules. The effect of Bureaucratic supervision on most workers is that they become apathetic and conform, doing the minimum amount of work required. Employee deviation from the rules is not tolerated, no matter what improvement in performance results. Literally, adherence to the system becomes more important than employee performance.

The **Autocratic** leader is a driving, dictator type who orders his subordinates about in a puppet-like fashion and expects complete compliance. The autocratic leader constantly oversees task performance, no matter how minor, and insists on it being done his way. The domineering, autocratic leader fails to motivate employees because they are allowed insufficient freedom and no discretion as to the manner in which a task is to be done.

Idiocratic managers pit one employee against another by privately telling each that he can do a better job than the other if he tries. This technique consists of attempting to motivate through various interpersonal forms of competition. His "game" is over when his employees realize how they are being used.

The classical Democratic leader is epitomized by a manager who attempts to create team spirit and a group approach. Together with his employees they develop group goals and decide how best they can be achieved.

Which leadership style is the best? Interestingly, there is no single leadership style that answers the demands of every situation. The effective supervisor will probably have to use all approaches, depending upon the employee, the work to be accomplished, and the occasion. No supervisor should develop a single stylized leadership approach if he wants to motivate different people effectively.

While no reputable behavioral scientist would deny the importance of money as a temporary motivator, research evidence indicates that money is not nearly as important a permanent motivating device as one might believe, and that several other motivational approaches promise more permanent results. These more permanent motivational approaches include employee participation, management by objectives, and "stretching."

Basic Supervisory Motivational Techniques

Employee Participation in the Decision-making Process This motivational approach supports the time-honored adage: "Shared decisions equal co-advocates," and helps to guarantee that each employee gets a "piece of the action" and thereby enjoys power and achievement, which McClelland[2] and Ghiselli[3] believe are the two main sources of motivation.

An important consideration here is that the manager must understand that going through the motions or tokenism is not the answer and will not work. The manager must develop a willingness to accept and put employee ideas and suggestions into organization operations, at least, initially, on a limited experimental basis.

Management by Objectives One of the major reasons that workers become bored and lose interest in their jobs results from job standardization where each job detail is engineered down to the finest details and demands rote performance on the part of the worker. Management by Objectives involves the supervisor explaining the objective of the operation and allowing the worker to decide the specific manner, within reasonable limits, in which the job would be done. This approach leaves something to the initiative of the worker and minimizes the deadly boredom of being oversupervised.

Stretching One of the greatest shortcomings of managers and instructors in all types of situations is to underestimate the capabilities and capacities of other people. The concept of *stretching,* as a motivational device, is simply a matter of challenging workers slightly beyond the normal estimate of their capabilities. This is not to be interpreted as frustrating workers with jobs that they cannot accomplish. Neither is stretching a matter of raising quotas. Rather, the objective is to assign more challenging work whenever possible for greater job satisfaction.

The Individualized Approach to Motivation

The individual approach to motivation means utilizing a leadership style and the motivating factors that fit the person, the job, the times, and the supervisor's objectives.

Behavioral science research tells us that it is acceptable, but only temporary, to motivate employees through appropriate leadership styles or by monetary rewards or incentives. For lasting results, managers must ultimately motivate employees according to their basic, human needs and interests, or by the satisfaction and challenge of their work.

Behavioral research indicates that people like to work, particularly when the work is challenging and is capable of motivating them by providing personal growth. Because of this, work-centered motivation is becoming increasingly popular as compared to person-centered motivation through the supervisor. Nevertheless, both person-centered and job-centered approaches to motivation are important.

Supervisory Communication

Cooperation is the key to a successful park/recreation operation but its achievement is never automatic. The supervisor is in a most strategic position to resolve or control conflicts that threaten effective cooperation as he interacts with his workers.

Developing and Maintaining Cooperation

If the supervisor is to be successful in bringing about cooperation, he must be an effective communicator.

Adequate communication is essential, particularly to an individual's sense of security and to his ability to adapt to conditions of stress and uncertainty. People are interested in developments that may affect their lives. Developments connected with a job are particularly threatening to one's economic and psychological security. Moreover, being informed is important and related to the need for recognition. We cannot shut off job-connected information and still expect employees to adapt to conditions of stress or to perform mightily without motivation.

Communication and Acceptance of Change

As effective as organizational communication might be, it is by its nature impersonal and represents a "shotgun" approach in communicating with employees. Bulletin boards and employee newsletters do serve a useful purpose, but they will never take the place of interpersonal communication between the supervisor and worker. Direct person-to-person communication is the critical link that must be preserved. Otherwise, organizational operation will suffer.

Interpersonal Communication

Often supervisors do not recognize that job instruction is a critical form of communication. Through job instruction the supervisor communicates with his workers about standards of work performance. He is literally showing his workers what he regards as acceptable performance in terms of quality, quantity, time, and safety in the work process.

Communication and Job Instruction

Another vital communication link related to job instruction has to do with regularly observing the employee to determine the effectiveness of his training job and the competence of the worker. Such worker appraisal provides the basis upon which the supervisor makes a recommendation for the employee upon completion of the probationary period.

The supervisor further communicates with the work force by inviting them to bring to his attention any aspect of the job process that should be changed.

Command of the art of listening is essential in effective supervision—the supervisor must be a patient and active listener. If he is to be successful in correcting the situation, he must listen carefully to the gripes and complaints that come from workers when something is wrong. To listen understandingly is not passive, but a very vigorous activity. It involves three distinct active steps: (1) Keep out of it—do not intrude physically, verbally, or mentally —shut up and listen! (2) Do not plan what you are going to say in response—don't think, listen. (3) Understand what is being felt as well as what is said—listen to *intent* as well as *content.*

Selection of Communication Media

For effective supervisory communication, a suitable choice of media must be made based upon the supervisor's communication strategy and objectives. Appropriate alternative media choices for supervisory communication are:

- *Written communications* are preferred whenever precise, detailed information or specific orders are involved. Unfortunately, written communications are often poorly done and may establish unintended barriers to interpersonal communication. Supervisors should recognize that exclusive use of written memoranda reduces person-to-person relationships that build understanding and cooperation.
- *Face-to-face, interpersonal communication* is most appropriate when the supervisor attempts to communicate toward changes in attitude, commitment, or motivation. Written memoranda between a supervisor and workers who have daily face-to-face contact is superfluous except in those instances when a written memo is necessary or is required as a back-up to a verbal communication.

Other Communication Considerations

Planning Your Communication

Before the supervisor attempts to communicate he or she should systematically plan the communication by answering the following questions.

- What are you communicating: a fact, order, information, or attitude?
- Why is the communication important or necessary?
- How should you deliver the communication—verbally, in person, by phone, or in writing?
- Where should you communicate—in your office, on the job site, in private?
- When should you communicate—now or later—will the timing be right?
- How do you understand your receiver—his point of view, bias, level of security or insecurity?

Is Your Communication Understood?

We communicate to gain cooperation through behavioral and attitudinal changes. However, our best efforts at communication may be wasted if we do not attempt to determine whether or not our message has been understood by the receiver. The supervisor can do this by asking questions which force the message recipient to reveal what he or she understands. The question "Do you understand?" is totally unacceptable because it will be inevitably answered with the socially acceptable answer "Yes" which gives you, the message sender, no idea as to what is understood. Only by encouraging the receiver to express reactions, by follow-up contacts, and by subsequent review of performance, can you obtain adequate "feedback." Only with this kind of information can the supervisor accurately judge whether or not the message has been understood properly.

Personnel Training

The volume of park and recreation maintenance work varies greatly from season to season in most instances. This variation obviously has a direct effect on the number of maintenance employees required to do the work at a particular time of the year. It is certainly neither practical nor economically feasible to employ a constant number of maintenance personnel on a year-round basis when there is insufficient work during certain seasons to justify a full staff. Many park and recreation organizations, therefore, are able to retain only key individuals around which to build their maintenance force during peak visitor-load seasons.

The seasonal nature of certain types of maintenance work results in the necessity to shift maintenance employees from one job to another according to varying demands.

Due to the need for flexibility among the year-round maintenance employees and the annual need for temporary full-time seasonal employees, there is the almost constant necessity to train new employees and to retrain permanent employees who serve on a year-round basis.

There are two basic aspects of maintenance employee training programs. One is employee orientation, which includes familiarizing the new employee with the maintenance manager, the worker's immediate supervisor, fellow workers, the work of the division, the new worker's job responsibilities, job performance standards, the work schedule, policies relative to visitor use, pay periods, personal appearance and grooming, vacation, sick leave, injury, absence, and tardy notification.

A checklist such as the example in Figure 3-5 is a practical device to help guarantee that each employee receives complete and uniform information during orientation.

The second major aspect of employee training focuses upon a program which is designed to improve employee knowledge, skills and attitudes related to job performance.

The individual responsible for maintenance personnel training programs is the maintenance manager, who may delegate training authority to members of the supervisory staff.

Certain fundamental questions arise with respect to personnel training. These include:

1. How are the training needs of employees determined?
2. What are some of the basic principles of learning?
3. What are the most effective sensory avenues of receiving and retaining information?
4. What is the best method for the trainer to use in instructing an employee to do a job?

Each of these questions will be considered in order.

Identifying Employee Training Needs

Detailed training can be developed upon fact finding which may be segregated into the following two categories:

NAME: _John Doe_ DATE: _5-23-76_

WHO'S WHO

Introduce employee to:
Department or Division Head ☑
Immediate Supervisor ☑
Fellow Workers ☑

WHAT'S WHAT

Work and organization of department:
The function of employee's specific unit

Job duties of new employee ☐

Job performance standards ☐

Method of securing supplies and equipment ☐

WORK SCHEDULE

Hours ☐   Lunch ☐
Overtime ☐   Coffee breaks ☐

PAYROLL INFORMATION

Pay periods ☐   Pay checks ☐

PERSONALS

Appearance and grooming ☐
Lockers ☐   Restrooms ☐
Transportation and parking ☐   Smoking ☐

TIME OFF

Vacation and holiday scheduling ☐
Sick and injury leave policies ☐
Responsibility of employee for notification when sick, injured,
late, etc. ☐

Figure 3-5 A Checklist for the Orientation of New Employees

- what the job requires in the way of skills and abilities,
- what skills and abilities the worker now possesses.

To obtain information about the skill and knowledge demands of the job, the trainer should first review the maintenance objectives and standards for the area, facility, or equipment which the worker is responsible for maintaining. In addition, the trainer should study job descriptions which indicate the kinds of work and skills demanded by that position. If job descriptions are not available, the trainer must proceed to prepare his own analysis of job requirements.

To discover what the workers can do or are doing, the trainer will want to consult various kinds of records of production, training backgrounds, and experience of individuals within the work group. The trainer might also proceed to arrange for trials or try-outs of performance on various kinds of equipment to determine the skills and abilities of employees. Finally, the individual responsible for training should observe the workers' methods and work habits on the job.

Basic Principles of Learning   A basic understanding of the trainee learning process is important to the success of any training endeavor. The following principles, while not comprehensive, provide a reasonable foundation upon which the trainer can launch his effort:

Learning progresses from the simple to the complex. The training program must be planned progress naturally from the simple skills, either physical or mental, to the more difficult or complex knowledge required.

Learning is based upon what is already known. The trainee must be able to relate new knowledge and skills to what is already known. The skilled instructor will develop a store of comparisons and analogies which will help the trainee understand what is being presented.

Repetition is necessary. In many cases, the learner will not understand all the new material completely when it is first presented.

The trainer must develop the habit of repeating it and presenting it in different ways to be sure it is thoroughly understood.

Learning must be used. Everyone tends to forget those items of knowledge and those skills which are not used regularly. The training program must provide opportunities to use what is gained.

Success is important. Knowledge not only must be used but must be used successfully to become permanent. The instructor should be careful to see that the trainee is successful in the application of new knowledge.

Incorrect habits must be changed. Where incorrect responses have been learned, the trainer must first show the learner why they are wrong or undesirable and then help build up a new pattern of response.

Learning can be transferred. A pattern of response or a fund of knowledge that has been developed to meet one situation can be used to solve a new problem or meet a new need. The training program should provide opportunities to develop this ability.

Learning does not always progress steadily. The instructor must be prepared to meet situations as when learning slows down for a period of time and then shows an upward trend. Individual trainees may have different patterns of progress, and the trainer must adjust to these.

Learning depends upon experience. The workplace training program should provide a variety of experiences in order to give the student the greatest possible number of opportunities to learn.

Individuals learn at different rates. Training programs must be flexible enough to allow each trainee to progress at the rate which is best for his own development.

Receiving and Retaining Information

To a considerable extent, learning depends on communication—communication from the trainer to the trainee in conveying information and ideas as well as communication from the learner to the trainer indicating the learner's understanding. The reception of information is largely dependent upon the sensory capacities of the individual. Of the five basic human senses, two of these, seeing and hearing, in most situations are the most effective. When conveying ideas and information, we tend to rely too much on the learner hearing what we have to say rather than relying on the capacity to see, which in combination with hearing is far more effective in the retention of information. Table 3-1 was developed as the result of a study done by the Industrial Extension Service, School of Engineering at North Carolina State University.

Table 3-1

*Relative Recall According to Sensory Avenues
of Receiving Information*

Method of Instruction	Recall After 3 Hours	Recall After 3 Days
A. Telling Alone	70%	10%
B. Showing Alone	72%	20%
C. Telling & Showing	85%	65%

The implication then for the effective instruction would be to de-emphasize the lecturing and telling, emphasize the showing and demonstrating, and also encourage the trainee to do the job. An extensive index of audio-visual aids for all phases of maintenance instruction is included in the appendix to this chapter.

Pattern for Instruction

A highly successful four-step method of instruction was developed for industrial purposes during World War II. This pattern of instruction provides a simple and practical approach to the trainer's task. The four-step pattern is based upon the principles of learning which were outlined earlier, and it emphasizes the fact that there must be two-way communication, between the trainer and the learner, both in the telling and in the doing.

Any trainer who is truly sincere and interested in improving instructional skills should follow the pattern for instruction outlined here.

- Prepare the trainee.
  Insure a learning situation by:
      putting the trainee at ease.
      finding out what the trainee knows.
      arousing the trainee's interest.
      placing the trainee correctly.
- Present the training.
  Stress key points by:
      telling,
      showing,
      explaining,
      demonstrating.
- Try out the trainee's performance.
  Be sure the trainee knows by:
      having the trainee perform the operation,
      having the trainee explain key points,
      correcting the trainee's errors,
      reinstructing the trainee.
- Follow up on the trainee.
  Practice is the key to good performance, therefore:
      put the trainee on his own,
      encourage questions from the trainee,
      frequently check the trainee's performance,
      taper off on viewing the trainee's performance.

In summary, then, the trainer must—

1. prepare the learner.
2. present the job or idea by telling, showing, and illustrating, one step at a time.
3. help the trainee apply the instruction until the habit is formed.
4. follow through to guarantee the success of the training.

Such instructional steps have application to all instructional situations whether the trainer is attempting to communicate an idea or to develop employee skills to do a particular job.

Opportunities outside the Local System

To further assist employees toward career development, the recreation/park organization should encourage participation of employees in relevant courses offered by trade schools, technical institutes, and institutions of higher learning that are close at hand and offer evening classes or correspondence courses. Maintenance equipment manufacturers periodically provide short training courses covering maintenance, operation, and repair of their products and will, in response to requests, provide such courses locally.

The highly successful *Park and Recreation Maintenance-Management School* is conducted annually by North Carolina State University. This school stresses the management of maintenance operations and utilizes the instructional services of outstanding practitioners in the field of park/recreation maintenance.

Employee participation in maintenance training programs away from the job can be best encouraged by paying the tuition and travel expenses and to continue salaries or wages during absences. Not only should employee attendance be stipulated prior to granting permission to attend, but the employee also should be required to share newly acquired knowledge, skills, and understandings with fellow employees and the manager upon return to the job. The responsibility here is two-fold: the employee must be willing to share what has been learned and the maintenance manager must schedule sufficient time for the employee to share this information.

One last step in the process is necessary if the maintenance manager is to impress his employees with the fact that he is genuinely serious and committed to the importance of employee training and career development. This last but most important step is to introduce the new ideas or methods brought back by the employee into organization operations on at least a limited basis until their value can be tested.

The building maintenance division should emphasize the importance of employees being aware of new maintenance methods and materials. Building maintenance trade publications should be made available to employees, with articles of particular significance routed either directly to employees or to supervisory personnel for presentation to employees by the supervisor.

Custodian Training   Since many custodians have received little formal training for their work, maintenance managers must place high priority on effective continuing training. Complicating the problem are the usual high turnover and frequent improvements in cleaning technology requiring revisions of methods and introduction of new materials. This means the custodial section must devote time to orientation, classroom instruction, on-the-job training and re-training, preparation and revision of cleaning manuals, and careful record keeping.

Good training starts even before the employee reports for work. It includes an orientation period during which a supervisor personally assists the new worker in the following ways.

1. Explain appropriate dress for the job assignment (preferably by phone before he reports for work the first day).
2. Introduce him to his fellow workers.
3. Define his duties clearly so that he knows exactly what is expected of him.
4. Explain basic rules and regulations governing employment such as those dealing with safety, accidents, smoking, drinking, and absenteeism.
5. Explain the length and nature of the probationary period, if one is in effect.
6. Show him where tools are located and show him the work area, locker room, cafeteria, and time clock.
7. Encourage him to seek help if he needs it, and tell him where to find it.
8. Tell him when and where he will receive his pay check.
9. Answer any question he may have.

It is not the purpose of this kind of orientation to teach all required job skills; that will come later. The purpose, at this point, is to create an impression of friendly, well organized, and efficient operation. Such first impressions can be surprisingly effective in encouraging receptive, cooperative attitudes among new employees. In many cases, trial and error is unavoidable because the new custodian must be put to work immediately.

Detailed instruction should come in two forms, on-the-job training and formalized classroom sessions. Because most cleaning jobs require a certain amount of manual dexterity and muscular coordination, actual supervised trials provide the most productive learning experiences for the novice. On-the-job training naturally consists of such supervised trials and errors, and classroom instruction should also include these experiences. In most cases trial and error starts early, simply because the new custodian starts working immediately. Therefore, it is imperative that he be given some instruction at the start to prevent the development of bad work habits and methods. It is important that more detailed instruction be given as soon as possible to help develop the most efficient approaches to various tasks.

For training sessions, choose employees who, through practice or talent, have become the best cleaners and ask them to demonstrate those operations which they have mastered. These sessions can be scheduled in the appropriate work areas before small groups of new workers. To get the message across, the supervisor should have novices attempt the operation on the spot under the scrutiny of the expert. This is the optimum teaching method for such information.

Because of the variety of tasks and materials the custodian must master, formal training sessions are also necessary in a well developed training program. These meetings, when well managed, serve to instruct custodians in basic topics such as the most efficient way to clean an activity room and in such esoteric matters as how various cleaning chemicals react with different surfaces. It is through these sessions that administrators and supervisors disseminate what they have learned about recent improvements in cleaning methods and technology. Such sessions can serve, therefore, both for instructing new employees and for retraining experienced workers.

For new employees, custodial managers will find it wise to provide some instruction in as many cleaning techniques and procedures as possible. (See Table 3-2, Suggested Outline for a Custodial Training Program.) Although not exhaustive, the list is extensive enough to serve as the basis for setting up a new training program. Though few employees will thoroughly master all methods and tasks mentioned, each should be familiar with all and expert in several. This familiarity improves cooperation among custodians, since each understands the problems his colleagues have to handle. Limited versatility creates flexibility that is essential if a custodial operation is to function successfully in the event of unexpected absences.

Since there is one most efficient way to handle each job and many less efficient methods, good training that effectively teaches custodians the right way will cut labor costs. To realize this potential saving, instructors must thoroughly cover each step of the major jobs mentioned in the Training Program Outline.

Table 3-2

A Suggested Outline for a Custodial Training Program

I. IMPORTANCE OF CUSTODIAL SERVICES WITHIN MAINTENANCE DIVISION

II. QUALIFICATIONS OF A GOOD CUSTODIAN

III. DEFINITIONS OF BASIC OPERATIONAL TASKS

IV. METHODS OF PERFORMING BASIC OPERATIONAL TASKS AND FREQUENCY OF PERFORMANCE
   A. Dry Dusting by Hand
   B. Wet Cleaning by Hand
   C. Dry Mopping
   D. Wet Mopping
   E. Sweeping
   F. Scrubbing
   G. Waxing
   H. Polishing
   I. Stripping

V. CLEANING SPECIAL EQUIPMENT, FIXTURES AND SURFACES
   A. Equipment and Fixtures
      1. Meeting Room Furniture
      2. Chalkboards
      3. Auditorium Seats
      4. Administrative Office Furniture
      5. Clerical Office Furniture:
         desks, tables, file cabinets
      6. Restrooms and Lounges:
         toilets, urinals*, wash bowls, waste receptacles
      7. Heating and Ventilating
      8. Light Fixtures*
      9. Waste Baskets
      10. Ash Trays
      11. Window Sills and Frames
      12. Doors and Frames
   B. Surfaces
      1. Floors:
         Wood, ceramic tile, terrazzo, composition, resilient, carpeted
      2. Walls:
         plastered, wood panelling, metal partitions, ceramic tile, cinder block

Table 3-2
(continued)

3. Ceilings:
   plastered, acoustical tile, removable panel
4. Metal and Plastic Surfaces:
   chrome, copper, brass, aluminum, stainless
   steel, formica, vinyl
5. Glass and Mirrors

VI. CLEANING PROCEDURES FOR BUILDING AREAS
  A. General Use Areas
    1. Lobbies-Entrances-Foyers
    2. Stairways and Stairwells
    3. Hallways-Corridors
    4. Elevators
  B. Specific Areas
    1. Meeting Rooms
    2. Laboratories
    3. Auditoriums
    4. Gymnasiums
    5. Restrooms and Lounges
    6. Administrative Offices
    7. Clerical Offices

VII. PEST CONTROL PRACTICES

VIII. CARE AND MAINTENANCE OF CUSTODIAL
    MATERIALS, TOOLS AND EQUIPMENT

IX. STANDARDS OF CLEANING AS MEASURED BY
    RESULTS AND OBSERVATION

*Detailed Job Sheets shown as Figures 3-6 & 3-7
Reproduced with the permission of The Association of Physical Plant Administrators and Colleges. Source: *A Basic Manual for Physical Plant Administration.* (Washington, D.C.: The Association, 1974), p. 150.

Figures 3-6 and 3-7 show suggested lesson plans for sessions on cleaning urinals and light fixtures.

The Maintenance Operations Manual

To supplement training, managers should prepare maintenance job description manuals. While a manual can never replace on-the-job and classroom instruction, it can serve other important needs. It is a readily available reference for the worker who cannot remember all the details of more complicated or less frequently performed jobs. A good manual will present for each task a numbered *sequence of operations* which explains, in order, each step to be

DETAILED JOB SHEET
CLEANING SPECIAL EQUIPMENT, FIXTURES AND SURFACES

RESTROOMS AND LOUNGES
DAILY CLEANING OF URINALS

TOOLS AND MATERIALS: Rubber Gloves   Dry Cloth
                      Small Bucket   Cleaning Agent
                      Sponge   Sanitizing Solution
                      Hand Mirror

SUGGESTED METHOD TO USE IN CLEANING URINALS:

1. Wearing rubber golves, wipe outer surface of urinal with sponge partially wrung out to prevent dripping.

2. Sprinkle cleaning agent on sponge and clean inside of urinal making sure all surfaces are clean.

3. Flush urinal.

4. Check with hand mirror to see if all inside surfaces are clean. If not, do the necessary cleaning with the sponge. Flush again.

5. Wring out sponge in sanitizing solution.

6. Continue above steps to complete battery of urinals.

7. Damp wipe exposed piping and valves with sponge. Do not use abrasives.

8. Polish with dry cloth the exposed piping and valves to keep chrome and/or brass fixtures bright and clean.

9. Return and store tools and materials properly for next use.

*Reproduced with the permission of The Association of Physical Plant Administrators of Universities and Colleges. Source: *A Basic Manual for Physical Plant Administration.* (Washington D.C.: The Association, 1974), p. 151.

Figure 3-6 A Detailed Job Sheet for Daily Cleaning of Urinals

DETAILED JOB SHEET
CLEANING SPECIAL EQUIPMENT, FIXTURES AND SURFACES

EQUIPMENT AND FIXTURES
LIGHT FIXTURES

TOOLS AND MATERIALS: Step Ladder or Scaffold
Container for holding dismantled fixtures
2 Pails   Metal Polish
Chemical Cleaner   Sponge or Cloth
Dry Cloth   Screw Driver
Dust Cloth   Pliers

SUGGESTED METHOD TO USE IN CLEANING LIGHT FIXTURES:

1. Put 2 gallons of warm water in each pail.
2. Add to one pail, 1/3 pint neutral chemical cleaner for the cleaning solution; the other pail of plain warm water is for rinse.
3. With tools and materials go to area of light fixtures to be cleaned.
4. Turn off electricity at MAIN SWITCH.
5. Set up ladder or scaffold with container fastened to platform near one side of first fixture in first row.
6. Climb ladder or scaffold with caution.
7. Loosen set screws holding shade or egg crating; use screw driver or pliers if too tight.
8. Remove shade or egg crating and lamp and place in container on platform.
9. Dust fixture with treated dust cloth.
10. Polish fixture; if discolored, use metal polish.
11. Carry shade or egg crating and lamp down ladder carefully.
12. Rinse shade or egg crating and lamp by dipping in rinse bucket.
13. Dry shade or egg crating with dry cloth.
14. Using precaution, climb ladder with shade and lamp and carefully place in container.
15. Replace lamp. Replace shade or egg crating to original position.
16. Tighten set screws sungly.
17. Climb down ladder and move to next fixture working progressively to end of row. Start second row from end just completed.
18. Change water as it becomes soiled.
19. Clean and store equipment properly for next use.

*Reproduced with the permission of The Association of Physical Plant Administrators of Universities and Colleges. Source: *A Basic Manual for Physical Plant Administration.* (Washington D.C.: The Association, 1974), p. 152.

Figure 3-7 A Detailed Job Sheet for Cleaning Light Fixtures

followed. Regular employees will not carry such manuals on their routine rounds, but new workers may need them, and supervisors can use such a complete inventory of operations to instruct new workers and to advise experienced ones.

All administrators should keep records of the instruction every member of the custodial staff receives. In addition, they should award certificates every time an employee satisfactorily completes another training course. Perhaps insignia, to be worn on uniforms, could be designed signifying the expertise acquired. Such touches stress the importance of training to employees and can even motivate them to perform at higher levels.

Records of Employee Training Performance

Employee Safety

The relationship between employee training and safety is a very close one. Reducing accidents is largely a problem of creating a safety-consciousness, which in turn is dependent upon educational and training efforts.

The development of this consciousness has become an increasing interest of both government and industry in recent years. Accidents are expensive and they benefit no one. When accidents are frequent, insurance rates increase and valuable men are lost for extended periods of time. The employee may find his physical well-being seriously impaired. Thus, there is rather unanimous agreement that safety-consciousness is most desirable.

The increasing recognition of management responsibility to develop a safety-consciousness means another big job for the supervisor. The supervisor is the one who must make such a program "click." Indeed, he must be sold on safety himself. It is not enough to give safety lip service at meetings, and then in between let matters take their natural course. Employees are quick to sense this.

Another Big Job for the Supervisor

To put over safety, a supervisor must believe in it and work at it so his men cannot mistake where he stands. He must regard safety this way: Efficient production is impossible without safe production. The supervisor must force himself for a time to look at production and service problems with an eye toward safety, and it will become second nature. Sooner than seems possible, a good safety outlook will become a habit.

Employee Accidents   The National Safety Council, in a 1962 survey of injury frequency, ranked park and recreation employees as receiving more than three times the average number of injuries of all industries reporting to the council.[4]

The survey also revealed that in a year one out of every 35 park and recreation employees receives a disabling injury, and that approximately two thirds of the park and recreation occupational injuries involved maintenance personnel.[5] See Figure 3-8.

Maintenance operations account for two thirds of the total park and recreation occupational injuries.

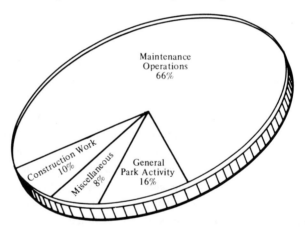

Figure 3-8 Park and Recreation Occupational Injuries

The Occupational Safety and Health Act

With the passage of the Occupational Safety and Health Act (OSHA) of 1970, public park and recreation maintenance managers began to discover what some industrial managers realized decades ago, that good safety is good business; it not only saves lives and limbs, it also saves time.

Although public employees are exempted by the act, Executive Order No. 11612 requires federal agencies, including the National Park Service, to develop effective and comprehensive occupational safety and health programs. Administration of the act by the various states also requires that comprehensive occupational safety and health programs applicable to all employees of the state and its political subdivisions be established. State, county, and municipal employers and employees would, therefore, be subject to virtually the same degree of official control as those in the private sector. However, such public employee protection is contingent upon each state submitting a plan to conduct its own Occupational Safety and Health Program and having that plan approved by the Secretary of Labor. See Table 3-3 for a roster of states that currently have approved OSHA plans. It must be understood that state implementation of approved OSHA plans varies greatly. The order of states as presented in Table 3-3 corresponds to the sequence in which Secretary of Labor approval for the state OSHA program was granted.

Table 3-3

State Implementation of Approved OSHA Plans

Approved State Occupational Safety and Health Plans as of 1976

Alaska	North Carolina	Connecticut
California	Oregon	Hawaii
Colorado	South Carolina	Nevada
Iowa	Tennessee	Indiana
Kentucky	Utah	Wyoming
Maryland	Vermont	Texas
Michigan	Virgin Islands	
Minnesota	Washington, D.C.	

**States That Have Withdrawn from Federally Approved
OSHA Programs
(Public employees are not covered.)**

Pennsylvania	New Jersey
Georgia	New York
North Dakota	Illinois
New Hampshire	Wisconsin

Secretary of Labor approval of any state OSHA plan requires the inclusion of a provision covering all state and local government employees. Park and recreation maintenance employees employed by private enterprises are automatically covered by the federal

OSHA act whether the act is administered by the federal government or if a state approved OSHA plan is in force. Any state that has federal approval for their OSHA plan is eligible for fifty percent federal funding to implement its program.

OSHA Coverage and Obligations of Federal Agencies and Their Employees

Section 19 of the law applies to all federal agencies and requires the heads of these agencies to conduct occupational safety and health programs consistent with standards developed under the act, including the maintenance of adequate records of occupational injuries and illnesses and the preparation of periodic reports for submittal to the Secretary of Labor. On July 26, 1971, the President signed Executive Order No. 11612 which further details the responsibilities and duties of heads of federal agencies and the Secretary of Labor in the administration of the act. Federal employees, in addition, have the responsibility to comply with safety and health standards, including rules, regulations, and orders promulgated under the act.

Duties   The law enumerates certain duties for both employers and employees. The employer has the general duty to furnish to each employee employment and a place of employment free from recognized hazards that are known, or likely, to cause death or serious physical harm.

The employer also has the duty to comply with occupational safety and health standards promulgated under the act and to obey other regulations adopted in administration of the act.

The duty of the employee is to comply with occupational safety and health standards and all rules, regulations, and orders issued pursuant to this act which are applicable to his or her own actions and standards.

Though both employer and employee have duties, prescribed penalties are invoked only against the employer. No legal penalties can be assessed against the employee.

As a practical matter, few employers are being charged with violations of the general-duty provision cited here. This means that the heart of the enforcement activity focuses on the safety and health standards promulgated by the Secretary of Labor.

OSHA spells out a number of rights held by employees. These fall under three main headings: **Employee Rights under OSHA**

- rights with respect to standards,
- rights with respect to access to information,
- rights with respect to enforcement.

1. The employee can participate in the standards-development process.
2. The employee must be kept informed of significant safety and health information, specifically of the law itself, of the summary of accident experience in the establishment, and of any safety violations alleged to exist in the establishment.
3. The employee must file complaints of violations with the Department of Labor or with compliance officers during inspections.
4. An employee or a representative of employees may accompany the compliance officer during an inspection.

If asked to do so, the Department of Labor is required to keep confidential the name of a complaining employee. Employers must not discriminate against employees exercising their rights under OSHA.

Standards are at the very heart of the safety process established by OSHA. The safety and health standards promulgated by the Secretary of Labor are designed to protect working people from occupational injury and illness. These standards are the principal criteria used by OSHA compliance officers when inspecting establishments. Safety and health standards are not an invention of the federal government. On the contrary, most of the OSHA standards are developed by nationally recognized standards-producing organizations established mainly by and for industrial management. **OSHA Standards**

Three types of injury/illness records must be maintained at each establishment: **OSHA Injury/Illness Records**

- a log of occupational injuries and illnesses,
- a supplementary record of occupational injuries and illnesses,
- an annual summary of occupational injuries and illnesses.

The log may be maintained on Form OSHA-100 or on any privately prepared equivalent. (See Exhibit 3-1 in the appendix to this chapter.)

The Supplementary Record may be maintained on Form OSHA-101 (see Exhibit 3-2) or on any other form (Workmen's Compensation, insurance company, etc.), which provides for the required information. The summary of occupational injuries and illnesses should be recorded on OSHA Form 102 (See Appendix 3-D). If the workers are widely scattered because of the nature of their work, records are maintained at some point of assembly—a garage, supervisor's office, etc.

OSHA Inspections   One of the key sections of the Occupational Safety and Health Act ensures OSHA compliance officers free entry into work establishments and access to certain records, which may provide information on working conditions related to occupational safety and health.

Section 8(a) of OSHA provides that the compliance officer, upon presenting appropriate credentials to the owner, operator, or agent in charge, is authorized—

- to enter without delay and at reasonable times any factory, plant, establishment, construction site, or other area, work-place or environment where work is performed by an employee of an employer;
- to inspect and investigate during regular working hours and at other reasonable times, and within reasonable limits and in a reasonable manner, any such place of employment and all pertinent conditions, structures, machines, apparatus, devices, equipment, and materials therein, and to question privately any such employer, owner, operator, agent, or employee.

Refusal to admit the compliance officer and any interference with his investigations can result in legal action and possible penalties.

The Opening   After the compliance officer has identified himself he should be
Inspection   met by a senior executive. He may ask for (and be given) certain
Conference   records that will assist him in his work. He will, in this conference, seek to evaluate the establishment's safety and health programs. An

employer's representative should be chosen to accompany the compliance officer on his inspection.

An authorized representative of the employees must also be given the opportunity to accompany the compliance officer during the course of an actual inspection. In a unionized establishment, arrangements for the selection of such a representative by the union should be made in advance to avoid delays. If there is no authorized employee representative, the compliance officer will interview employees from time to time on his inspection tour, the employee interviews must not be interfered with by the production schedule. Neither may the employer discriminate, in any way, against an employee for anything said or shown to the compliance officer.

The Inspection

The route and duration of the inspection will be determined by the compliance officer. He can go where he chooses, talk to whom he wishes, take photos, make instrument readings, and examine records.

A point of controversy in connection with the inspection has been the matter of pay for employees who represent the employees during the inspection. In general, the law does not require the employer to pay the employee for the time spent accompanying a compliance officer. However, there may be cases when non-payment would be considered discriminatory, as, for example, when an establishment that has previously compensated employees for making safety inspections suspends the practice for a particular employee.

The Closing Inspection Conference

After the inspection (and/or review of records), the compliance officer closes the visit by conferring with the employer or a representative. During this conference, the compliance officer will discuss any apparent violations he has noted, and he may discuss with the employer the nature and implementation of corrective measures. He will notify the employer of any alleged violations for which he will recommend that a citation be issued.

OSHA Violations

Alleged violations would fall under one or more of the following three headings:

- General Duty,
- Safety and Health Standards,
- Regulations.

Few citations for violation of the general duty clause in OSHA are currently being issued. For the most part, OSHA limits citations to alleged violations of standards or regulations. However, the general duty clause is part of the law, and any employer may be charged with its violation.

Citations may allege violations of any of the following types:

- **Imminent Danger** The act defines imminent danger as, "Any conditions or practices in any place of employment which are such that a danger exists which could reasonably be expected to cause death or serious physical harm immediately or before the imminence of such danger can be eliminated through the enforcement procedures otherwise provided by this act."
- **Non-Serious Violation** If a condition exists, which the compliance officer believes is likely to cause injury but not death or serious physical harm, or if the employer did not know of the hazard, the violation will be considered non-serious. A tripping hazard on a level surface would be an example.
- **De Minimix Violation** This term is used for a violation that has no immediate or direct relationship to safety or health. An example would be the lack of partitions for individual toilet facilities.
- **Willful Violation** A violation is willful if the employer either intentionally and knowingly violated the act or, even though he did not know he was violating the act, he was aware that a hazardous condition existed, and he made no reasonable effort to eliminate the condition.
- **Repeated Violation** A repeated violation is one for which a second citation is issued for violation of the same standard or the general duty clause. This differs from a failure-to-abate violation in that the repeated violation occurs after the original violation was abated.

A citation may be issued to the employer for violations of safety and health standards by employees. The employer is considered responsible for requiring employees to comply with standards. An example would be the failure of employees to wear personal protective equipment required by the standards. Employers must take all necessary steps to assure employee safety compliance.

Unfortunately, OSHA is based upon standards primarily developed by and for the private sector of industry and does not relate to many of the special problems of park and recreation employee safety. In addition, OSHA standards relate to physical conditions of an industrial nature. More development is needed in the areas of work procedures and employee safety instruction. OSHA simply does not go far enough.

Employee Safety Training

Unsafe acts along with unsafe conditions are the two major sources of accidents. One of the major causes of unsafe acts is lack of knowledge or skill. The remedy is training. It is the supervisor's job to see that employees within his work group are properly trained to perform their jobs in a safe manner. This obviously presupposes the supervisor's ability to teach. In brief, there are two widely used techniques for training workers how to perform their jobs in a safe and efficient manner. One is Job Safety Analysis (JSA) and the other Job Instruction Training (JIT). When these two techniques are combined and properly utilized, employees learn to perform their jobs safely.

Job Safety Analysis is a procedure for breaking a job down into steps, determining the hazards involved, and the recommended safe procedures for performing each step of the job. In its final form, it is a written guide as to how to do a job safely.

Job Instruction Training is a highly successful four-step method for teaching job skills. Supervisors should be capable in the use of this procedure. (See *Pattern for Instruction* in the *Personnel Instruction* section of this chapter.) When JIT is used in connection with the steps in the JSA, it becomes a very effective technique for safety training.

Courses offered through correspondence are often utilized in connection with individual or home study. The advantages of individual study are to be found in the fact that the trainee can set his or her own pace and set a study schedule that is most convenient.

The National Safety Council offers two safety training courses for supervisors—"Supervising for Safety," and "Supervisor's Guide to Human Relations." These courses are available through the Safety Training Institute of the National Safety Council, 425 N. Michigan Avenue, Chicago, Illinois, 60611.

Special Employee Safety Problems

A broad spectrum of safety problems and hazards are to be found in the park and recreation maintenance field.[6] While all problems and hazards will not pertain to a given operation, the alert manager will analyze his situation and direct his staff to institute the safety control measures that are appropriate. Special safety problems and hazards of park and recreation situations include the following.

Temporary and Seasonal Employees

Park and recreation organizations have many seasonal and part-time employees according to peak visitor seasons. The temporary employee group is largely made up of students with little work experience and safety training and older retired or semi-retired workers who are often in a state of poor health. When orientation and training time for the inexperienced temporary employee is limited, it is wise to develop a concise safety training packet to be mailed to the worker prior to his reporting to work with the admonition to study the material in preparation for a test on the material when he reports. In the case of the older temporary employee, for correct job placement, it would be wise to double check for physical limitations and the health status of the individual either by a health examination or a check into his previous work performance.

Language Barriers to Safety

Some temporary or seasonal employees may be functionally illiterate and, therefore, unable to read or write. Others may be handicapped by their inability to understand English and communicating in a foreign language. Under such circumstances, it would be wise to prepare employee job safety instructions in both English and the foreign language(s) in question.

Workers in Isolated Locations

Due to the size of many recreation areas, maintenance and construction workers must often work alone or in small groups at locations isolated from emergency medical aid. Such employees should be trained in proper use and care of safety equipment for their job assignment. Employees who must work alone, particularly in isolated areas, should be self-reliant, trained in first aid, and fully capable of recognizing potential hazards to themselves and to the public. A hazard reporting system should be established as well as an accident reporting procedure.

Employees doing maintenance and construction on roads and in parking lots are exposed to the hazards of moving vehicles in addition to the normal accident exposure from operating vehicles. Whenever possible, advance warning signs, barricades, and flagmen should be used. Tool carts and vehicles may be placed between oncoming or passing traffic and the work point, in addition to but not in lieu of, barricades and flagmen. Flasher units, signs, and traffic cones should be used to warn and channel traffic for worker protection. Trucks and other maintenance and construction vehicles that may have to stop or impede traffic should be equipped with special rotating or blinking lights. Advance warning lights placed well ahead of the work site are imperative so that motorists can anticipate the operation. Flagmen, who are used to direct traffic, should wear high visibility (orange) vests and safety hats. Vests must be reflectorized for night use.

Vehicles and Traffic Hazards

Park/recreation maintenance and construction requires the use of a wide variety of hand and portable power tools, most of which are potentially dangerous when put into the hands of inexperienced employees. Tools range from a pair of common hand pliers to power saws and powerful hydraulic equipment. Special training and supervision are required for the safe use of tools. The National Safety Council indicates that the following minimum requirements for the use of tools should be observed:

Tools and Equipment

1. *Provide and use the right tool for the job.* Quality tools should be provided, and employees should be trained and instructed to use the right tool for a given job. Electrical tools should bear the listings of the Underwriters Laboratories (UL) label and be either of the double insulated type or electrically grounded through three wires and grounded circuits.

2. *Tools should be well maintained and kept in safe condition.* Procedures should be established for employees to report and turn in defective, unsafe tools, electrical equipment, and extension cords. A record system for regular tool and equipment inspection and maintenance should be established. Centralized tool control is desirable and will help ensure uniform inspection and maintenance.

3. *Supervisors should train and supervise employees in the correct use of tools for each job.* Such training is especially important for electrical equipment and power tools because of the danger of fatal shock and permanently disabling injuries. Hand cutting tools such as axes, saws, chisels, and knives, must be kept sharp for proper functioning, and the user must be trained in the proper use of these to avoid accidents.

4. *Tools should be stored in a safe place.* Serious accidents occur because tools have fallen from overhead places or individuals are injured as a result of carrying sharp or pointed tools in pockets or leaving them where sharp points or cutting edges are exposed.

Protective Equipment

Safety glasses should be provided and worn by employees using any hand or power tool when there is a danger of flying chips, sparks, or other hazards to the eyes.

Steel-toed safety shoes protect the feet from heavy objects that might fall or roll over a worker's toes. Additional protection to the instep is provided by metatarsal guards. Safety hats should be worn to protect workers' heads from falling objects. Heavy gloves should be worn to protect hands and wrists when handling sharp or rough material, but gloves should not be worn around moving machinery where rotating parts might catch the glove and pull the hand into danger. Rubber gloves, aprons, and splash resistent goggles should be worn when handling corrosive chemicals and toxic pesticides and herbicides. In addition to other protective equipment, air filtering respirators should be worn by all personnel involved in paint, herbicide and pesticide spraying operations.

Rubbish Removal

Collection and removal of garbage and refuse in parks usually does not involve use of heavy duty compactor trucks with the dangerous shearing action of the compactor blade. However, a variety of injuries, such as strains and overexertion, are constant hazards to the unwary park refuse collector. For this reason it is necessary to establish lifting, loading, and lowering procedures and train workers on the safety size and weight range of materials to be handled. Whenever possible, mechanical loading equipment should be used to handle refuse containers that cannot be safely handled by two men.

Refuse containers should be no larger than the 32–33 gallon size (preferably of open mesh) or 20 gallon size if they are to be handled by one man only. Fifty-five gallon steel drums are still used by some park systems as refuse containers. Because of their heavier weight and bulk, at least two men should handle them. Holes for water drainage purposes should be punched or drilled in the bottom of solid containers.

Supervisors should train employees in proper lifting methods by means of posters, motion pictures, and printed material. Refuse collection truck drivers should be trained in safety procedures to protect members of their crews and the public. Well-understood signals between the driver and the crew must be developed for proper teamwork in stopping, backing up, and picking up containers. A guide should stand near the rear of the truck to direct the driver.

If trucks must stop on roads and at driveways, they should be equipped with warning lights and caution signs. Local and state vehicle codes for lighting and signals should be followed

Mowing Operations

Safety requirements for walk-behind and riding mowers, both rotary and reel type, are given in OSHA Standards (29 CFR, Section 1910.243). According to the National Safety Council's Public Employee Guide, *Street and Highway Maintenance,* the main safety points to consider in mowing operations are—

1. Keep both hands on the handlebars or steering wheel.
2. Two or more mowers working in tandem should: (a) stay at least 15 feet apart, and (b) side-by-side mowing should be forbidden.
3. Always look out for "blind" spots.
4. Operators should wear head, eye, and foot protection.
5. On large tractor-mower combinations (a) units must have heavy roll-over bars; (b) operators must wear safety belts; (c) operators should mow as far as possible from people to minimize the danger of the mower striking and throwing objects hidden in the turf; and (d) chain or other types of curtain guards should be installed around rotary mowers as further protection from objects thrown by the mower blades.
6. Because of the danger of amputation, operators should be instructed never to unclog or adjust a mower until the power is turned off.

7. To avoid fire and explosion, the motor should be turned off and allowed to cool before refueling.

8. Tractor-mowers that travel on roads or highways should conform to all local and state regulations and should be equipped with flasher lights, high visibility flags, and slow-moving-vehicle signs.

Landscaping   Landscaping can involve a variety of power and hand tools ranging from shovels to portable chain saws. Power equipment such as a chain saw is exceptionally dangerous to the inexperienced or untrained users. Hedge trimmers, axes, machetes, and hand saws can also cause painful injury and can be used safely only if employees are thoroughly trained and the tools themselves are kept in safe condition and good repair. For anything but the lightest landscaping, safety hats, safety shoes, and safety glasses should be worn. Safety belts and ropes used in tree trimming should be inspected daily for wear. Trees should be felled, and heavy timber should be cut only by trained foresters or others thoroughly familiar with the hazards of the equipment and heavy work involved. All of the precautions for tractor mowing are even more critical in the operation of a "bush hog" for cleaning brush, especially in rocky and rough terrain.

Seven Steps to Safety

Before any effective employee safety hazard control program can be developed, the maintenance manager must be genuinely committed to the importance of employee safety. The maintenance manager must realize that:

1. accidents can be prevented,
2. accident prevention costs less than the costs of accidents,
3. safety is just good management and efficient operation.

While the humanitarian aspects of safety cannot be disregarded, the economic aspects of insurance costs, medical expenses, efficiency, and public and employee relations demand attention in the accident control program. Accident prevention requires no complicated or unwieldy organization; it can and should be integrated into all phases of recreation maintenance operations and management.

If the maintenance manager will follow the hazard control measures outlined in the following "Seven Steps to Safety," he will have made an excellent start in his program of employee safety:

1. The maintenance manager must want to stop accidents. He cannot initiate a safety program half-heartedly, but he must sincerely want to stop accidents and be willing to exert the total energy necessary to accomplish this.
2. Assign someone to help on details. Assign a good supervisor to become informed on applicable safety standards established by OSHA, training, accident reporting, and program activities.
3. Locate the hazards—watch for things that cause accidents. Accident statistics will assist in locating safety hazards. Encourage employees to suggest safer ways of doing maintenance work.
4. Make the job safe. Remove hazards. Make machines, equipment, and operations as fool-proof as possible. Examples of safety equipment are guards for saws, goggles for grinding equipment, and welding masks.
5. Control employee work habits. Teach the safe ways of doing the job. Enforce compliance with safety regulations and make new rules when necessary.
6. Keep simple safety records. Uncover accident causes, check progress, and compare experience with others. Simple records consist of an accident report form and an accident analysis chart. Finally, recognize that records will help reveal injury hazard areas.
7. Get employees into the act. Involve first-line supervisors and grass roots employees. Make them safety conscious. Solicit their suggestions and utilize their ideas. Devote staff meeting time to safety. Brainstorm and develop innovative approaches to the employee safety program.[7]

Evaluating Employee Performance

Supervisors tend to handle personnel selection, indoctrination, and training fairly well, but then totally shirk their responsibility to the new worker once he is on the job. The excuse often given by the supervisor is that the satisfactory worker is capable of caring for himself so "I spend my time with the marginal-problem cases."

The enlightened supervisor recognizes that there are great potential dividends to be received by working with all employees, particularly the good workers. He realizes that it is important to build on the strengths of his work group, rather than on the weaknesses. Therefore, it is imperative that the supervisor avoid the arm-chair approach to reviewing employee performance. Rather, he should spend maximum time on the job site personally observing employee performance and getting direct feedback on irritations that affect good performance. By operating in this manner, the supervisor does not have to depend upon periodic spot ratings that tend to produce a distorted picture of employee performance. Instead, the supervisor's employee appraisal is continuous, informal, and routine to the point that it is an accepted part of work life rather than "snoopervision," which is resented. In reality, the seeming informal appraisal of employee performance must be carried on in a more precise, systematic manner than it might outwardly appear.

The Why of Ratings   A written record of employee performance is essential if the supervisor is to be capable of making objective, defensible recommendations regarding training, transfer, dismissal, promotion, or permanent appointments for each employee. Literally, the supervisor must rate each employee, and this is not an easy task. The accuracy of a given rating depends upon many things including the rating skills and immediate disposition of the rater, his range of contact with the individual being rated, and the tangibility of the traits under consideration. On the last point word meanings play a part. The level of abstraction influences the range of possible differences in opinion.

In short, it must be admitted that ratings are by nature rather ambiguous, awkward, and imprecise. Perhaps it would be convenient if production records, examination results, and seniority rules were adequate to relieve the supervisor from the necessity of using ratings. But they cannot, and there is no evidence that they ever will. A great many decisions and actions in the course of human relationships depend upon a matter of opinion. Instead of decrying this fact, time and attention should be given to finding a means of putting such opinion on a more systematic and factual basis.

Where Ratings   Ratings can be applied to two areas of a relationship between the
May Be Used   supervisor and the worker: (1) organization control, which is the traditional emphasis, and (2) individual worker guidance. Assuming that there is a formal rating system calling for evaluations at several

specified times, take a probationary worker as a hypothetical case in point. Does this worker turn out a reasonable quantity of work? Does he waste too much material or damage equipment excessively? Does he get to work on time? Does he have a number of questionable absences? Does he cooperate with others? Does he ask for advice when he needs it?

The answers to these questions serve organization control purposes directly. They also provide guidance for managerial actions that affect the central aspirations of our probationary worker—training, transfer, dismissal, permanent appointment, promotion, and so on. It would be unrealistic to deny their frustrating potentials to the employee. However, it would be equally unrealistic to ignore the importance of systematic answers to such questions for the furtherance of legitimate organization goals. But, the answer in each case has equal potential as a basis for praise of the individual where the facts warrant it. Each answer can provide constructive guidance to the individual and the supervisor as well.

If there is a formal worker evaluation system in a given situation, it may be quite unsuited to what the supervisor sees as being appropriate, but it is unlikely that he can do anything about it. Whether or not there is an official personnel rating system, the supervisor should not lose sight of the fact that he personally has to make judgments and recommendations. One thing the supervisor can do, regardless of rating system conditions, is to guard against bias and error in his ratings.

Guarding against Bias and Error

The first step is to learn what these hazards are. Bias is an inclination toward a conclusion as you approach the problem. Sometimes it may be based upon reason; but, where it is completely unreasonable, it is called prejudice. Prejudice ignores facts or applies irrelevant facts to the situation at hand in order to support an emotionally satisfying conclusion. Prejudice obviously has an unfair influence upon rating results, but rational bias may be equally harmful. Moreover, there is sometimes a fine line between rational bias and rationalization of prejudice.

The danger in rational bias is that it may cause a supervisor to rate a person as he was and not as he is. For example, a worker might be absent three times without good cause. The next time he is absent, it would not be unreasonable for the supervisor to assume he was "goofing off" again. Yet, the fourth time he might have an entirely valid reason for absence. Thus, even when bias seems reasonable, it is most important to check the case by fact finding and situational thinking.

Even as bias may cause discrimination among individuals on rational but insufficient grounds, prejudice causes irrational discrimination. Its basis may be conscious or unconscious. While it is very unlikely that the supervisor can do much about the latter, he can control conscious prejudice by looking for it. He should simply check his ratings against these questions: "Am I making this judgment on the basis of the real individual or on the basis of race, religion, or ethnic background? Furthermore, "Do I make the judgment because the individual is a man, or a woman?" It is most important to recognize that positive and negative discrimination is unjust. No individual deserves special favor any more than he or she deserves unfair condemnation.

Generalized Rating Errors

Apart from the rather specific influence of bias upon the ratings of given individuals or groups, many raters commonly evidence generalized errors in their rating efforts. The most common rating errors[8] can be grouped in these classifications: (1) leniency, (2) the halo effect, (3) central tendency, (4) contrast, and (5) association.

Leniency is far and away the most common rating error and gives a highly overrated picture of the employee's performance, thus destroying any potential the rating might have for constructive employee guidance.

The Halo Rating Error occurs when the rater is particularly impressed (negatively or positively) by one particular trait, characteristic, or area of employee performance and tends to allow this impression to overinfluence rating the individual in other areas of performance.

The Central Tendency Error often results from the rater not being personally familiar with a particular trait, characteristic, or area of performance as required for rating on a particular employee-rating form or scale. The rater often covers his ignorance by then giving the employee an average or central rating.

The Contrast Error can be described as a supervisor rating an employee in comparison with himself. To avoid contrast error, the rater must become circumspect and determine if he is rating on the basis of expecting all employees to be like him.

The Association Error takes many forms; among these are:
(1) failure on the part of the rater to distinguish semantically
among terms that describe different rating traits or characteristics,
(2) the tendency for a rater to rate adjacent traits on a scale more
consistently than those that are separated by a greater distance on
the form, and (3) rater fatigue or irritation associated with leniency
or severity in rating. To minimize association error related to fatigue, particularly when forced to use a complex time-consuming
rating form, the rater would be wise to rate all employees on the
same trait before going on to the next item.

How Can The Supervisor Become More Systematic? More
systematic rating depends upon the development or reinforcement
of two attitudes by the supervisor: (1) that evaluation is a continuous responsibility, and (2) that conscious effort is necessary to
improve the evaluation. Without these attitudes, forms and procedures have little value.

**Approaches to
Rating**

The "Employee Performance Record"[9] devised by Flanagan and
Burns is an approach with great potential for increasing the supervisor's systematic attention to the evaluation problem. This technique does not require the supervisor to make the traditional overall judgments required by a twenty or thirty item rating scale of
ambiguous or imprecise characteristics or traits. Instead, the supervisor needs only to record his day-to-day observations of *exceptional* (not routine) worker performance in specific on-the-job incidents. It is these continuing factual records of both outstanding
effective and outstanding ineffective specific performance that provide the basis for whatever opinions or recommendations the supervisor may have to express periodically, or on special occasions, regarding the employee.

**The Employee
Performance Record**

The Employee Performance Recording Form which the
supervisor utilizes to record the exceptional incidents of worker
performance is essentially one that provides equal space for the
recording of effective behavioral incidents on one half of the cen-
terline of the form, and incidents of ineffective behavior on the
other half. See Figure 3-9. The feature of recording incidents of
effective as well as ineffective behavior provides a constructive positive basis for post-appraisal interviewing as well as a negative basis.

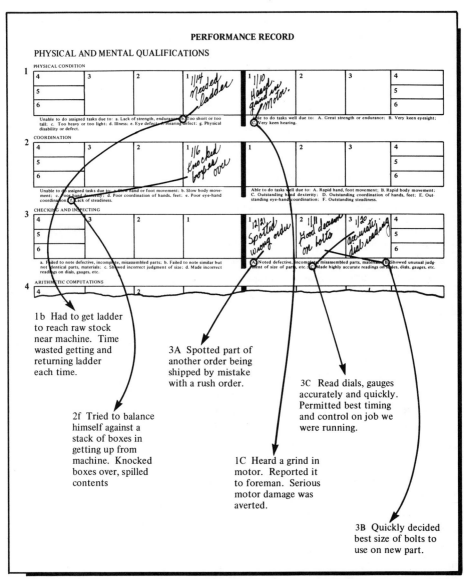

PERFORMANCE RECORD

PHYSICAL AND MENTAL QUALIFICATIONS

1b Had to get ladder
to reach raw stock
near machine. Time
wasted getting and
returning ladder
each time.

3A Spotted part of
another order being
shipped by mistake
with a rush order.

3C Read dials, gauges
accurately and quickly.
Permitted best timing
and control on job we
were running.

2f Tried to balance
himself against a
stack of boxes in
getting up from
machine. Knocked
boxes over, spilled
contents

1C Heard a grind in
motor. Reported it
to foreman. Serious
motor damage was
averted.

3B Quickly decided
best size of bolts to
use on new part.

Source: John C. Flanagan and Robert K. Burns, "The Employee Performance Record: A New Appraisal and Development Tool," *Harvard Business Review,* (Sept.-Oct. 1955), pp. 98-99.

Figure 3-9   An Illustrated Section of the Employee Performance Record

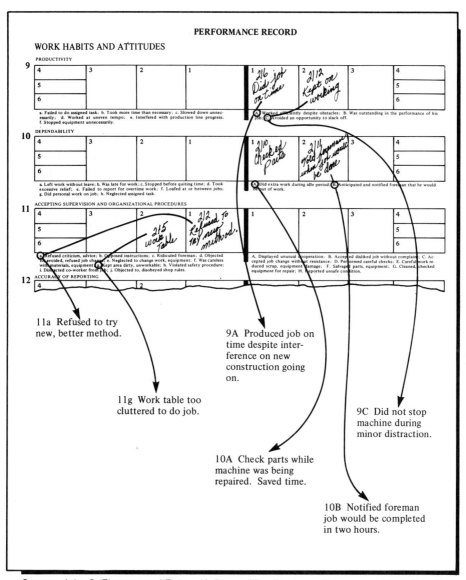

Source: John C. Flanagan and Robert K. Burns, "The Employee Performance Record: A New Appraisal and Development Tool," *Harvard Business Review*, (Sept.–Oct. 1955), pp. 98-99.

Figure 3–9 (Continued)

The remainder of the Employee Performance Recording Form is developed by the supervisor according to the categories and subcategories of responsibility for the employee's particular job. For example, a broad category of job responsibility might be entitled "Physical and Mental Qualifications." This category might then be broken down into: (1) physical condition, (2) coordination, (3) checking and inspecting, (4) arithmetic computation, (5) learning and remembering procedures and instructions, (6) judgment and comprehension, (7) understanding and repairing mechanical devices, and (8) improving equipment and showing inventiveness. Another broad category of job responsibility might be "Work Habits and Attitudes" with a further breakdown of (1) productivity, (2) dependability, (3) accepting supervision and organizational procedures, (4) accuracy of reporting, (5) response to departmental needs, (6) getting along with others, (7) demonstrations of initiative, and (8) assuming responsibility. Space must be provided on the Employee Performance Recording Form for the brief recording of incidents (both commendable and undesirable) that occurred within a particular category of job responsibility.

The supervisor then classifies the incidents according to the category guidelines that the form provides.

The principles advanced in the Flanagan and Burns rating system are most useful. It is important to emphasize that a supervisor have a daily record of actual behavioral performance in terms of incidents. But, this definitely should not be perceived by the workers as a "black book" routine. Positive as well as negative incidents must be recorded to get the true picture.

It is unwise to make a show of this system during a workday. Instead, the supervisor should consider the events of each day at its close, then record the exceptional, non-routine incidents. He should not put off recording until next week or even tomorrow; there is great hazard that the bad will then predominate over the good, or that the supervisor will forget the bad done by the worker whom he already favors and the good work by the worker with whom he is little acquainted or whom he dislikes.

The Trait-Oriented Employee Rating Form

A trait- or characteristic-oriented employee rating form is presented in Figure 3-10. This rating is quite different from the Flanagan-Burns "Employee Performance Record" in that it encourages the rating of the employee on the basis of general traits or characteristics rather than specific situational behavior. Several major difficulties arise in connection with the use of such a form.

First, the form encourages recording of general perceptions of the ratee in pre-established categories rather than specific instances of behavioral performance. This often results in the inability of the rater at the request of the "ratee" to identify specific instances of performance that supposedly were the basis of a "low" rating. Obviously, mutual respect, trust, and confidence suffer in such situations. Second, the form does not provide the opportunity for the rater to indicate "insufficient opportunity to observe" and thus evaluate an individual in one or more categories. This then forces the supervisor to guess and probably give an "average" rating because he is not sure. Third, employee evaluations should be continuous, not sporadic. Customarily employee evaluations by the supervisor must be completed and turned in once or twice a year. With pre-established trait or characteristic rating categories, there is a marked tendency for the supervisor to wait until just before the deadline to complete the form and turn it in. This leaves the supervisor in the unenviable position of having to recall incidents that may have occurred months previously and which are only dim recollections that invite rating bias and encourage other types of generalized rating errors.

The Flanagan-Burns Employee Performance Record tends to minimize the rating problems mentioned. However, the Trait-Oriented Employee Rating Form does have some advantages that undoubtedly account for its popularity and high incidence of use. First, the Trait-Oriented Employee Rating Form does not require the manager or supervisor to develop job rating categories that are specific to the worker's job. This makes it initially easier for the supervisor, but certainly not easier when he is called upon to provide information of employee performance which is specific to the job in question. Second, the Trait-Oriented Employee Rating Form requires only that the rater "check" the appropriate level (i.e., unsatisfactory, average, excellent) of his estimate. He is not required first to identify the category of work responsibility within which the exceptional behavior occurred and then briefly record what the employee did and the result of the behavior. In short, registering a check mark is immediately easier for the rater. However, the check mark is often a marginal basis for a promotion or discharge recommendation.

METROPOLITAN RECREATION DISTRICT
Employee Performance Rating Report

NAME_____ DEPARTMENT_____ POSITION_____

SECTION A   DATE OF REPORT_____

PERFORMANCE FACTORS	UNSATISFACTORY	BELOW STANDARD	STANDARD	GOOD	EXCEPTIONAL
RELIABILITY	☐ ☐ Frequently reports late, is absent or leaves early, lacks proper attention to duty.	☐ ☐ Occasionally tardy with without reason, attendance irregular which hinders performance.	☐ ☐ Usually on time, average attendance and work performance.	☐ ☐ Always on time. Diligent in duties.	☐ ☐ Always on time and spends extra time on job to improve himself. Very diligent in duties.
KNOWING THE JOB AND WORK QUANTITY	☐ ☐ Displays inadequate ability despite constant and proper instruction.	☐ ☐ Limited knowledge of job. Does not work to capacity.	☐ ☐ Average knowledge of job and work habits.	☐ ☐ Knows all phases of job. Works to capacity.	☐ ☐ Knows all phases of job and strives to improve. Far above expectations.
INTEREST AND WORK ATTITUDE	☐ ☐ Dislikes work, no enthusiasm, needs constant direction and watching.	☐ ☐ Interest spasmodic, rarely enthusiastic. Needs considerable supervision.	☐ ☐ Normal amount of interest in work. Some enthusiasm. Conscientious but needs regular supervision.	☐ ☐ Interested in work. Usually enthusiastic. Only occasional supervision required.	☐ ☐ High interest in work, very enthusiastic, always dependable in highest degree. Minimum supervision.
COOPERATION AND RELATIONSHIP WITH PEOPLE	☐ ☐ Does not work well with or assist others in department. Antagonistic.	☐ ☐ Seldom works with others. Occasionally will assist them if required to do so.	☐ ☐ Generally works well with others. Frequently offers assistance.	☐ ☐ Quick to volunteer in department projects, assignments; works well with and assists others.	☐ ☐ Always inspires good teamwork. Exceptional in projects and assignments.
JUDGMENT	☐ ☐ Poor sense of values, makes poor, impractical decisions.	☐ ☐ Jumps to conclusions, makes decisions which should be referred to supervisor.	☐ ☐ Decisions and judgment dependable on routine matters.	☐ ☐ Uses common sense. Most decisions acceptable.	☐ ☐ Sound judgment and decisions always based on thorough analysis.
QUALITY OR WORK	☐ ☐ Makes constant mistakes. Inaccurate and makes errors. Cannot work under pressure.	☐ ☐ Work not neat, or not consistently up to required standard.	☐ ☐ Generally up to minimum standards in work. Works normally under pressure.	☐ ☐ Work generally neat and well arranged. Makes accurate and adequate decisions when required to do so.	☐ ☐ Work constantly neat and very well arranged. At best during pressure periods. Very accurate in all phases.
INITIATIVE	☐ ☐ Needs much attention. Lacks self reliance and drive. Needs too much prodding.	☐ ☐ Rarely suggests; good follower. Relies heavily on others.	☐ ☐ Progressive. With encouragement often offers sound suggestions to improve job	☐ ☐ Resourceful. Develops assignments ably; makes new or original contributions.	☐ ☐ Looks for and takes on additional tasks. Highly ingenious. Improves standards. Self starter with sound ideas.

COMMENTS: This space to be used for additional remarks for any above or below standard performance. If below standard, remarks should
state what specific action is being taken to improve rating.

Figure 3-10 A Trait-Oriented Employee Rating Form

SECTION B   SECTION B TO BE COMPLETED FOR SUPERVISORY EMPLOYEES ONLY

PERFORMANCE FACTORS	UNSATISFACTORY	BELOW STANDARD	STANDARD	GOOD	EXCEPTIONAL
LEADERSHIP	☐ ☐ Lacks full support and cooperation of sub-ordinates. Easily prejudiced and maintains poor discipline.	☐ ☐ Enjoys only passive support and cooperation. Not sufficiently objective or impersonal in business relations.	☐ ☐ Obtains good support and cooperation. May encounter occasional difficulties in relationships with subordinates; not of serious nature, however.	☐ ☐ Strong leader who has willing support and cooperation. Rarely experiences even minor difficulties.	☐ ☐ Outstanding example of leadership. Always has enthusiastic support and cooperation of subordinates.
PERFORMANCE OF DEPARTMENT	☐ ☐ Requires close supervision. Often has problems and is behind schedule.	☐ ☐ Work occasionally lags. Requires more than normal supervision.	☐ ☐ Performs well with reasonable promptness under normal supervision.	☐ ☐ Consistently reliable under normal conditions. Department does special as well as required work with minimum supervision.	☐ ☐ Work always on schedule even under most difficult circumstances. Little or no supervision needed.
ORGANIZATION AND PLANNING OF WORK	☐ ☐ Frequently unable to assemble data for sequence of work.	☐ ☐ Can only follow existing procedures involving routine details.	☐ ☐ Capable of good planning of normal work, but needs guidance on major changes or projects.	☐ ☐ Needs little guidance in any assignment. Well organized.	☐ ☐ Clearly sees objectives. Planning and organization always outstanding.
DELEGATION OF RESPONSIBILITY	☐ ☐ Over burdens self with unnecessary detail giving rise to conflicts between subordinates as to responsibilities.	☐ ☐ Does not delegate wisely. Subordinates have too much or too little authority. Sometimes lacking a clear understanding of what is expected of him.	☐ ☐ Generally does an adequate job of delegating. Subordinates know in most cases just what their responsibilities are.	☐ ☐ Subordinates have better than average knowledge of their functions and relationships.	☐ ☐ Excellent judgment in delegating responsibility. Subordinates know what is expected of them at all times.

COMMENTS: This space to be used for additional remarks for any above or below standard performance. If below standard, remarks should state what specific action is being taken to improve rating.

SECTION C

1. In your opinion is employee properly placed in right job? Yes ___ No___ If "No," what type of work do you feel he is best suited for?_____
_____

2. Has employee expressed a desire for any other type of work with the Park District? Yes___ No___ If so, what position or in what department?_____

3. Do you consider the employee a candidate for promotion at this time? Yes___ No___ If "No," in the near future? Yes___ No___ To what job do you feel he could be advanced? _____

4. Has employee expressed dissatisfaction with his rate of promotion? Yes___ No___

5. What steps are presently being taken or are planned to prepare employee for promotion? (If "None" also state reason.) _____

OVERALL RATING ☐   ☐ ☐   ☐ ☐   ☐ ☐   ☐ ☐   ☐
                    UNSATISFACTORY   BELOW STANDARD   STANDARD   GOOD   EXCEPTIONAL

Employee's Signature _____ Date _____ Supervisor's Signature _____ Date_____

Figure 3-10 (Continued)

Worker Evaluation: Worth the Price?

Employee evaluation is time consuming and, thus, expensive. However, its potential value as a basis for permanent assignment, promotions, pay adjustments, employee training, validation of recruiting, and other personnel selection procedures justifies the cost if the information recorded is objective and valid.

The Diagnostic Post-appraisal Interview

Rating results must be communicated back from the supervisor-rater to the worker-ratee if employee resistance to rating is ever to be overcome. Certainly, secrecy in keeping rating results from the employee can only cause suspicion and distrust which shatters mutual understanding and respect. The post-appraisal interview should be approached from the standpoint of a private positive review of the worker's job performance with emphasis on correction and assistance to the worker rather than criticism and censure. Potentially, the diagnostic post-appraisal interview is that time when the supervisor-rater can demonstrate the value of personnel rating to the employee by accentuating the positive.

Data provided by the Flanagan-Burns Employee Performance Record provides excellent post-appraisal discussion information of both effective and ineffective employee job behavior and serves both worker guidance and job control requirements.

Maier[10] points out that post-appraisal interviews can be approached by the supervisor in three different ways: (1) the tell-and-sell approach, (2) the tell-and-listen style, or (3) the problem-solving type. Unless the supervisor is dealing with an uncooperative surly employee, he would most likely employ the tell-and-listen or problem-solving interview approaches which put stress on the supervisor's role as a listener. This encourages the worker to explain himself and work out solutions to his own problems. Such an outcome develops employee self-confidence and a feeling of trust and mutual respect between the worker and his supervisor.

One of the problems that must be overcome with a performance rating system is the tendency of a supervisor not to discuss an employee's work performance at any other time other than at the end of a performance rating period. In most cases a performance rating report is completed on the employee twice a year, but sometimes only once a year. A supervisor should not make the mistake of letting an employee go for that period of time without a discussion of those items which should be discussed at the time of occurrence. For instance, if an employee has been late to work three or four times, the supervisor should immediately talk with the employee rather than make a notation of all the lateness and identifying it much later during the time of the performance rating report. The performance report is an overall evaluation of the employee during a particular time period and should in no way hinder the supervisor in performing day-to-day responsibilities.

Employee Discipline

Positive worker self-discipline is reflected in the combination of the willingness to carry out supervisory instructions, abide by known work rules, and inhibit any personal behavior that might undermine the achievement of organizational objectives. Positive worker self-discipline usually results from fair and carefully established work rules and regulations, which are clearly understood and accepted.

Constructive work group discipline generally rests upon a foundation of well-established policies executed through consistent supervisory practices. This most desirable situation usually occurs only when there is a clear listing of reasonable work group rules and the penalties for their violation are clearly understood by all workers. A systematic method for instructing employees as to work rules and job performance standards must be established.

There must also be a well-established procedure for fact finding as a basis for prompt disciplinary decision making prior to the taking of any disciplinary action. It is important to note that the supervisor may be involved with a great many disciplinary actions, ranging from a minor reprimand to legal prosecution for illegal job-associated activity. While it is probable that other personnel in the organization hierarchy will also be involved in decisions regarding cases of severe breaches of discipline, nevertheless, it is imperative that the supervisor possess documented detailed records of worker behavior as a basis for the action taken. From the standpoint of positive motivation, supervisory warnings that prevent more serious breaches of discipline are preferable to more punitive measures. This is particularly true where the penalty visits hardship on the worker's family through economic deprivation.

Reprimands

In any reprimand situation, according to Sherwood, "The emphasis should be placed upon cooperative effort to avoid repetition of the incident rather than upon 'bawling out.' "[11] The employee should be given the opportunity to discuss the problem with the supervisor personally so that the worker has the chance to clear up any supervisory misunderstanding. In the majority of cases it is the way that the supervisor reprimands a worker that is more important than what he does. The supervisor must handle the situation with extreme caution or run the risk of terminating any future mutual trust, respect, or two-way communication with the employee.

When approaching the worker, the supervisor must clearly establish which rules or regulations were broken. The supervisor should also interpret the consequences of the employee's act or failure to act. The reprimand should be given by the supervisor in private, allowing the worker ample opportunity to make a positive response.

What about Transfer? Unfortunately, the military game of "shape up or ship out" has also been played in civilian governmental service and in private industry. While there are several legitimate uses for transfer, such as meeting fluctuating workloads or increasing worker versatility, "There is little that can be said for the quality of supervision which 'passes on' its problem cases."[12]

Labor Relations

The maintenance supervisor is rarely involved in making final decisions relative to the union contracts and policies. However, the importance of the maintenance supervisor's day-to-day relationship with the union should not be underestimated. The maintenance supervisor is on the firing line when it comes to handling grievances, taking disciplinary action, and adhering to other terms of the union agreement. Mistakes made at this point can be costly and this is precisely why supervisors and foremen must carry out management's policies and abide by the union contract to the letter.

Management Actions to Assist Supervisors in Labor Relations Job Descriptions should be developed by the park/recreation organization prior to entering into a collective bargaining agreement with the union. It is highly important that these job descriptions include the proviso that the employee may perform other tasks assigned. Such a provision in job descriptions, when included in the union agreement, guards against management being "boxed in" and unable to utilize services of employees when needed for emergency or non-emergency jobs not included in the job description.

A grievance procedure, which is simply a means for settling worker dissatisfactions through established channels should be developed by the park/recreation organization even if an employee union does not exist in the situation.

Supervisory training for functional union understanding should be provided by the park/recreation organization if there is to be the realistic expectation of supervisory success in handling union complaints and grievances.

Such a training program should include—

1. Familiarizing the supervisor with the collective bargaining laws of your state and local jurisdiction and keeping supervisory personnel aware of new legislation.
2. Developing detailed supervisory understanding of the local collective bargaining agreement so as to avoid mistakes in abiding by the terms of the union contract.
3. Familiarizing the supervisor with the local employee grievance procedure from the first step through the last.
4. The proper way for the supervisor to handle an employee grievance.

Grievances are important managerial problems and they demand prompt action, regardless of how trivial the complaint may appear from the factual side. A grievance is a sign that something is irritating a person. Low morale, lack of job satisfaction, and complaining are contagious. The first line supervisor is the key to locating symptoms of employee dissatisfaction. He must learn to be a good listener and to spot nonverbal complaints. Skill in interviewing and counseling will aid in finding the underlying causes of employee dissatisfaction. It should be recognized that behavior patterns may be symptoms of other problems unrelated to employment. Also, grievances, as expressed by the individual, often do not point to the heart of the problem. Management and union practices and employees' personality differences all have some effects on grievances.

Although there are always likely to be grievances wherever people are employed, competent managers can do much to prevent situations that precipitate grievances. (Prevention is the proper approach.)

Management must do the following:

a. anticipate grievances,

b. have a well-defined procedure for handling them,

c. take care of them promptly.

A four step approach for the proper handling of grievances utilized by the Aluminum Company of America[11] includes the following:

Receive the Grievance Properly   This includes listening intently, taking notes, and generally impressing the complainant with your concern, and, finally, either making a decision then or advising the worker when he can expect an answer from you.

Get the Facts   Gather all facts on the assumption that the case will have to be defended before an appeals board. Systematically check records that might dispute or support the facts as reported. Check personnel regulations. Verify the facts with other workers. Review the complaining employee's record. Reconcile any conflicting facts before making a decision.

Take Action   Any action that would make "right" any "wrong" situation caused by the supervisor or any other member of management might be included here—"going to bat" for a wronged employee if the facts warrant it or explaining to the worker why he was wrong if the facts indicate this. Remain calm and advise the worker how to proceed with the next step of the grievance procedure if he threatens to appeal. The supervisor should do nothing that would be detrimental to him at the hearing of the case. The supervisor should communicate in a dated written memorandum to his supervisor all facts in the situation.

Follow up   Involved here is the supervisor making certain that his decision or planned action resulting from the grievance has been carried out, thus minimizing the possibility of other grievances coming from the same source.

5. Familiarizing supervisors with the employee appeal procedure. Appeals arise from supervisory decisions, particularly those involving disciplinary penalties. When the employee does appeal a supervisory grievance decision, it is important for the supervisor to recognize that appeal boards usually require two types

of proof. These are identified by Pfiffner[14] as (1) specific evidence of offenses or work rule infractions at particular times, dates, and places, (2) assurance via facts and systematic records that the supervisor has exercised consistent efforts to warn, caution, help, and rehabilitate the worker.

In an appeals situation, the strength of the supervisor's case, in addition to his handling of the grievance, often rests upon his entire range of supervisory skills including communication, counselling, training, and evaluation habits. Inconsistencies in employee evaluation, sarcastic communications, prejudicial treatment, and failure to inform workers of appeal rights all work against the supervisor and invite the appeal board to reverse the supervisor's decision or reprimand the action.

Review Questions

1. What approaches might be helpful for recruiting capable skilled maintenance tradesmen for the recreation maintenance organization?

2. What is motivation?

3. Money has been identified as a temporary motivator. Identify and describe sound techniques or methods that have great potential as permanent motivators.

4. As a supervisor, how would you attempt to motivate each employee in your work group?

5. What single leadership style is best for motivating all employees?

6. Identify the advantages of interpersonal communication between the supervisor and the worker compared to written organizational communication from management to worker.

7. Employee orientation should include certain elements. What are these?

8. What are the basic principles of learning upon which the job trainer can rely?

9. Describe the relative effectiveness of telling and showing and the combination of telling and showing regarding the human reception and retention of information.

10. Describe the highly effective four-step pattern of instruction developed by industry during World War II.

11. As a supplement to training, explain the utility of maintenance operations manuals.

12. Reducing employee accidents rests largely upon what major factor?

13. Describe the scope of park/recreation occupational injuries as compared with the average of all industries.

14. What is the extent of injuries to park/recreational maintenance operations personnel as compared with total park/recreation occupational injuries?

15. What is OSHA? How does it influence local governmental public park/recreation maintenance employees?

16. Describe the problem of employee safety with temporary and

seasonal employees. Indicate what steps can be taken to minimize the problem.

17. Describe the minimum safety requirements recommended by the National Safety Council for the use of tools by maintenance personnel.

18. Personal protection equipment for maintenance personnel should include what equipment?

19. What is the purpose(s) of employee ratings?

20. Describe rater bias and prejudice. Indicate what the rater might do to avoid bias and prejudice.

21. The most common employee rating errors are leniency, the halo effect, the central tendency, contrast and association errors. Describe the cause and influence of each and indicate what the rater might do to minimize their effects.

22. Outline the advantages of using the Flanagan-Burns Employee Performance Record rather than a Trait-Oriented Employee Rating Form.

23. Describe the purpose and proper procedure of the Diagnostic Post-Appraisal Interview.

24. Outline the four-step approach that a supervisor may use in properly handling an employee grievance.

25. Describe the two basic requirements necessary to provide the foundation upon which constructive work group discipline can develop.

26. Describe the proper supervisory steps to be taken when reprimanding a worker and, also, the criteria to be followed to determine whether or not to transfer the reprimanded worker.

Notes to Chapter 3

1. James C. McChesney, "Personnel Policies—Including an Outline and Sample Personnel Policy Manual for Parks and Recreation Departments," *Management Aid Bulletin* no. 63 (Wheeling: National Recreation and Park Association, 1966), p. 40.

2. David McClelland, *Studies in Motivation* (New York: Appleton, Century, Crofts, 1955).

3. E. Ghiselli, M. Haire, and E. Lawler, *Managerial Thinking: An Int. Study* (New York: Wiley Company, 1966).

4. National Safety Council, *Public Employee Safety Guide—Parks and Recreation* (Chicago, 1974), pp. 4-5.

5. Ibid., p. 4.

6. Ibid., pp. 6-13.

7. Ibid., pp. 16-17.

8. David E. Sterle and Mary R. Duncan, *Supervision of Leisure Services* (San Diego: San Diego State University Press, 1973), p. 87.

9. John C. Flanagan and Robert K. Burns, "The Employee Performance Record: A New Appraisal and Development Tool," *Harvard Business Review,* September-October 1955, pp. 95-102.

10. R. R. Maier, *Principles of Human Relations,* 6th ed. (New York: John Wiley and Sons, 1959), pp. 403-9.

11. Frank P. Sherwood and Wallace H. Best, *Supervisory Methods in Municipal Administration* (Chicago: International City Managers Association, 1958), p. 223.

12. Ibid., p. 223

13. Aluminum Company of America, "A Four-Step Approach to Handling Grievances," *Effective Communication on the Job,* Joseph M. Dooher and Vivienne Marquis, eds. (New York: American Management Association, 1956), p. 207

14. John M. Pfiffner, *The Supervision of Personnel,* 2nd ed. (Englewood Cliffs, New Jersey: Prentice-Hall, Inc., 1958), p. 368.

Bibliography

American Management Association. "The Ten Commandments of Good Communications." Prepared by the Staff of the AMA Executive Communications Course, New York, 1955.

American Park and Recreation Society. *The Supervisor's Workshop.* Prepared and edited by the Staff of the National Foremans Institute, Waterford, Connecticut, 1968.

Buechner, Robert D. *Public Employee Unions—Organizations—A Manual for Park and Recreation Officials. Management Aid Bulletin no. 81.* Arlington, Virginia. National Recreation and Park Association, 1969.

Flanagan, John C. and Burns, Robert K. "The Employee Performance Record: A New Appraisal and Development Tool." *Harvard Business Review,* September-October 1955.

Herzberg, Fredrick. *"One More Time—How Do You Motivate Employees." Harvard Business Review,* January-February 1968.

Horney, Robert L. *Administrative Development Series, Part I and Part II. National Recreation Association Management Aid Bulletins* nos. 91 and 92. Arlington, Virginia, 1972.

International City Managers Association. *Effective Supervisory Practices.* International City Managers Association, Chicago, 1965.

Kloske, Robert E. "Supervising Maintenance Personnel—Communication, Discipline-Evaluation." A monograph prepared for the Park and Recreation Maintenance Management School, North Carolina State University. Raleigh, 1972.

Mayfield, Harold. "In Defense of Performance Appraisals." *Harvard Business Review,* March-April, 1960.

McChesney, James C. *Personnel Policies—Including an Outline and Sample Personnel Policy Manual for Park and Recreation Departments.* National Recreation and Park Association Management Aid Bulletin no. 63. Arlington, Virginia, 1966.

Owens, Rhodell E. "Supervising Maintenance Personnel—Personnel Manuals." A monograph prepared for the Park and Recreation Maintenance Management School, North Carolina State University. Raleigh, 1973.

Owens, Rhodell E. "Supervising Maintenance Personnel—Career Development—Training, Education and Employee Evaluation, Guidance and Counselling." A monograph prepared for the Park and Recreation Maintenance Management School, North Carolina State University. Raleigh, 1974.

Paul, William; Robinson, Keith; Herzberg, Fredrick. "Job Enrichment Pay-Off," *Harvard Business Review,* March-April, 1969.

Puryear, Jack. "Supervising Maintenance Personnel—Understanding Personnel, Motivation, Incentives and Morale." A monograph prepared for the Park and Recreation Maintenance Management School, North Carolina State University. Raleigh, 1972.

Sterle, David E., and Duncan, Mary E. *Supervision of Leisure Services.* San Diego State University Press, San Diego, 1973.

Sternloff, Robert E. "Conducting Education Programs for Leisure

Service Personnel." A position paper prepared for and adopted by the National Council of the National Recreation and Park Association, Arlington, Virginia, 1973.

Strong, Lydia. "Do You Know How to Listen?" *Effective Communication on the Job.* Joseph M. Dooher and Vivienne Marquis, eds. American Management Association, New York, 1956.

Sherwood, Frank P. and Best, Wallace H. *Supervisory Methods in Municipal Administration.* International City Managers Association, Chicago, 1958.

Weber, George O. ed. and Fincham, Michael W. *A Basic Manual for Physical Plant Administration.* The Association of Physical Plant Administrators of Universities and Colleges, Suite 510, Dupont Circle, Washington, D.C., 1974.

Appendix

Index to Visual Aids

The following list of films and audio-visual aids for park and recreation maintenance management was selected from a longer and more comprehensive list compiled for the broader field of environmental sanitation and maintenance management education and training. This comprehensive listing and index to visual aids was developed by the:

Environmental Management Association
1710 Drew Street
Clearwater, Florida 33515

Permission for use of this Environmental Management Association material was granted by Harold C. Rowe, Executive Director.

While a listing does not constitute endorsement of any particular film, the authors are confident that this index will prove especially valuable as a training aid in the search for more efficient maintenance operations and better employee relations.

Orders for films, whether on a free loan, rental, or sales basis, should be made *directly* to the source indicated for each film. **127**

Table of Contents

How To Use This Index

1. Films are grouped by subject matter.
2. Films are also indexed alphabetically by title.
3. Sources of films are identified in each film listing by alphabetical code. The source index of distributors is contained on pages 153-159.
4. Symbols used in film listings to indicate size and type of film are:

   MP — Motion Picture
   FS — Film Strip
   TR — Overhead Transparency
   TFR — Television Film Recording
   VTR — Video Tape Recording (closed circuit television)
   16mm — 16 millimeter film
   35mm — 35 millimeter filmstrip or slides

A sample listing and symbol interpretation is as follows:

   THE WINNING COMBINATION
   MP, 16mm, Sound, Color, 10 Mins. Tackles the difficult supervisory job of motivating subordinates to cooperate with the company's efforts to reduce waste and control costs. (BNA)

LINE 1: Title of film (and Film Number if available)
LINE 2: Type and size of film, sound or silent, black & white or color, and running time in minutes; description of film contents with the film source following (in parenthesis).

5. Films are classified under the heading in which it is felt they have the greatest bearing.

General Notes on Film Usage

1. Rental and purchase prices of films fluctuate and, therefore, are not included.
2. Films for loan or rental should be requested well in advance of the scheduled showing. When ordering, include alternate showing dates as well as the Film Number (if applicable).
3. Check your projection equipment before ordering films. Be sure you have the right equipment for the right film (i.e., film-strips cannot be shown on motion picture equipment) before ordering films. Improper equipment or planning will damage and delay your program and purpose.

Index to Films by Subject

Communications

AVOIDING COMMUNICATION BREAKDOWN

MP, 16mm, Sound, Color, 24 Mins. Calls attention to warning signals of defective communication. (BNA)

CHANGING ATTITUDES THROUGH COMMUNICATION

MP, 16mm, Sound, Color, 24 Mins. Understanding change will help create acceptance of new policies. (BNA)

COMMUNICATION FEEDBACK

MP, 16mm, Sound, Color, 24 Mins. Shows that effective communication is impossible if feedback is ignored, distorted, avoided, or simply not perceived. (BNA)

THE EXTRA STEP

MP, 16mm, Sound, Color, 33 Mins. Emphasizes good business principles in telephone usage. (AT&T)

HOW TO IMPROVE MANAGEMENT COMMUNICATIONS

I. *Motivation by Communication*
MP, 16mm, Sound, B&W, 26 Mins. Explores communications as an integral part of the motivating process. (AMA)

HOW TO IMPROVE MANAGEMENT COMMUNICATIONS

II. *Communications Downward*
MP, 16mm, Sound, B&W, 20 Mins. Develops an understanding of the importance of downward communications, particularly in increasing employee confidence and awareness. (AMA)

HOW TO IMPROVE MANAGEMENT COMMUNICATIONS

III. *Communications Upward*
MP, 16mm, Sound, B&W, 26 Mins. Identifies and analyzes common blocks to upward communications; helps apply a new approach in conveying information to top management. (AMA)

HOW TO IMPROVE MANAGEMENT COMMUNICATIONS

V. *On Listening*
MP, 16mm, Sound, B&W, 11 Mins. Designed to challenge your listening ability with an actual test. (AMA)

HOW TO IMPROVE MANAGEMENT COMMUNICATIONS

VII. *How to Think and Speak on Your Feet*
MP, 16mm, Sound, B&W, 28 Mins. Deals with the dynamics of communication with others. (AMA)

IF AN ELEPHANT ANSWERS

MP, 16mm, Sound, Color, 26 Mins. Demonstrates the hazards that many businesses can face due to inept or careless telephone usage. (AT&T)

A MESSAGE TO NO ONE (MIS–748)

MP, 16mm, Sound, Color, 24 Mins. An adult philosophical study of "listening" and not listening habits; failure to hear through inattention, boredom, and discourtesy. (NMAC)

PERSON TO PERSON COMMUNICATION

MP, 16mm, Sound, Color, 14 Mins. Analyzes the major barriers in face-to-face communication; specific practical methods for overcoming them. (RFI)

PRODUCTION 5118 (MIS–746)
MP, 16mm, Sound, Color, 30 Mins. The study of one man's attempts to clearly communicate his ideas to others. (NMAC)

Community Relations

COMPANY MANNERS
MP, 16mm, Sound, Color, 30 Mins. Points out that cooperation of employees in every phase of operation is essential for maintaining good relations between the company and its publics. (AAR)

Detergents

HOW WE CAN CLEAN UP DERMA-TITIS
FS, 35mm, Sound, Color, 12 Mins. Skin care safety provisions for fighting this occupational disease. (SDA)

THE PURSUIT OF CLEANLINESS
MP, 16mm, Sound, Color, 14-1/2 Mins. Explains the evolution and importance of cleanliness, how soap and detergents work, their contributions to environmental health. (SDA)

Food Sanitation

BASIC SANITATION
Slides, Sound, Color, 15 Mins. Discusses the prevention of spoilage and foreign materials in commercially prepared foods. (GPC)

DINING ROOM SANITATION
MP, 16mm, Sound, Color, 8 Mins. Shows techniques of sanitary food handling in the dining room and stresses the responsibility of personnel both to look and to be clean. (NEM)

KITCHEN HABITS (M–148g)
MP, 16mm, Sound, Color, 12 Mins. Shows the importance of developing good habits relating to food sanitation. (NMAC)

General Interest

HERITAGE OF SPLENDOR
MP, 16mm, Sound, Color, 18 Mins. Emphasizes the importance of America's outdoor areas as a natural resource for recreation and the citizen's obligation to preserve them. (KAB)

OLD AS THE HILLS
MP, 16mm, Sound, Color, 28 Mins. Depicts man's progress through the years and his dependence upon nature for all that he has discovered in developing our modern way of life. (NOR)

Handicapped Personnel

EMPLOYEES ONLY (#411)
MP, 16mm, Sound, B&W, 13-1/2 Mins. Dramatically documents the completely successful integration of the physically handicapped into all

phases of a large company's activities. (SMI)

Health

IMPORTANCE OF SANITATION
MP, 16mm, Color, 22 Mins. Shows the importance of sanitation in society today, of people employed in sanitation and their critical role in the continuing battle for health and cleanliness. (ISSA)

IT MUST BE THE NEIGHBORS (M-1171)
MP, 16mm, Sound, Color, 14 Mins. Emphasizes the relationship between good premises sanitation and freedom from mosquitoes, flies, cockroaches, and rodents. (NMAC)

OCCUPATIONAL DISEASES (FMIS-672)
FS, 35mm, Sound, Color. Classification and description of such occupational diseases as lead poisoning, silicosis, and dermatoses are discussed. (NMAC)

PUBLIC HEALTH (Series No. 11550)
FS, 35mm, Color. A survey of the scope of public health centers at local, national, and international levels emphasizes the concept that germs are everybody's business. (EBEC)

PUBLIC HEALTH ASPECTS OF THE OCCUPATIONAL ENVIRONMENT
FS, 35mm, Sound, Color. Discusses health hazards faced by workers in various occupations and suggests the implications of these hazards for the public official. (NMAC)

THE WATCH ON HEALTH (M-1061)
MP, 16mm, Sound, Color, 13-1/2 Mins. Describes briefly the historic high points and current programs of the Public Health Service. (NMAC)

YOU AND GOOD HEALTH
FS, 35mm, Sound, Color, 7 Mins. Illustrates the need to keep physically fit for peak performance. (VLI)

Housekeeping—General

CASE OF THE CLUTTERED CORNER
MP, 16mm, Sound, B&W, 10 Mins. How clutter and poor housekeeping contributes to accidents. (NSC)

DOWN AT THE OFFICE
MP, 16mm, Sound, B&W, 10 Mins. Discusses importance of good housekeeping in offices and commercial building operations. (NSC)

HOUSEKEEPING's PLACE ON THE TEAM
FS, 35mm, Sound, Color, 7 Mins. Relates the need for different departments and how housekeeping fits in to complete the team. (VLI)

KEEP IT CLEAN FOR SAFETY'S SAKE
Slides, Color, Script provided. Discusses housekeeping chores such as keeping aisles clear, eliminating tripping hazards, storing tools and rags. (NSC)

Housekeeping—Hotel

THE MAGIC TOUCH Part I
FS, 35mm, Sound, Color, 15 Mins.
Shows the importance of the maid's
role in a successful operation; correct
procedures following standard practices are detailed. (AHMA)

THE MAGIC TOUCH Part II
FS, 35mm, Sound, Color, 15 Mins.
Continues in detail the making up of
rooms and shows how to handle
special and emergency situations.
(AHMA)

Human Relations

EXAMINING THE WILL TO WORK
MP, 35mm, Sound, Color, 14 Mins.
Motivational documentary for those
who wish to encourage self-evaluation, continuing education, on-the-job
training and self-development at all
levels. (RFI)

GETTING AHEAD: THE ROAD TO
SELF-DEVELOPMENT
MP, 16mm, Sound, Color, 28 Mins.
Motivational documentary for those
who wish to encourage self-evaluation, continuing education, on-the-job
training and self-development at all
levels. (RFI)

THE HERITAGE OF THE UNCOMMON
MAN
MP, 16mm, Sound, Color, 28 Mins.
Encourages people to take a bigger
look at their potential and their op-
portunities. (BNA)

I JUST WORK HERE
MP, 16mm, Sound, Color, 17 Mins.
This attitude-formation film encourages your people to create a more favorable organizational image and improve their attitudes toward the job.
(RFI)

JUDGING PEOPLE
MP, 16mm, Sound, B&W, 23 Mins.
Explains and illustrates the process of
reaching more accurate estimates of
ability, personality, intelligence, character, and potential. (RFI)

MEANINGS ARE IN PEOPLE
MP, 16mm, Sound, Color, 24 Mins.
Demonstrates how misunderstandings
occur by presenting reenactments in
typical at-work situations. (BNA)

1004 SUTTON ROAD (MIS 747)
MP, 16mm, Sound, Color, 30 Mins.
Describes how attitude toward a job
influences the degree of success
achieved. (NMAC)

PLACING THE RIGHT MAN ON THE
JOB (OE-156)
MP, 16mm, Sound, B&W, 13 Mins.
Cases of five different workers, unsatisfactory in particular jobs, who are
reassigned to other jobs more suitable
to their abilities and capacities. (GSA)

THAT'S NOT MY JOB
MP, 16mm, Sound, Color, 26 Mins.
Builds cooperation by encouraging
people to learn how their work relates
to the work of others and how together they contribute to the purpose
of the organization. (RFI)

YOU, YOURSELF, INCORPORATED
MP, 16mm, Sound, Color, 24 Mins.
Demonstrates that the only real development is self-development; motivated men make progress and profits. (BNA)

Institute of Sanitation Management

WHAT IS ISM?
Slides, 35mm, Color, Script provided. A documentary on the history, concept and services of the Institute of Sanitation Management. (ISM)

Man and the Environment—General

CITIES IN CRISIS: A MATTER OF SURVIVAL
MP, 16mm, Sound, Color, 18 Mins. Examines causes, effects, and possible solutions to the problem of air, water, and land pollution. Stresses threats to health and existence of man. (UEVA)

CITIES IN CRISIS: WHAT'S HAPPENING
MP, 16mm, Sound, Color, 21 Mins. Exposes the crass and ugly in contemporary and urban life. Deals with traffic jams, smog, and ghettos in the megalopolis. (UEVA)

THE HOUSE OF MAN—OUR CHANGING ENVIRONMENT
MP, 16mm, Sound, Color, 17 Mins. Reveals the waste of resources in urban and rural areas; comparison of progress through wasteful methods and intelligent preservation of resources. (EBEC)

LET'S KEEP AMERICA BEAUTIFUL
MP, 16mm, Sound, Color, 14 Mins. Presents the litter problem against a backdrop of some of the country's most beautiful landscapes. (KAB)

THE LITTERBUG
MP, 16mm, Sound, Color, 8 Mins. Donald Duck is the star of the picture which shows various types of litterbugs in action. (KAB)

NO TIME FOR UGLINESS
MP, 16mm, Sound, Color, 26-1/2 Mins. Some good and not-so-good features of American Cities. (AIA)

THE THIRD POLLUTION (No. AM–1904)
MP, 16mm, Sound, Color, 23 Mins. Depicts existing practices of solid waste disposal and describes various approaches to improving these practices. (NMAC)

WEALTH OF THE WASTELAND
MP, 16mm, Sound, Color, 27 Mins. Story of research to recycle waste minerals and metals from domestic trash and refuse. (BOM)

Water Pollution

CLEAN WATER IS EVERYBODY'S BUSINESS (FMIS–825)
FS, 35mm, Silent, Color. Describes development of the nation's water pollution problem, measures taken to correct the situation. (NMAC)

IT'S YOUR DECISION—CLEAN WATER
MP, 16mm, Sound, Color, 14-1/2 Mins. An up-to-the-minute report on

the nation's water crisis; the effect of people, prosperity, and products. (SDA)

LIVING WITH TODAY'S WATER
MP, 16mm, Sound, Color, 26 Mins. Explores the causes and effects on to-day's water pollution; how a water-works operation removes some of it. (MIPS)

THE NEW RIVER
MP, 16mm, Sound, Color, 23 Mins. Shows the use of water in industry and how it returns to the stream or river in a usable condition. (APA)

PENNIES FOR HEALTH
MP, 16mm, Sound, Color, 13-1/2 Mins. Community project for pollu-tion control. (NWI)

PIPELINE TO THE CLOUDS
MP, 16mm, Sound, Color, 33 Mins. Comprehensive exploration of the sources of water, water treatment, and ways of supplying an abundant quantity of water. (NAPHCC)

PURE WATER AND PUBLIC HEALTH
MP, 16mm, Sound, Color, 28 Mins. Dramatizes the water supply prob-lems in a hypothetical community. (CIPRA)

THE RIVER MUST LIVE
MP, 16mm, Sound, Color, 21 Mins. A frightening study of what happens when a river is overloaded with more waste than it can absorb and the con-sequences to those who have to de-pend on it. (SOC)

TROUBLED WATERS
MP, 16mm, Sound, Color, 28 Mins. Pollution in the U.S. (USSPWC)

WATER—WEALTH OR WORRY FOR AMERICA
MP, 16mm, Sound, Color, 24 Mins. Emphasizes long-term advance plan-ning necessary for enough water; facts on industrial usage; the growing de-mand for water and restricted usage. (CIPRA)

Air Pollution

AIR OF DISASTER (M-1419-X)
MP, 16mm, Sound, Color, 50 Mins. A visit to the U. S. Public Health Service Air Pollution Laboratory at Cincin-nati, Ohio, demonstrates research on auto exhaust emissions. (NMAC)

AIR POLLUTION AND YOU (F-1528-X)
FS, 34mm, Color, Guide provided. Outlines the basic problem of air pol-lution, its principal effects on health and property, and some approaches to its control. (NMAC)

THE ANSWER IS CLEAR
MP, 16mm, Sound, Color, 14 Mins. Discusses the aspects of air pollution and progress made in reducing ex-haust smoke and odor. (MTPS)

BEWARE OF ILL WINDS (F-1745-X)
FS, 35mm, Color, Guide provided. Describes the regional approach to controlling air pollution under the provisions of the Federal Air Quality Act. (NMAC)

BEWARE THE WIND (M-1707-X)
MP, 16mm, Sound, Color, 22 Mins. The origins and evolution of the world wide affliction of dirty air not

only in American cities but in various European capitals as well. (NMAC)

ILL WINDS ON A SUNNY DAY (MIS-984)

MP, 16mm, Sound, Color, 29 Mins. Traces the growth of America from a rural agricultural society to the urbanized, industrial nation of today. Demonstrates the problem of air pollution. (NMAC)

IT'S THE ONLY AIR WE'VE GOT (M-1431-X)

MP, 16mm, Sound, Color, 25 Mins. Tells the story of Pittsburgh's continuing fight against air pollution. (NMAC)

ON A CLEAR DAY YOU CAN ALMOST SEE TERMINAL TOWER (M-1712-X)

MP, 16mm, Sound, Color, 22 Mins. Documentary studying Cleveland's air quality problem in a frank and low-keyed manner. (NMAC)

OUR AIR

MP, 16mm, Sound, Color, 18 Mins. Explains the major causes and describes the various efforts now being made to minimize air pollution. (MIPS)

THE POISONED AIR (M-1418-X)

MP, 16mm, Sound, Color, 50 Mins. Representatives from the motor vehicle industry explain Detroit's position with regard to air pollution from cars, trucks, and buses. (NMAC)

SOMETHING IN THE WIND (TFR-1308-X)

MP, 16mm, Sound, B&W, 30 Mins. This three-part documentary presents a compelling picture of pollution in the twin Kansas City areas. (NMAC)

THIS BUSINESS OF AIR (No. M-1420-X)

MP, 16mm, Sound, Color, 30 Mins. A documentary on air pollution in the St. Louis area. (NMAC)

TO CLEAR THE AIR

MP, 16mm, Sound, Color, 22 Mins. The roles that industry, government and individuals can play in the fight for cleaner air. (APE)

WITH EACH BREATH (M-1430-X)

MP, 16mm, Sound, Color, 30 Mins. Against a background of the general air pollution problem, the film depicts New York State's approach to air pollution. (NMAC)

Maintenance—General

AUTO-SCRUBBERS

MP, 16mm, Sound, Color, 9 Mins. Discussion by building operations staff members about two types of auto-scrubbers. (VA)

THE BIG DIFFERENCE

MP, 16mm, Sound, Color, 17 Mins. Research behind maintenance products. (SCJ)

CARPET LIFE IS IN THE CARE

FS, 35mm, Sound, Color, 10 Mins. Classification of carpet dirts, methods of removal on a daily and periodic basis. (HSCE)

FOR SAFETY'S SAKE

MP, 16mm, Sound, B&W, 15 Mins.

How to use, inspect, and care for portable power drills, grinders, saws, and electrical tools. (AAR)

HAND TOOLS
Slides, Color, Script provided. Illustrates carrying, storing, maintaining, and using common hand tools. (NSC)

HOW TO SELECT THE RIGHT GRINDING WHEEL
MP, 16mm, Sound, Color, 30 Mins. Grinding wheel markings clearly explained; also step-by-step procedure in selecting wheels. (NOR)

IT'S THE BREAKS (#2302)
MP, 16mm, Sound, Color, 13 Mins. The story of LEXAN polycarbonate sheet for glazing, the toughest transparent material ever developed; benefits for schools, plants, and public buildings against vandalism. (SMI)

MAINTENANCE PAINTING: AN ENGINEERING APPROACH TO LOWER COSTS
MP, 16mm, Sound, Color, 26 Mins. A discussion on the importance of pre-planning and design to insure lower paint maintenance costs. (HI)

MAXIMUM SECURITY
MP, 16mm, Sound, Color, 10 Mins. Illustrates the role of locking devices in glass doors as they relate to the security of a building. (ARMC)

SEWER CLEANING AND MAINTENANCE
MP, 16mm, Sound, Color, 35 Mins. Preventive maintenance program on main sewer lines. (RMC)

SYSTEMS, SAVINGS AND YOU
MP, 16mm, Sound, Color, 12 Mins. Lays the foundation for a study of proper maintenance techniques in general. (KNA)

Maintenance—Facilities

BETTER WASHROOM MAINTENANCE
MP, 16mm, Sound, Color, 9 Mins. Illustrates importance for establishing regular programs of washroom maintenance. (SCJ)

GREENER ON YOUR SIDE
MP, 16mm, Sound, Color, 23-1/2 Mins. A professional approach on methods and products used in grounds care, especially grass. (HI)

HEY CHARLIE, IT'S TIME TO WASH THE WALLS AGAIN
FS, 35mm, Sound, Color, 7-1/2 Mins. A "how to" production to show the user how he can bring speed and efficiency to a disagreeable and time-consuming task. (GWC)

AN OUNCE OF PREVENTION
MP, 16mm, Sound, Color, 8 Mins. Maintenance short cuts to keep floors, walls, desks, and other surfaces clean. (SCJ)

Maintenance—Floors

CARE AND MAINTENANCE OF CONCRETE, MARBLE AND TERRAZZO FLOORS
MP, 16mm, Sound, Color, 19 Mins.

Shows the proper procedure for taking care of hard surface floors. (MCP)

THE CARE AND MAINTENANCE OF RESILIENT TILE FLOORS

FS, 35mm, Sound, Color, 12 Mins. Tells the story of the care and maintenance of 5 types of resilient floors. (MCP)

THE CLEANING AND MAINTENANCE OF RESILIENT FLOORS

MP, 16mm, Sound, Color, 22 Mins. Methods of cleaning and maintenance of resilient floors; sweeping and mopping techniques, operating floor machines and vacuums. (ISSA)

DAILY FLOOR MAINTENANCE

MP, 16mm, Sound, Color, 9 Mins. Various daily and periodic floor cleaning situations experienced by the building operations janitor. (VA)

FINISHING GYM FLOORS

MP, 16mm, Sound, Color, 8 Mins. Procedures for removing old finishes; sealing, finishing, and maintaining gym floors. (SCJ)

FINISHING THE FLOOR

Slides, Color, Script provided. Illustrates proper maintenance procedures for the application of a floor finish. (SCJ)

THE FINISHING TOUCH

MP, 16mm, Sound, Color, 8 Mins. Illustrates procedures and equipment for stripping and finishing resilient floors. (SCJ)

FLOOR FINISHING

VTR, 6 Mins. Shows a technique suitable for the application of a non-

buffable floor finish; the spray buff technique for touch-up of scuff marks is demonstrated. (AIR)

FLOOR MACHINES

MP, 16mm, Sound, Color, 5-1/2 Mins. Shows the safe use of a standard floor machine and includes maintenance and storage procedures. (VA)

FLOOR REFINISHING

MP, 16mm, Sound, Color, 24 Mins. Outlines the two most common refinishing techniques. (VA)

FLOOR SEALING

VTR, 5 Mins. A procedure for applying a liquid sealer to a prepared floor is detailed; pitfalls to be avoided are explained fully; two methods of application are demonstrated. (AIR)

FLOORS THAT SAY WELCOME

FS, 35mm, Sound, Color, 14 Mins. Deals with basic fundamentals of intelligent use and care of equipment in maintaining resilient floors. (GWC)

FLOOR STRIPPING

VTR, 16 Mins. Two methods of stripping a floor are demonstrated; the double bucket method and the watering can/wet vacuum method. (AIR)

FLOOR WAXING

VTR, 8 Mins. A complete procedure for waxing a floor with a buffable, slip-resistant wax is demonstrated. (AIR)

THE INSTALLATION, FINISHING AND MAINTENANCE OF GYM FLOORS

FS, 35mm, Sound, Color, 10 Mins. The correct installation of gym floors, the procedure for finishing, including painting of the lines, and the maintenance of a gym floor after it is properly sealed. (MCP)

MAINTAINING BUFFABLE FLOOR FINISHES

Slides, Color, Script provided. Illustrates proper maintenance procedures to correctly maintain buffable floor finishes. (SCJ)

MODERN FLOOR MAINTENANCE

MP, 16mm, Sound, Color, 15 Mins. Techniques of resilient floor maintenance, including care of equipment. (WGL)

PREPARING THE FLOOR

Slides, Color, Script provided. Illustrates proper maintenance procedure for preparing floors for finish application. (SCJ)

PROPER CARE OF HARD FLOORS

FS, 35mm, Sound, Color, 30 Mins. Guide to treatment and maintenance of all types of masonry, brick, and stone flooring. (HSCE)

PROPER CARE OF RESILIENT FLOORS

FS, 35mm, Sound, Color, 20 Mins. Defines types of resilient floors, the tools and equipment needed in sealing, waxing and maintenance, and the proper cleaning procedure. (HSCE)

PROPER CARE OF WOOD FLOORS

FS, 35mm, Sound, Color, 30 Mins. Complete steps for scrubbing, refinishing and sealing gymnasiums. (HSCE)

SCOTCH-BRITE SYSTEMS

FS, 35mm, Sound, Color, 20 Mins. Offers good information on the spray cleaning method of floor maintenance. (3M)

SPRAY BUFFING FOR MAINTAINING FLOOR FINISHES

Slides, Color, Script provided. Proper maintenance procedures for spray buffing. (SCJ)

THE TREATMENT AND MAINTENANCE OF CONCRETE FLOORS

FS, 35mm, Sound, Color, 12 Mins. Illustrates the proper method of cleaning, etching and sealing concrete floors and maintenance of those floors after they have been sealed. (MCP)

YOUR TERRAZZO OR OXYCHLORIDE FLOOR AND HOW TO MAINTAIN IT

FS, 35mm, Sound, Color, 12 Mins. Shows the installation of terrazzo floors, the proper method of cleaning, sealing and waxing of these floors and the maintenance of them after they are put to use. (MCP)

Personnel Management

CALL 'EM ON THE CARPET

MP, 16mm, Sound, B&W, 12 Mins. Covers the important matter of correcting faults without incurring ill will. (AAR)

A CASE OF INSUBORDINATION (4 Parts)

MP, 16mm, Sound, Color, 20 Mins. each. One incident as it is perceived by the employee, the supervisor, a witness, and an arbitrator. (RFI)

THE ENGINEERING OF AGREEMENT
MP, 16mm, Sound, Color, 21 Mins. Demonstrates both directive and non-directive techniques that are basic to obtaining cooperation and handling of differences of opinions. (RFI)

EVERY MINUTE COUNTS (OE 161)
MP, 16mm, Sound, B&W, 10 Mins. Problems a new supervisor has handling lateness, loafing, and absenteeism; and how he learns to deal with individual cases. (GSA)

FRAGILE—HANDLE FEELINGS WITH CARE
MP, 16mm, Sound, B&W, 12 Mins. How workers react to various changes, orders and safety rules. (AAR)

GET A GRIP ON YOURSELF
MP, 16mm, Sound, B&W, 15 Mins. Motivational film showing how feelings and emotions can undermine determination. (AAR)

THE MARVELOUS MOUSETRAP
MP, 16mm, Sound, Color, 24 Mins. There are vital relationships between the quality of each individual's work, the size of company profits, and the job security of all employees. (BNA)

THE MOTIVATION TO WORK
I. *The Modern Meaning of Efficiency*
MP, 16mm, Sound, Color, 25 Mins. Explains why it is no longer efficient to break down jobs into components so simple that "even a child could do it." (BNA)

THE MOTIVATION TO WORK
II. *KITA, or What Have You Done For Me Lately?*
MP, 16mm, Sound, Color, 25 Mins. An in-depth analysis of what the "hygiene" portion of the "motivation-hygiene" theory actually is. (BNA)

THE MOTIVATION TO WORK
III. *Job Enrichment in Action*
MP, 16mm, Sound, Color, 25 Mins. Solution to the motivation problems; demonstrations on how it is done. (BNA)

THE MOTIVATION TO WORK
IV. *Building a Climate for Individual Growth*
MP, 16mm, Sound, Color, 25 Mins. Analysis of real growth as compared with mere status symbols as measures of advancement. (BNA)

THE MOTIVATION TO WORK
V. *The ABC Man: The Manager in Mid-Career*
MP, 16mm, Sound, Color, 25 Mins. Helps to identify and to overcome the problems of the manager faced with mid-career obsolescence. (BNA)

THE NEW TRUCK DILEMMA
MP, 16mm, Sound, Color, 25 Mins. Gets the vital message of fairness in decision-making across to your people, using the powerful tool of role-playing in case study. (BNA)

PEOPLE DON'T RESIST CHANGE
MP, 16mm, Sound, Color, 22 Mins. Tells management how to make needed changes in work procedures by enlisting the cooperation of those affected. (BNA)

THE REAL SECURITY

MP, 16mm, Sound, Color, 24 Mins. Illustrates the cause and cures of "mental retirement" and organizational lethargy. (BNA)

SHOWDOWN (M-1213)

MP, 16mm, Sound, Color, 13 Mins. An "open-end" film presenting the problematical situation of the new young supervisor and the older marginal worker. (NMAC)

SOMETHING TO WORK FOR

MP, 16mm, Sound, Color, 30 Mins. Reveals what work means to people and how managers can motivate employees to improve productivity and raise work standards. (RFI)

THE TROUBLE WITH ARCHIE

MP, 16mm, Sound, Color, 23 Mins. Attacks the problems behind job assignments that fail; discusses perceptual differences and their influence on work relations and job performance. (RFI)

Pest Control

AREA POISONING [M-37.1-f(2)]

MP, 16mm, Sound, B&W, 9 Mins. Discusses the uses of such rodenticides as red squill, ANTU, arsenic trioxide. (NMAC)

BIOLOGY AND CONTROL OF THE COCKROACH (M-426)

MP, 16mm, Sound, Color, 14 Mins. Recognition and control of the cockroach; new insecticides for the control of cockroaches which are resistant to chlordane. (NMAC)

BIOLOGY AND CONTROL OF DOMESTIC FLIES (M-628)

MP, 16mm, Sound, Color, 15 Mins. Public health importance, biology, environmental control of common species of domestic flies. (NMAC)

BIOLOGY AND CONTROL OF DOMESTIC MOSQUITOES (M-357)

MP, 16mm, Sound, Color, 22 Mins. Stresses the need for control of domestic mosquitoes. (NMAC)

CHEMICAL BIOCIDES

MP, 16mm, Sound, Color, 6 Mins. Illustrates the lethal effects of a chemical pesticide. (TGFC)

ENEMIES OF MAN

MP, 16mm, Sound, B&W, 20 Mins. Live action pictures of household pests. (WKPC)

FLY CONTROL THROUGH BASIC SANITATION (4-090)

MP, 16mm, Sound, Color, 9 Mins. Shows conditions which favor fly breeding and outlines specific procedures for control. (NMAC)

GETTING THE BUGS OUT

MP, 16mm, Sound, Color, 9 Mins. The insect problem—where to look for them and how to eliminate them. (SCJ)

HEALTH HAZARDS OF PESTICIDES (M-204)

MP, 16mm, Sound, Color, 14 Mins. Emphasizes the potential public health hazards resulting from the widespread use of pesticides. (NMAC)

MOSQUITO AND ITS CONTROL
MP, 16mm, Sound, Color, 11 Mins. Details of the mosquito's anatomy and its breeding and feeding habits. (CIF)

PESTICIDES—FUNDAMENTALS   OF PROPER APPLICATION (#758)
MP, 16mm, Sound, Color, 16 Mins. Outlines the basic working parts of spray equipment from the tank to the nozzle. (SMI)

RAT KILLING [M-37.1-f(1)]
MP, 16mm, Sound, B&W, 13 Mins. Emphasizes three aspects of rat control—sanitation techniques, rat-proofed buildings, and rat killing. (NMAC)

RATPROOFING (M-37.1e)
MP, 16mm, Sound, B&W, 10 Mins. Explains methods and materials to be used in the ratproofing of buildings. (NMAC)

RATS DEFY MAN
MP, 16mm, Sound, 10 Mins. How rats enter and infest buildings. (WKPC)

RATS, MICE AND YOU (2 Parts)
MP, 16mm, Sound, Color, 20 Mins. Covers habits and characteristics of rats and mice; shows control methods. (FWS)

SANITATION TECHNIQUES IN RAT CONTROL (M-37.1d)
MP, 16mm, Sound, B&W, 12 Mins. Explains the importance of controlling rats by cutting down their food supply; suggests various methods of garbage and refuse storage and removal. (NMAC)

Plant Layout and Construction

INCINERATION (M-353)
MP, 16mm, Sound, Color, 13 Mins. Discusses principles of incineration. (NMAC)

LITTER NO MORE
MP, 16mm, Sound, Color, 8 Mins. Demonstrates mobilization, plant installation, maintenance, and pick up for dumping refuse containers. (MHI)

MUNICIPAL   SEWAGE   TREATMENT PROCESSES (M-6)
MP, 16mm, Sound, B&W, 13 Mins. Explains processes of sewage treatment. (NMAC)

REFUSE   DISPOSAL   BY   SANITARY LANDFILL (M-228)
MP, 16mm, Sound, Color, 13 Mins. Construction, equipment, selection of sites, operation of sanitary landfills. (NMAC)

TRICKLING FILTERS
MP, 16mm, Sound, Color, 16 Mins. Construction of a trickling filter using little hand labor without tile breakage. (NCSA)

Safety—General

ACCIDENTS DON'T HAPPEN
MP, 16mm, Sound, B&W, 11 Mins. Describes industrial work hazards and shows the dangers of carelessness on and off the job. (AAR)

ACCIDENTS   DON'T   JUST   HAPPEN (MIS-362)
MP, 16mm, Sound, B&W, 14 Mins.

Discusses and demonstrates underlying factors that cause accidents. (NMAC)

BEFORE IT'S TOO LATE

MP, 16mm, Sound, Color, 13-1/2 Mins. Emphasizes the importance of using seat belts in vehicles and subtly stresses the fact that seat belts do save lives. (AT&T)

THE BREAKING POINT

MP, 16mm, Sound, Color, 24 Mins. A safety loss-and-damage film which points out that the common cause of accidents produces a common result—damage to people and things. (AAR)

A GRAY DAY FOR O'GRADY

MP, 16mm, Sound, B&W, 15 Mins. Shows the necessity and importance of all levels of supervision accepting responsibility in preventing injuries. (AAR)

GROWING PAINS

MP, 16mm, Sound, Color, 33 Mins. Emphasizes the importance of a mature attitude toward safety among plant workers. (NCSA)

NO ONE ELSE CAN DO IT

MP, 16mm, Sound, B&W, 13 Mins. Deals with a foreman's responsibility for the safety of his subordinates. (AAR)

ON EVERY HAND

MP, 16mm, Sound, Color, 10 Mins. Depicts a variety of hazards to hands and tells how to avoid them. (NSC)

SAFETY AND THE FOREMAN SERIES
I. *Fact Finding, Not Fault Finding*

MP, 16mm, Sound, B&W, 12 Mins. Cites foreman's responsibility for checking equipment, working conditions, etc. (NSC)

SAFETY AND THE FOREMAN SERIES
II. *Foresight, Not Hindsight*

MP, 16mm, Sound, B&W, 12 Mins. How foremen can help eliminate hazards before they cause accidents. (NSC)

SAFETY AND THE FOREMAN SERIES
III. *No One Else Can Do It*

MP, 16mm, Sound, B&W, 12 Mins. Foreman's responsibility for making safety work; safety as a major production tool. (NSC)

SAFETY AND THE FOREMAN SERIES
IV. *What They Don't Know Can Hurt*

MP, 16mm, Sound, B&W, 12 Mins. Need to show workers right way of doing a job and to correct them when wrong. (NSC)

TO LIVE IN DARKNESS

MP, 16mm, Sound, B&W, 13 Mins. A dramatic case portrayal of three men who lost their eyesight through carelessness. (AAR)

WORK SMART, STAY SAFE

FS, 35mm, Sound, Color, 10 Mins. How accidents are caused on the job; highlights of safe work habits. (NRA)

YOUR RICHEST GIFT

MP, 16mm, Sound, Color, 10 Mins. Demonstrates to workers their share of the responsibility for their safety from eye injury. (AFI)

Safety—Fire

THE ANGRY FLAME
FS, 35mm, Sound, Color, 10 Mins.
Fire hazards in foodservice operations, techniques on fighting them if they break out; prevention. (NRA)

READ THE LABEL—AND LIVE
MP, 16mm, Sound, Color, 9 Mins. Explains why warning labels should be read; how to distinguish flammable products; safe handling practices for paint thinners, cleaning compounds, insecticides. (NFPA)

YOUR CLOTHING CAN BURN
MP, 16mm, Sound, Color, 13 Mins. Tells which fabrics are safest, which are easily ignited, causes and prevention of clothing fires. (NFPA)

Safety—First Aid

FIRST AID NOW
MP, 16mm, Sound, Color, 28-1/2 Mins. Shows what to do in case of burns or broken bones; how to control internal and external bleeding; and how to administer mouth-to-mouth resuscitation when breathing has stopped. (JJ)

Safety—Material Handling

HOW TO AVOID MUSCLE STRAIN
MP, 16mm, Color, 15 Mins. Diagrammatic illustration of muscle strains and motion studies. (BSI)

HOW TO LIFT PROPERLY
FS, 35mm, Sound, Color, 6-1/2 Mins. The proper use of body mechanics to prevent injury and eliminate strain. (VLI)

LIFT WITH YOUR HEAD
FS, 35mm, Script provided. Teaches and reminds employees how to avoid back injuries due to lifting; shows wrong and right way to lift and how to reach. (AHMA)

MANUAL LIFTING AND HANDLING
Slides, Color, Script provided. How to lift objects without straining or injuring the back; how to prevent falls or collisions. (NSC)

A NEW WAY TO LIFT
MP, 16mm, Sound, Color, 10 Mins. Describes new lifting technique designed to eliminate painful back injury. (NSC)

YOU CAN HANDLE IT
MP, 16mm, Sound, B&W, 10 Mins. Demonstrates safe material handling methods, lifting, carrying, stacking, etc. (NSC)

Safety—Safety Programs

MARGIN OF SAFETY
MP, 16mm, Sound, B&W, 22 Mins. Explains the need for safety measures in industry; the adoption of safety rules. (MIPS)

SAFETY BEGINS WITH YOU
FS, 35mm, Sound, Color, 9-1/2 Mins. Teaches a new employee how acci-

dents can be prevented while using equipment during routine work day. (VLI)

SAFETY IS IN ORDER

MP, 16mm, Sound, Color, 10 Mins. Discusses the relationship of housekeeping and maintenance to safety. (NSC)

Sanitation—General

DOUBLE BUCKET TECHNIQUES

VTR, 7 Mins. The double bucket technique, using one mop, is demonstrated. (AIR)

MOPS

MP, 16mm, Sound, Color, 9-1/2 Mins. Shows the preparation, use, maintenance, and storage technique of the "Urbana" dust mop and wet mop. (VA)

THE SCHOOL BUS: SPRAY TECHNIQUE

VTR, 12 Mins. A sanitation procedure for a school bus is demonstrated, including the use of a spray/fogger unit. (AIR)

Sanitation—Facilities

COLOR IT CLEAN

MP, 16mm, Sound, Color, 20 Mins. Follows an area janitor through the daily toilet cleaning procedures. (VA)

CONSERVE YOUR ENERGY

FS, 35mm, Sound, Color, 15 Mins. Step-by-step procedures for cleaning washrooms. (HUN)

INTRODUCTION TO SWIMMING POOL SANITATION (M–402)

MP, 16mm, Sound, Color, 24 Mins. An introduction to swimming pool sanitation. Lecture. (NMAC)

KEEP IT CLEAN

MP, 16mm, Sound, Color, 30 Mins. Floor care and rest room cleaning are featured with emphasis on step-by-step procedures and the importance of the proper maintenance of these areas. (HUN)

THE LOCKER AND SHOWER ROOMS: HOSE PROPORTIONATOR TECHNIQUE

VTR, 27 Mins. One of the fastest methods of applying a detergent-disinfectant solution to area with floor drains is to use a hose proportionator, coupled with a garden hose. (AIR)

THE LOCKER AND SHOWER ROOMS: SPRAY TECHNIQUE

VTR, 33 Mins. Shows how a locker and shower room can be totally cleaned and disinfected with the use of a pump tank spray unit. (AIR)

THE REST ROOM: DOUBLE BUCKET TECHNIQUE

VTR, 34 Mins. Shows step-by-step procedures for establishing a total sanitary environment in your rest room; utilizes the double bucket technique and cotton-head mops. (AIR)

THE REST ROOM: HOSE PROPORTIONATOR TECHNIQUE

VTR, 22 Mins. Shows a complete sanitation procedure for cleaning toilet bowls, urinals, commodes, sinks, mirrors, walls and floors in the rest room areas. (AIR)

THE REST ROOM: SPRAY TECHNIQUE

VTR, 37 Mins. Use of a pump tank sprayer for product application; emphasizes the ability to reach inaccessible areas. (AIR)

SPRAY CLEANING RESTROOMS

FS, 35mm, Sound, Color, 12 Mins. Importance of proper maintenance of floors and fixtures in restrooms. (HSCE)

THE SWIMMING POOL: HOSE PROPORTIONATOR TECHNIQUE

VTR, 11 Mins. A fast and efficient method for keeping the swimming pool perimeter free from dirt and germs is demonstrated. (AIR)

TOILET TECHNOLOGY

MP, 16mm, Sound, Color. Procedures and methods for the care of restrooms and locker room facilities.

Suggestion Systems

IMAGINATION AT WORK

MP, 16mm, Sound, Color, 21 Mins. Illustrates how anyone can do more creative thinking; stimulates suggestion program, methods improvement and problem-solving. (RFI)

IMPROVING THE JOB (OE 163)

MP, 16mm, Sound, B&W, 9 Mins. A supervisor asks an employee for work-improvement suggestions. (GSA)

Training—General

CASH ON THE BARREL HEAD

MP, 16mm, Sound, Color, 20 Mins. Drives home some hard facts about the value of an employee's company-provided benefits "package." (BNA)

COLLECTIVE BARGAINING—*You Are There at the Bargaining Table*

MP, 16mm, Sound, B&W, 50 Mins. Designed to show management, supervisory, and plant personnel how collective bargaining actually works. (AMA)

CREATIVITY

MP, 16mm, Sound, B&W, 21 Mins. Demonstrations exploring the effects on creativity of such common blocks as lack of curiosity and repressive effects of stereotyped training and education; suggestions on how to overcome them. (AMA)

PERFORMANCE STANDARDS—*Setting Standards of Performance*

MP, 16mm, Sound, B&W, 31 Mins. Establishment of a foundation and framework for a productive meeting on setting standards of performance. (AMA)

PREVENTING WASTE

MP, 16mm, Sound, Color, 8 Mins. Motivates all personnel to "think waste" and gives a few pointers on some of the little things that add up to significant loss. (NEM)

QUALITY MOTIVATION

Slides, Sound, Color, 16 Mins. Methods of improving employee morale, safety, reducing waste, downtime and increasing productivity. (GPC)

YOU'RE COMING ALONG FINE
MP, 16mm, Sound, Color, 23 Mins. Provides many insights into the appraisal process. (RFI)

Training—Induction and Orientation

A GOOD BEGINNING
MP, 16mm, Sound, Color, 10 Mins. Demonstrates and compares the correct techniques with the wrong way to induct and train employees on new jobs. (BNA)

INSTRUCTING THE WORKER ON THE JOB (OE 155)
MP, 16mm, Sound, B&W, 14 Mins. How not to instruct a new worker and the results of poor on-the-job instruction; in contrast, how such instruction should be done. (GSA)

Training—Management

AN EXTRA 5 KNOTS
I. *The Communication of Purpose*
MP, 16mm, Sound, B&W, 40 Mins. Distinguishes between what people work at and what people work for. (RFI)

AN EXTRA 5 KNOTS
II. *The Strength of Leaders*
MP, 16mm, Sound, B&W, 40 Mins. Explores four characteristics common

to all leaders and traces the effects of each on motivation. (RFI)

AN EXTRA 5 KNOTS
III. *The Functions of Management*
MP, 16mm, Sound, B&W, 40 Mins. Reveals what specific questions a manager must answer if his people are to give him that "extra 5." (RFI)

ARE YOU EARNING THE RIGHT TO MANAGE OTHERS?
MP, 16mm, Sound, Color, 28 Mins. Every manager has to "earn the right" to be a strict, non-nonsense supervisor by building a "supportive" relationship with subordinates. (BNA)

BREAKING THE DELEGATION BARRIER
MP, 16mm, Sound, Color, 30 Mins. For managers who have difficulty in giving their people sufficient responsibility and authority. (RFI)

COMMUNICATING MANAGEMENT'S POINT OF VIEW
MP, 16mm, Sound, Color, 24 Mins. Shows how managers can become more skillful in the aspect of communication techniques. (BNA)

DELEGATION
MP, 16mm, Sound, B&W, 21 Mins. Examines the three main aspects of delegations: responsibility, authority, and accountability. (AMA)

THE EFFECTIVE EXECUTIVE
I. *Managing Time*
MP, 16mm, Sound, Color, 25 Mins. Demonstrates why every executive needs to know where his time goes

and how to plan more effective use of it. (BNA)

THE EFFECTIVE EXECUTIVE

II. *What Can I Contribute?*

MP, 16mm, Sound, Color, 25 Mins. Any organization is really a group of specialists working together as a team. (BNA)

THE EFFECTIVE EXECUTIVE

III. *Focus on Tomorrow*

MP, 16mm, Sound, Color, 25 Mins. Yesterday's successes linger on beyond their productive life and become "investments in managerial ego." (BNA)

THE EFFECTIVE EXECUTIVE

IV. *Effective Decisions*

MP, 16mm, Sound, Color, 25 Mins. Shows how effective executives utilize constructive dissent to make sure that each decision is the best choice of alternatives. (BNA)

THE EFFECTIVE EXECUTIVE

V. *Staffing for Strength*

MP, 16mm, Sound, Color, 25 Mins. Effective executives never ask, "What can my subordinates not do?" They ask, "What can they do uncommonly well?" (BNA)

GENERAL MANAGEMENT—*Managing a Manager's Time*

MP, 16mm, Sound, B&W, 24 Mins. A different view of where and how a manager spends half his time. (AMA)

HOW GOOD IS A GOOD GUY?

MP, 16mm, Sound, Color, 21 Mins. Explores why some leaders fail to get the respect of their people; how to be fair yet firm. (RFI)

LEADERSHIP—*Leadership Characteristics*

MP, 16mm, Sound, B&W, 23 Mins. Examination of the type of authority a person can exercise in getting work done through people. (AMA)

THE MAKING OF A DECISION

MP, 16mm, Sound, Color, 32 Mins. Motivates managers to follow a rational process in their decision making. (RFI)

MANAGEMENT BY OBJECTIVES

MP, 16mm, Sound, Color, 27 Mins. Offers many important "how-to's" in applying a program using this technique. (BNA)

MANAGEMENT FILM CLASSICS

II. *The Principles of Organization*

MP, 16mm, Sound, B&W, 36 Mins. Establishes and explores the ten basic principles of organization. (AMA)

MANAGEMENT FILM CLASSICS

III. *How the Organization Affects the Man*

MP, 16mm, Sound, B&W, 35 Mins. The influence of the organization on the man in terms of the true elements which motivate him. (AMA)

MANAGEMENT FILM CLASSICS

IV. *The Relationship Between Line and Staff*

MP, 16mm, Sound, B&W, 35 Mins. Unveils the rightful place and prerogative of line and staff in the communication chain. (AMA)

MANAGEMENT FILM CLASSICS
V. *Education and Training of Future
Managers*
MP, 16mm, Sound, B&W, 47 Mins.
Probes the four basic skills which
should be taught in developing future
managers. (AMA)

MANAGEMENT, MOTIVATION & THE
NEW MINORITY WORKER
MP, 16mm, Sound, Color, 43 Mins.
Deals frankly and openly with the
problems encountered by foremen
and supervisors in handling hard-core
employees. (RFI)

MANAGERS IN ACTION
III. *Management the Simple Way*
MP, 16mm, Sound, B&W, 30 Mins.
Six simple steps to good management.
(AMA)

MANAGERS IN ACTION
V.   *Keep the Pressure Down*
MP, 16mm, Sound, B&W, 30 Mins.
A frank discussion of one of the
toughest problems facing a manager: how to correct employee performance. (AMA)

MANAGERS IN ACTION
X.   *Management Refueling*
MP, 16mm, Sound, B&W, 30 Mins.
Explores the resources available to
the man who would get the greatest
satisfaction out of his management
activity. (AMA)

MANAGERS IN ACTION
XI.   *How Do I Know I'm a Pro?*
MP, 16mm, Sound, B&W, 30 Mins.
A discussion of several basic quali-

ties of the thoroughly professional
manager. (AMA)

MANAGERS IN ACTION
XIII. *An Enlightened Manager*
MP, 16mm, Sound, B&W, 30 Mins.
What is an enlightened manager? A
personal answer to this provocative
question. (AMA)

MANAGERS IN ACTION, SERIES II
II.   *Setting Your Target*
MP, 16mm, Sound, B&W, 30 Mins.
Examines the principles of long-
range planning and how to gain the
perspective for successful planning
of any kind. (AMA)

MANAGERS IN ACTION, SERIES II
III. *What's the Job?*
MP, 16mm, Sound, B&W, 30 Mins.
Discussion of job descriptions and
an organization chart, their importance, basic functions and principles. (AMA)

MANAGERS IN ACTION, SERIES II
V.   *Skull Practice*
MP, 16mm, Sound, B&W, 30 Mins.
The best tools for conducting a job
appraisal interview. (AMA)

MANAGERS WANTED
MP, 16mm, Sound, Color, 28 Mins.
Brings into focus problems which
influence the career development of
every manager. (RFI)

STYLES OF LEADERSHIP
MP, 16mm, Sound, Color, 26 Mins.
Helps managers find the right balance
between effective control and the

meaningful involvement of their people. (RFI)

TOUGH-MINDED MANAGEMENT

I. *Management by Example*
MP, 16mm, Sound, Color, 25 Mins. A tough-minded manager is not solely a disciplinarian, but one whose primary drive is to build himself, his subordinates, and his organization. (BNA)

TOUGH-MINED MANAGEMENT

II. *The Man in the Mirror*
MP, 16mm, Sound, Color, 25 Mins. Discusses a manager's behavior off the job as well as on the job. (BNA)

TOUGH-MINDED MANAGEMENT

III. *The Fully Functioning Individual*
MP, 16mm, Sound, Color, 25 Mins. One must grow, challenge himself, and have the courage to stick his neck out to support the organization; in return for the right to expect growth opportunities and fair appraisal. (BNA)

TOUGH-MINDED MANAGEMENT

IV. *The Fully Functioning Organization*
MP, 16mm, Sound, Color, 25 Mins. There must be a "grand design" which sets the style and tone of the entire organization. (BNA)

Training—Supervisory

THE CASE OF THE MISSING MAGNETS
MP, 16mm, Sound, Color, 10 Mins. Helps supervisors to understand that

"a taut ship" goes hand-in-hand with human relations in building a highly motivated team. (BNA)

THE CHALLENGE OF LEADERSHIP
MP, 16mm, Sound, Color, 10 Mins. Designed to help supervisors identify and analyze the qualities which make a leader. (BNA)

INSTRUCTIONS OR OBSTRUCTIONS
MP, 16mm, Sound, Color, 10 Mins. Will give supervisors many useful hints on how to handle the difficult job of communicating verbally with subordinates. (BNA)

IT'S AN ORDER
MP, 16mm, Sound, B&W, 12 Mins. Illustrates that unless supervisors give orders clearly the worker will not be able to carry them out efficiently and safely. (AAR)

LISTEN, PLEASE
MP, 16mm, Sound, Color, 10 Mins. Emphasizes the importance of listening in a supervisory job. (BNA)

MAN IN THE MIDDLE
MP, 16mm, Sound, B&W, 28 Mins. The story of the average supervisor caught in the middle between his boss, the union, and his subordinates. (RFI)

OVERCOMING RESISTANCE TO CHANGE
MP, 16mm, Sound, Color, 30 Mins. Shows supervisors how to recognize the emotional factors which breed resistance to change.

SUPERVISING WORKERS ON THE JOB (OE 157)

MP, 16mm, Sound, B&W, 10 Mins. Illustrates good and poor methods of supervision; the dangers of "snooper-vising." (GSA)

THE WINNING COMBINATION

MP, 16mm, Sound, Color, 10 Mins. Tackles the difficult supervisory job of motivating subordinates to coop-erate with the company's efforts to reduce waste and control cost. (BNA)

WORKING WITH OTHER SUPER-VISORS (OE 153)

MP, 16mm, Sound, B&W, 8 Mins. Shows how a supervisor fails because he does not recognize the importance of working harmoniously with other people, especially his fellow super-visors. (GSA)

Source Index

Association of American Railroads   **AAR**
American Railroads Building
Washington, DC 20036

Advance Chemical Company   **ACC**
333 Fell Street
San Francisco, CA 94102

Association Films, Inc.   **AFI**
600 Grand Avenue
Ridgefield, NJ 07657

American Hospital Association   **AHA**
840 North Lake Shore Drive
Chicago, Il 60611

American Hotel & Motel Association   **AHMA**
888 Seventh Avenue
New York, NY 10019

American Institute of Architects   **AIA**
Documents Division
1735 New York Avenue, N.W.
Washington, DC 20006

Airkem, a Division of Airwick Industries, Inc.   **AIR**
111 Commerce Road
Carlstadt, NJ 07072

AMA   American Management Association
The American Management Association Bldg.
135 West 50th Street
New York, NY 10020

ANA   ANA-NLN Film Library
267 West 25th Street
New York, NY 10001

APA   American Paper Institute
260 Madison Avenue
New York, NY 10016

APE   American Petroleum Institute
1271 Avenue of the Americas
New York, NY 10020

ARMC   Adams Rite Manufacturing Company
1425 Grand Central Avenue
Glendale, CA 91201

AT&T   American Telephone & Telegraph Company
192 Broadway
New York, NY 10038
(Contact your local Bell Telephone Business Office)

BNA   BNA Films
5615 Fishers Lane
Rockville, MD 20852

BOM   Bureau of Mines
U. S. Department of Interior
4800 Forbes Avenue
Pittsburgh, PA 15213

BSI   Bray Studios, Inc.
630 Ninth Avenue
New York, NY 10036

CIF   Coronet Instructional Films
65 East South Water Street
Chicago, IL 60601

CIPRA   Cast Iron Pipe Research Association
Suite 323, Executive Plaza East
1211 West 22nd Street
Oak Brook, IL 60521

Chemical Specialties Manufacturers Association   **CSMA**
50 East 41st Street
New York, NY 10017

Diversey Chemical Company   **DIV**
212 West Monroe Street
Chicago, IL 60606

The Dow Chemical Company   **DOW**
Audio-Visual Center
Midland, MI 48640

Encyclopaedia Britannica Educational Corporation   **EBEC**
425 North Michigan Avenue
Chicago, IL 60611

U.S. Fish & Wildlife Service   **FWS**
Predator and Rodent Control Branch
Washington, DC 20025

National Audiovisual Center (GSA)   **GSA**
Washington, DC 20409

Gerber Products Company   **GPC**
445 State Street
Fremont, MI 49412

Geerpres Wringer Company   **GWC**
P.O. Box 658
Muskegon, MI 49443

Health Education Service   **HES**
P.O. Box 7283—Capitol Station
Albany, NY 12224

Hercules, Inc.   **HI**
Wilmington, DE 19899

Henry Strauss & Company   **HSC**
31 West 53rd Street
New York, NY 10019

Hillyard Sales Company—Eastern   **HSCE**
St. Joseph, MO 64502

Huntington Laboratories, Inc.   **HUN**
P.O. Box 710
Huntington, IN 46750

ISM   Institute of Sanitation Management
             1710 Drew Street
             Clearwater, FL 33515

ISSA   International Sanitary Supply Association
             5330 North Elston Avenue
             Chicago, IL 60630

JJ   Johnson & Johnson
             Consumer Services Department
             New Brunswick, NJ 08903

KAB   Keep American Beautiful, Inc.
             99 Park Avenue
             New York, NY 10016

KNA   "Kex" National Association
             7100 Baltimore Avenue
             College Park, MD 20740

LBD   Link-Belt Division, FMC Corporation
             Public Relations Department
             Film Library
             Prudential Plaza
             Chicago, IL 60601

LSAA   Linen Supply Association of America
             P.O. Box 2427
             Miami Beach, FL 33140

MCP   Multi-Clean Products, Inc.
             2277 Ford Parkway
             St. Paul, MN 55116

MHI   Material Handling Institute
             1326 Freeport Road
             Pittsburgh, PA 15238

MSPSD   Modern Talking Picture Service
             1212 Avenue of the Americas
             New York, NY

NAPHCC   National Association of Plumbing, Heating and Cooling
             Contractors
             1016 20th Street, N.W.
             Washington, DC 20036

National Canners Association   **NCA**
1133 20th Street, N.W.
Washington, DC 20036

National Crushed Stone Association   **NCSA**
1415 Elliot Place, N.W.
Washington, DC 20007

National Educational Media, Inc.   **NEM**
3815 West Chauenga Boulevard
Hollywood, CA 90028

National Fire Protection Association   **NFPA**
60 Batterymarch Street
Boston, MA 02110

National Medical Audiovisual Center (Annex)   **NMAC**
Station K
Atlanta, GA 30324

Norton Company   **NOR**
New Bond Road
Worcester, MA 01606

National Restaurant Association   **NRA**
Educational Materials Center
1530 North Lake Shore Drive
Chicago, IL 60611

National Safety Council   **NSC**
425 North Michigan Avenue
Chicago, IL 60611

National Water Institute   **NWI**
420 Lexington Avenue
Room 1250
New York, NY 10017

Office of Civil Defense   **OCD**
The Pentagon
Washington, DC 20310

Single Service Institute   **PCCI**
250 Park Avenue
New York, NY 10017

RFI   Roundtable Films, Inc.
       321 South Beverly Drive
       Beverly Hills, CA 90212

RMC   Rockwell Manufacturing Company
       Flexible Pipe Tool Division
       415 Zangs Boulevard
       Dallas, TX 75208

SCJ   S. C. Johnson & Son, Inc.
       Service Products Division
       Racine, WI 53403

SDA   The Soap and Detergent Association
       Industrial & Institutional Division
       475 Park Avenue South
       New York, NY 10016

SOC   Shell Oil Company
       Film Library
       450 North Meridian Street
       Indianapolis, IN 46204

SMI   Sterling Movies, Inc.
       43 West 61st Street
       New York, NY 10023

TC   Tranex Corporation
       P.O. Box 116
       Garden Grove, CA 92642

TGFC   Tennessee Game and Fish Commission
       Film Library
       1600 Lock Road
       Nashville, TN 37207

3M   3M Company
       3M Center
       St. Paul, MN 55101

UEVA   Universal Education and Visual Arts
       221 Park Avenue, South
       New York, NY 10003

USDA   Motion Picture Service
       Office of Information

U.S. Department of Agriculture
Washington, DC 20250

U.S. Senate Public Works Committee   **USSPWC**
Room 4204
New Senate Office Building
Washington, DC 20510

Visual Aids   **VA**
University of Illinois
Champaign, IL 61820

Vestal Laboratories, Inc.   **VLI**
Division of W. R. Grace & Company
4963 Manchester Avenue
St. Louis, MO 63110

Walter G. Legge Company, Inc.   **WGL**
101 Park Avenue
New York, NY 10017

Wil-Kil Pest Control, Inc.   **WKPC**
522 West North Avenue
Milwaukee, WI 53212

LOG OF OCCUPATIONAL INJURIES AND ILLNESSES

Case or file no.	Date of injury or initial diagnosis of illness. If diagnosis of illness was made after first day of absence enter first day of absence. (mo./day/yr.)	Employee's Name (First name, middle initial, last name)	Occupation of injured employee at time of injury or illness	Department to which employee was assigned at time of injury or illness	DESCRIPTION OF INJURY OR ILLNESS		EXTENT AND OUTCOME OF INJURY OR ILLNESS					
					Nature of injury or illness and part(s) of body affected (Typical entries for this column might be: Amputation of 1st joint right forefinger Strain of lower back Contact dermatitis on both hands Electrocution—lightning)	Injury or illness code See codes at bottom of page.	Fatalities Enter date of death (mo./day/yr.)	Lost Workday Cases		Nonfatal Cases Without Lost Workdays		
								Enter workdays lost due to injury or illness (see instructions on back.)	If after lost workdays, the employee was permanently transferred to another job or was terminated, enter a check in the column below	If no entry was made in columns 8 or 9, but the injury or illness did result in: medical treatment, other than first aid, or; diagnosis of occupational illness, or; loss of consciousness, or; restriction of work or motion; Enter a check in the column below	If a check in column 11 represented a transfer or termination, enter another check in column 12
1	2	3	4	5	6		7	8	9	10	11	12

Company Name _____

Establishment Name _____

Establishment Location _____

Injury Code

10 All occupational injuries

Illness Codes

21 Occupational skin diseases or disorders
22 Dust diseases of the lungs (pneumoconioses)
23 Respiratory conditions due to toxic agents
24 Poisoning (Systemic effects of toxic materials)
25 Disorders due to physical agents (other than toxic materials)
26 Disorders due to repeated trauma
29 All other occupational illnesses

Exhibit 3-1

Supplementary Record of Occupational Injuries and Illnesses

EMPLOYER

1. Name _____

2. Mail address _____
   _____(No. and street)_____(City or town)_____(State)

3. Location, if different from mail address _____

INJURED OR ILL EMPLOYEE

4. Name _____ Social Security No. _____
   ____(First name)_____(Middle name)_____(Last name)

5. Home address _____
   _____(No. and street)_____(City or town)_____(State)

6. Age _____   7. Sex: Male_____ Female_____ (Check one)

8. Occupation _____
   (Enter regular job title, *not* the specific activity he was performing at time of injury.)

9. Department _____
   (Enter name of department or division in which the injured person is regularly employed, even though he may have been temporarily working in another department at the time of injury.)

THE ACCIDENT OR EXPOSURE TO OCCUPATIONAL ILLNESS

10. Place of accident or exposure _____
    _____(No. and street)_____(City or town)_____(State)
    If accident or exposure occurred on employer's premises, give address of plant or establishment in which it occurred. Do not indicate department or division within the plant or establishment. If accident occurred outside employer's premises at an identifiable address, give that address. If it occurred on a public highway or at any other place which cannot be identified by number and street, please provide place references locating the place of injury as accurately as possible.

11. Was place of accident or exposure on employer's premises? _____ (Yes or No)

12. What was the employee doing when injured? _____
    (Be specific. If he was using tools or equipment or handling material,
    _____
    name them and tell what he was doing with them.)
    _____

13. How did the accident occur? _____
    (Describe fully the events which resulted in the injury or occupational illness. Tell what
    _____
    happened and how it happened. Name any objects or substances involved and tell how they were involved. Give
    _____
    full details on all factors which led or contributed to the accident. Use separate sheet for additional space.)

OCCUPATIONAL INJURY OR OCCUPATIONAL ILLNESS

14. Describe the injury or illness in detail and indicate the part of body affected. _____
    (e.g.: amputation of right index finger
    _____
    at second joint; fracture of ribs; lead poisoning; dermatitis of left hand, etc.)

15. Name the object or substance which directly injured the employee. (For example, the machine or thing he struck against or which struck him; the vapor or poison he inhaled or swallowed; the chemical or radiation which irritated his skin; or in cases of strains, hernias, etc., the thing he was lifting, pulling, etc.)
    _____
    _____

16. Date of injury or initial diagnosis of occupational illness _____.
    (Date)

17. Did employee die? _____ (Yes or No)

OTHER

18. Name and address of physician _____

19. If hospitalized, name and address of hospital _____
    _____

    Date of report _____ Prepared by _____
    Official position _____

Exhibit 3-2

SUPPLEMENTARY RECORD OF
OCCUPATIONAL INJURIES
AND ILLNESSES

To supplement the Log of Occupational Injuries and Illnesses (OSHA No. 100), each establishment must maintain a record of each recordable occupational injury or illness. Workmen's compensation, insurance, or other reports are acceptable as records if they contain all facts listed below or are supplemented to do so. If no suitable report is made for other purposes, this form (OSHA No. 101) may be used or the necessary facts can be listed on a separate plain sheet of paper. These records must also be available in the establishment without delay and at reasonable times for examination by representatives of the Department of Labor and the Department of Health, Education and Welfare, and States accorded jurisdiction under the Act. The records must be maintained for a period of not less than five years following the end of the calendar year to which they relate.

Such records must contain at least the following facts:

1) *About the employer*—name, mail address, and location if different from mail address.

2) *About the injured or ill employee*—name, social security number, home address, age, sex, occupation, and department.

3) *About the accident or exposure to occupational illness*—place of accident or exposure, whether it was on employer's premises, what the employee was doing when injured, and how the accident occurred.

4) *About the occupational injury or illness*—description of the injury or illness, including part of body affected; name of the object or substance which directly injured the employee; and date of injury or diagnosis of illness.

5) *Other*—name and address of physician; if hospitalized, name and address of hospital; date of report; and name and position of person preparing the report.

SEE *DEFINITIONS* ON THE BACK OF OSHA FORM 100.

Exhibit 3-2 (Continued)

Summary

Occupational Injuries and Illnesses

Establishment Name and Address:

Injury and Illness Category		Fatalities	Lost Workday Cases			Nonfatal Cases Without Lost Workdays*	
			Number of Cases	Number of Cases Involving Permanent Transfer to Another Job or Termination of Employment	Number of Lost Workdays	Number of Cases	Number of Cases Involving Transfer to Another Job or Termination of Employment
Code 1	Category 2	3	4	5	6	7	8
10	Occupational Injuries						
21	*Occupational Illnesses* Occupational Skin Diseases or Disorders						
22	Dust diseases of the lungs (pneumoconioses)						
23	Respiratory conditions due to toxic agents						
24	Poisoning (systemic effects of toxic materials)						
25	Disorders due to physical agents (other than toxic materials)						
26	Disorders due to repeated trauma						
29	All other occupational illnesses						
	Total—occupational illnesses (21-29)						
	Total—occupational injuries and illnesses						

*Nonfatal Cases Without Lost Workdays—Cases resulting in: Medical treatment beyond first aid, diagnosis of occupational illness, loss of consciousness, restriction of work or motion, or transfer to another job (without lost workdays).

Exhibit 3–3

Summary
Occupational Injuries and Illnesses

Every employer is required to prepare a summary of the occupational injury and illness experience of the employees in each of his establishments at the end of each year within one month following the end of that year. The summary must be posted in a place accessible to the employees. The form on the reverse of this sheet is to be used.

Before preparing the summary, review the log to be sure that entries are correct and each case is included in only one of the classes identified by columns 8, 9, and 11. If an employee's loss of work days is continuing at the time the summary is being made, estimate the number of future work days he will lose and add that estimate to the work days he has already lost and include this total in the summary. No further entries need be made with respect to such cases in the next summary.

Occupational injuries and the seven categories of occupational illness are to be summarized separately. Identify each case by the code in column 7 of the log of occupational injuries and illnesses.

The summary from the log is made as follows (for occupational injuries, code 10—follow the same procedure for each of the illness categories):

Fatalities. For cases with code 10 in column 7, count the number of entries (date of death) in column 8.

Lost Workday Cases, Number of Cases. For cases with code 10 in column 7, count the number of *entries* in column 9.

Number of Cases Involving Transfer or Termination. For cases with code 10 in column 7, count the number of check marks in column 10.

Number of Lost Workdays. For cases with code 10 in column 7, *add* the entries (lost workdays) in column 9.

Nonfatal Cases Without Lost Workdays, Number of Cases. For cases with code 10 in column 7, count the checks in column 11.

Number of Cases Involving Transfer or Termination. For cases with code 10 in column 7, count the checks in column 12.

Total each column for occupational illnesses and then, on the last line for occupational injuries and illnesses combined.

Compare the sum of entries in the total line for columns 3, 4, and 7 with the total number of cases on the log. If the summary has been made correctly, they will match.

Exhibit 3-3 (Continued)

Chapter 4

The Maintenance of Buildings

and Structures

Introduction

Park and recreation building and structure maintenance becomes more and more important with each passing day. Park and recreation buildings and structures represent millions of dollars in initial construction with replacement costs estimated annually at a growing 10 percent over and above original construction costs. The necessity of systematic quality maintenance to guard against premature need for building and structure replacement is obvious.

This chapter is organized to cover the three major aspects of building and structure maintenance: (1) building structure and systems maintenance, (2) preventive maintenance, and (3) custodial or housekeeping maintenance.

The building maintenance organizational chart presented as Figure 4-1 illustrates this organizational arrangement.

It is important to note that the principles of building maintenance, as presented, apply not only to large building structures but also to smaller buildings and structures such as picnic shelters, campground washhouses, swimming-pool locker, shower, and toilet areas, vacation cabins, snack bars, and to certain aspects of outdoor partial structures such as amphitheaters and campfire seating circles.

Should the building maintenance division be able to hire only two men, exclusive of custodial personnel, one of them should be a general purpose maintenance man capable of working on several building structural components. The other man should be capable of providing general care of the systems within the building.

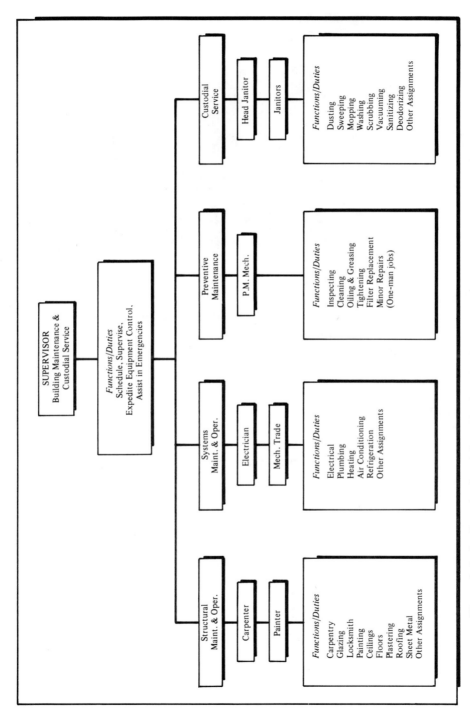

Figure 4–1 An Organizational Chart for Building Maintenance for a Park and Recreation System

Preventive maintenance is especially important for outdoor facilities that are heavily used by the public.

Organization and Staffing

In a small park/recreation system, the maintenance staff often consists of a handful of generalists—men who are multi-skilled. Their supervisor is often the overall maintenance manager. To develop a building maintenance staff to serve a small recreation system, the maintenance manager should begin by hiring the following basic corps of tradesmen:

- *a carpenter,* one who is competent enough to handle cabinet making, furniture repair, glazing, screening, puttying, caulking, latches and locks;
- *an electrician,* trained in and capable of handling both lighting and power;
- *a mechanic,* who also can work as a plumber and steamfitter;
- *a painter,* who can also glaze, putty, caulk, spackle, and lay asphalt and vinyl asbestos floors, install insulation around pipes, and who is familiar and reasonably capable in handling most kinds of surface coatings and coverings.

The staff should be augmented as additional personnel are required. A carpenter's helper and a second mechanic would be of great benefit. (The second mechanic will allow the department to divide pipe work into heating and cooling; for technical reasons, one man is seldom strong enough in both fields.)

Structural and Systems Maintenance

Significant improvements continue to be made in almost every category of building structures and systems materials, and the maintenance materials and methods necessary for these. Building maintenance requires an organization capable of emergency, preventive, and corrective work on a wide variety of structures and systems. Building structural work is highly diversified in that it includes roofs, walls, windows, doors, floors, and foundations. Structural maintenance work requires personnel skilled in handling lumber, masonry, concrete, mortar, flashings, wall and floor coverings, and a variety of other structural maintenance and repair materials.

Systems to be maintained include wiring, ducts, pipes, elevators and escalators built into a structure. Maintenance of such systems requires personnel skilled in heating and ventilating, air conditioning, plumbing, electrical lighting, gas, compressed air, fire alarms, and sprinklers. Other specialists needed, in order of descending importance, are a combination roof and sheet metal mechanic, a mason, a machinist, and a welder.

Building maintenance staff organization in small recreation systems is usually quite simple, with individual tradesmen reporting directly to the maintenance manager, a building superintendent, or possibly a shop foreman.

Maintenance Standards for Buildings

Building maintenance standards are the established level at which the structure should be maintained to assure maximum, overall economy consistent with its functional requirement. For example, a warehouse scheduled for removal within five years should not be maintained at the same standard or level of maintenance as a warehouse scheduled for retention for twenty-five years. Consequently, more than one level or standard of building maintenance may be developed and approved for use by the recreation system policy-making authority. Multiple level building maintenance standards developed by the National Park Service are presented in the appendix to this chapter.

Basic Approaches to Structure and Systems Maintenance

Two basic philosophies prevail in the general maintenance field and often clash in connection with building maintenance. These are corrective maintenance and preventive maintenance. The first philosophy emphasizes reacting to maintenance problems after they occur rather than anticipating them. Although reaction to a problem is an important part of any complete maintenance program, it should never compromise an organization's total program as is sometimes the case when maintenance funds are inadequate. Inevitably, this leads to crisis maintenance, which, ultimately, is the most expensive kind of program. Preventive maintenance emphasizes the identification and elimination of potential problems before they disrupt building operations. An effective preventive maintenance program does require an initial outlay of time and money for proper organization. However, it normally repays the original cost many times over by minimizing potential damage, reducing emergency overtime work, and eliminating expensive rush purchasing.

Preventive Maintenance

Preventive maintenance, the key to minimizing emergency repair work, is merely establishing a procedure for identifying potential breakdowns and making adjustments or small repairs, thus avoiding the costs of major repairs and unscheduled shutdowns. Identification of the need for preventive maintenance is not established by gazing into a crystal ball, but, rather, through the development and institution of systematic inspection procedures. Reduced to its basic elements, preventive maintenance consists of identification of maintenance needs through inspecting and proceeding to clean, lubricate, tighten, adjust, and replace worn or damaged parts when necessary. Preventive maintenance includes such items as:

building surfaces, exterior and interior	light bulbs
closet doors	light fixtures
door hinges	mechanical rooms
drains	motors
exhaust fans	pumps
fan belts	shower valves
faucets	toilets
filters	

Preventive maintenance job assignments for each recreation/park organization must be tailored according to buildings and equipment, their number, types, and ages. To develop accurate job assignments and instructions, the building maintenace supervisor or his delegate—possibly a preventive maintenance mechanic—must develop a complete list of all preventive maintenance tasks. The preventive maintenance tasks inventory should include instructions to the mechanic as to how he should proceed. For example:

Preventive Maintenance Job Inventory

- Inspect buildings in area and report all deficiencies you cannot correct to the work control desk.
- keep mechanical rooms clean and orderly at all times.
- Tighten or adjust door closers and window locks and hinges.
- Replace burned-out light bulbs and fluorescent tubes.
- Open clogged toilets and drains with plunger or hand auger. If fixture requires power auger or must be disassembled, report it to the work control desk.
- Repair leaking water faucets and shower heads.

Such jobs are not assigned according to a regular schedule, but are done whenever a preventive maintenance mechanic discovers them during his rounds, or whenever a building occupant reports them. After inspecting the reported problem, the preventive maintenance mechanic should either correct the condition himself or report it to the work control desk. To guide him, the preventive maintenance supervisor should stress the importance of not attempting jobs requiring considerable time, a high level of expertise, or additional men.

Organizing various maintenance jobs into a work schedule is one of the most difficult aspects of establishing a preventive maintenance program. Once the work inventory for equipment maintenance has been compiled, the main problem is integrating tasks into the daily and weekly maintenance work routines. While most preventive maintenance men can remember their normal daily and weekly tasks, few can be expected to remember such infrequent tasks as monthly valve testings, semi-annual greasings, and even annual cleaning or replacement of parts.

Once routine or preventive jobs have been defined from equipment manuals, they should, thereafter, be filed for easy reference. Two filing techniques have proven quite effective as reminders of infrequent maintenance tasks.

1. Reminder Tab File
    This procedure utilizes a card file consisting of one card for each piece of equipment needing preventive maintenance. Each card identifies a piece fo equipment according to its location and lists each type of maintenance required, indicating recommended frequency, replacement parts, lubrications, and supplies needed. Space is provided opposite each preventive maintenance job to record performance dates. Colored code tabs are attached to cards to identify daily, weekly, monthly, semi-annual, and annual jobs. By checking this file regularly, the preventive maintenance mechanic can find when each job was done last and quickly determine when the next one is due. See Figure 4-2.

2. Frequency Code Cards
    This alternative procedure requires a different card for each preventive maintenance task. Different card colors indicate task frequency (weekly, monthly, semi-annual, etc.). Each card includes cross-references to all other work needed. More cards are required under this system, but this allows more room for listing important data, parts and supplies, and for recording dates when work is accomplished.

To supplement information from card files, the preventive maintenance man can use floor space diagrams, community and park maps to further organize his work routine. Maps and diagrams of his work area will allow the preventive maintenance man to locate all his major equipment maintenance jobs and mark the diagrams and maps, using a color code that complements the card file system. The preventive maintenance mechanic can then plan to

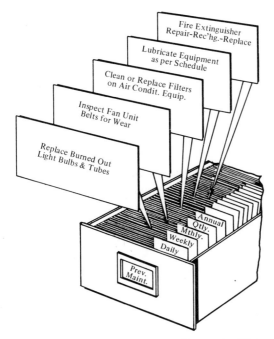

Figure 4-2 Reminder Tab File for Preventive Maintenance

take the most time-saving routes to follow on different days. Since many jobs are not done daily, several routes are necessary. Even though his routes vary frequently, time spent mapping the best route is still time well spent. Such planning saves wasted steps and reminds the preventive maintenance man to carry appropriate tools and supplies with him.

Preventive Maintenance Personnel

The effective preventive maintenance mechanic is a trouble shooter who possesses a variety of skills. Ideally, preventive maintenance mechanics will come from a broad, multi-trade background and bring with them expertise for analyzing equipment breakdowns, estimating work, coping with emergencies, and understanding operating instructions for complex electrical and mechanical equipment. Of equal importance, they should have initiative and be men who can be relied on to work independently and perform competently. They must also recognize their own limitations and not attempt jobs requiring excessive time, greater skill than they possess, or additional personnel.

Locating men with these qualities is not easy, training them is difficult, and keeping them is even more difficult, especially since skilled specialists generally command higher salaries and greater esteem. Some organizations, therefore, have tried to upgrade the job by establishing a separate higher job classification for preventive maintenance mechanics and paying good men what they deserve.

Preventive Maintenance Work Assignments

Area maintenance and crew maintenance are two widely used methods for accomplishing preventive maintenance work. Many organizations combine these two approaches to benefit from the advantages of each.

Area Maintenance Utilizing the area maintenance method, the preventive maintenance mechanic is basically responsible for a clearly defined area. One system, for instance, may assign each preventive maintenance man a specific number of buildings. Another system may assign a maximum number of gross square feet of specific building floor space per preventive maintenance mechanic. The appropriate assignment depends upon the conditions in each system. The preventive maintenance mechanic may set up a small shop for his area where he keeps building plans, manuals, records, tools, and regularly used parts and supplies. The major tasks of the preventive maintenance mechanic include: inspecting, cleaning, lubricating, adjusting, and making small repairs—tasks which are closely related and generally accomplished on the job site. The equipment job inventory establishes the limits of the mechanic's work responsibility.

The potential advantages of the area method of preventive maintenance include more thorough coverage, resulting in early discovery of developing problems, and on-the-spot repairs that save paperwork and travel time. Area maintenance personnel become familiar with local problems and peculiarities of the area, its equipment, and its occupants. Area maintenance allows for flexibility in scheduling, which averts schedule conflicts with special recreation programs and events. Area maintenance also establishes the basis upon which personal job commitment grows. When a worker is solely responsible for an area, he usually develops considerable pride in its condition.

It is the single man working alone that creates the greatest limitation to area maintenance. Unless the job is within easy reach and can be handled by one man without need for additional personnel or special tools, a crew or contractor must be called in. The preventive maintenance mechanic can replace most light bulbs, but he must call in a contractor or special crew with tall ladders for bulb replacement in high ceilings. When the hand auger or plunger will not work to clear a toilet drain, a plumber with a special power tool must be summoned. Door hinges can be tightened by the preventive maintenance mechanic; but, repairs to locks require a locksmith.

Crew Maintenance   The crew approach to maintenance tends to overcome the limitations inherent in the single-man area method. Utilizing this approach, a crew combines to cover a larger zone. In a small system, the area might include all recreation buildings. The crew supervisor spends much of his time organizing the preventive maintenance work: inspecting, making job lists, ordering parts and supplies, assigning men, and reviewing their work. His ability as an organizer spells the difference between effective and ineffective crew maintenance.

A crew has flexibility and can complete more jobs than a single worker. Assuming good supervision, only the necessary number of men would be assigned to handle each job; in some instances, everyone on the crew might work alone to accomplish individual assignments. In other situations the entire crew might be assigned to a single project. Further flexibility comes from the relative ease with which a crew compensates for absences.

Certain disadvantages and complications are associated with crew maintenance. One disadvantage relates to crew members not becoming as familiar with the larger crew territory and its troubles as the single mechanic. Team coverage makes the fixing of responsibility for unsatisfactory performance more difficult. A major complication with crew maintenance is the difficulty in assigning proper numbers of crew personnel. There is a tendency where there is a crew to assign two or more men even if a job does not warrant them, resulting in featherbedding and economic loss to the organization.

Both area and crew maintenance are best served when a small shop serving as a base of operations is established for each major area of   **Preventive Maintenance Shop** the recreation/park system. The preventive maintenance shop should contain—

- maintenance and operating equipment manuals provided by the manufacturer;
- technical drawings, including the "as-built" architectural, structural, electrical, and mechanical prints for each building in the area;
- records, inventories of equipment and preventive work to be done and logs of work completed;
- supplies, a small stock of repair parts and maintenance materials most frequently used;
- tools, those usually found in the preventive maintenance mechanic's kit include such items as wrenches, a bulb extractor, an electric drill, a flashlight, a set of screwdrivers, pliers, a water key, toilet plunger and auger, fuse puller, a grease gun, a hammer, and so on.

Preventive Maintenance Records

In addition to keeping equipment and work inventories and work schedules, the maintenance mechanic should maintain concise daily records of all work completed for each piece of equipment. Major equipment jobs should be noted in two places—on a dated tag attached to the equipment and on the inventory record kept in the maintenance shop. These records, if properly kept, complete a work history for all equipment in the area.

Maintenance personnel also should record all work for the department's work control system. Figure 4-3 shows a form for reporting work time expended and materials used. In the time consumption charged to each job, the mechanic includes time allowed for planning, ordering supplies, travel, clean-up, and record keeping. Since maintenance workers also use time for planning, tool care, record keeping, coffee breaks, resupply, and the like, a shop time allowance of perhaps 15 percent of the work day is acceptable, generally.

Maintenance of Equipment and Supplies for Buildings

The use and availability of proper maintenance equipment and maintenance supplies greatly influences the adequacy of a building and structure maintenance program. New and improved mainten-

RECREATION/PARK SYSTEM

PM AREA _____ DATE _____

Work Categories	Bldg. No.		Bldg. No.		Bldg. No.		Bldg. No.	
	Time Hrs.	Material Cost	Time Hrs.	Material Cost	Time Hrs.	Material Cost	Time Hrs.	Material Cost
Air Conditioning								
Carpentry								
Electrical								
Heating								
Painting								
Plumbing								
Roofing								
Ventilation								
Other Specify*								
TOTAL								

Signed _____

*Refers to vacations, sick leave, shop time, etc.

Figure 4-3 Preventive Maintenance Daily Work Report

ance equipment and supplies become available almost continuously. Certainly it would be foolhardy to accept at face value every new maintenance product that comes along through the assumption that it is better than what we have been using. A much safer and defensible approach would be to test the many new products offered on the market today on a limited basis prior to our accepting any one of them as a total replacement. The old adage, "Be not the first by whom the new are tried or yet the last to lay the old aside," seems to be quite appropriate as a guide to follow when adopting new maintenance supplies such as cleaning agents. With changes in cleaning technology developing so rapidly, the recreation maintenance manager should assign one man to review current maintenance publications and to investigate new developments that might prove economical in future operations. Manufacturers of maintenance supplies readily provide information and assistance regarding the proper use of their products and in the development of justifications for new purchases.

The maintenance manager might want to consider the formula developed by the National Association of Bank Auditors and Comptrollers. This association estimates that every daily savings of ten minutes labor by a $5,000 a year employee justifies a $1,000 expenditure for equipment.

Criteria for Purchasing Equipment

Personnel Prior to purchasing a particular piece of maintenance equipment, competent operating personnel must be available to operate the equipment. Should operating personnel not be available, the possibility of having the maintenance service provided on a contractual basis should be investigated.

Frequency of Use Should the maintenance equipment item under consideration be required only on an occasional basis, then it would be well to investigate the possibility of occasionally renting such equipment when it is needed.

Replacement Parts and Repair Service A major consideration in the selection of maintenance equipment would be the immediate availability of parts and repair service so as to minimize the "down" time of the equipment in question.

Equipment Storage Space Sufficient proper storage for maintenance equipment is essential to minimize deterioration and accelerated repairs due to improper storage. That sufficient storage space should be provided in advance of acquiring maintenance equipment is obvious.

Equipment Versatility In appraising expensive equipment, maintenance managers in recreation/park systems should make special note of the machine's versatility. Some floor cleaning pieces, for example, can clean, scrub, buff, and even vacuum. Every additional job that a tool can handle bolsters the economic justification for purchasing it. Some of the greatest economies can come in the area of floor maintenance, a job that consumes 30 to 40 percent of the custodial budget.

Equipment Size Prior to selecting a particular brush, broom, or machine, analyze each size available. A 19-inch disk floor machine, for instance, may cost 15 percent more, but it will cover 25 percent more area. The size of the equipment must also be correlated with characteristics of the area. A 48-inch broom will obviously cover twice as much space as a 24-inch broom, but it may prove too cumbersome for cramped hallways and stairs.

Equipment Standardization Standardization is important because it simplifies repair and replacement of key parts. It also reduces stock room costs and confusion, since parts for only one type of each machine need be stored. According to one expert, standardization is valuable enough to justify giving those companies featuring it a 5 to 10 percent advantage in a competitive bidding situation.

The following basic list of custodial maintenance equipment is recommended for building custodial care in a small recreation/park system:

Custodial Maintenance Equipment

1. floor machines, 18"
2. vacuum cleaner, domestic type
3. vacuum cleaner, industrial type with attachments

4. floor machine, large, capable of scrubbing large areas (gymnasiums)
5. wall washing machine
6. carpet-pile-lifter machine

Evaluation of Supplies
Maintenance supplies, because of their regular use, usually represent costly budget items. It is most important, therefore, that the various kinds of maintenance supply items available to accomplish a particular maintenance task be evaluated as to their efficiency and appropriateness for the type and location of the building or facility being maintained.

Standardization The benefits of standardization in the use of maintenance supplies may be experienced in standardized personnel training and financial saving in terms of ordering greater quantities at lesser costs. Standardization has practical application in the area of maintenance equipment in that the problem of replacement parts and repair service for multiple pieces of equipment of the same brand greatly simplifies the problem.

Stockpiling of Maintenance Supplies Stockpiling supplies, as well as some building and construction materials, can prove to be economical. Certainly there is potential time to be saved in being able to immediately schedule maintenance work without having to wait for parts and materials to be ordered and delivered. However, it must be recognized that adequate storage must be available, together with personnel who are responsible for a system of inventory control to ensure availability and to prevent overstocking of particular items. In addition, control over environmental factors such as heat, cold, ventilation, light, and dampness is essential in any successful stockpiling effort.

Stockpiling can result in lower prices being paid through the practice of contracyclical purchasing; that is, to purchase items during periods of depressed prices. The proximity to a supplier is another important consideration as to whether or not you should stockpile. If your supplier is close at hand, in most instances it would be wise to use his storage facilities if yours are limited or nonexistent. The type and amount of maintenance equipment and supplies will vary with each building and structure and its pattern of use. Careful analysis and sound planning will result in the saving of substantial costs.

Custodial or Housekeeping Services

Today's building custodial work is, by necessity, the responsibility of a specialist knowledgeable in the use of the latest maintenance equipment materials and techniques. No longer is the building custodian a manual laborer who sells the services of his muscles. The effective building custodian is now a specialist who understands the chemistry of cleaning agents, the synthetics and plastics involved in building and furniture construction, an engineer who understands the proper use and care of power equipment, the businessman who wisely and economically spends the maintenance dollar for top quality results. Of equal importance is the fact that the modern day building maintenance custodian must serve effectively as a public relations man, a policeman, a trainer of other employees, and the guardian of public health and safety in and around the building or structure for which he is responsible.

Custodial Cleaning Standards

A seemingly resonable and logical way for the housekeeping manager to commence with a cleaning operation would be to first establish standards or levels of cleanliness and then deduce what finances, manpower, equipment, and supplies are necessary to achieve them. Unfortunately, the housekeeping manager rarely enjoys the opportunity to start from scratch. Instead, he usually inherits an ongoing operation where standards are determined by past funding levels. Unfortunate also is the fact that the housekeeping manager rarely finds logically developed and widely accepted standards to apply to his situation.

Most authorities recommend that every recreation system develop its own building-cleaning standards without explaining what these standards should be or how they should be discovered. The discussion of cleaning standards is usually concluded with the statement that each agency establish standards according to "organizational or community preference."

In practice, there are two kinds of cleaning standards: general and specific. General standards usually apply to the whole recreation/park system or to individual recreation buildings, and it is usually the members of the recreation system governing board who decide which level of cleanliness—fair, good, or excellent—will be met under current budgetary restrictions. Specific cleaning standards apply to the frequencies and methods used for specific cleaning tasks. To accomplish a change in general standards, the custodial division alters the specific standards. For example, as part of a program to upgrade a recreation system from fair to good, the custodial manager might require all hallways to be damp-mopped three times weekly instead of once weekly and all rugs and carpets to be vacuumed daily rather than weekly.

General and specific cleaning standards require the establishment of performance categories such as fair, good, or excellent. It is essential that each category be clearly defined in specific, although arbitrary, performance levels. This is the job of the custodial manager. Note the Housekeeping Standards which appear in the appendix to Chapter 4.

The manager of a well organized custodial division will be able to show the recreation system governing board how much time (and therefore how much money) will be needed to provide each level of cleaning for every major kind of building area. Table 4-1 illustrates how such a major area cleaning time list might be developed for recreation center buildings. Methods utilized for determining cleaning performance times are discussed later in this chapter.

Table 4-1

Achievement levels of cleaning for major areas in a hypothetical recreation center building

	Excellent	Good	Fair
Center Office	12 min.	10 min.	8 min.
Center Gymnasium	25	20	15
Center Shower & Locker Room	30	25	20
Center Lounge	20	15	10
Center Meeting Room	17	15	10
Small Library	21	15	10
Fixture Bathroom	23	20	20
Equipment & Supply Room (150 sq. ft.)	7	5	3

When the custodial manager inherits an ongoing cleaning service with implicit standards based on past funding, he should avoid altering the operation and defining explicit standards until he knows, rather precisely, how well the current service is operating. To evaluate the current service, the manager would do well to determine how both the building custodians and the building occupants appraise the existing program.

Such an evaluation can be conducted on the basis of two prepared questionnaires. The first questionnaire would require custodial personnel to describe the tasks for which they believe they are responsible, noting the frequency of execution and self-evaluation of the effectiveness of their job performance. A second questionnaire would then be prepared and distributed to recreation building occupants requesting that they describe the cleaners' work and rate the results as good, fair, or poor.

From an analysis of the information provided by this evaluation, the custodial manager can get a fairly accurate indication of the work being done as well as a fairly reliable estimate of the actual cleaning standards being achieved. This information then should provide an initial basis for recommendations to the system administrator and the system policy-making body for service expansion or reduction and a policy statement establishing cleaning standards.

Custodial Staffing

For the custodial manager, a policy statement from the policy-making body that establishes general cleaning standards will greatly simplify the practical problems of determining staff needs. A cleaning standards policy will provide a goal for cleaning frequencies and methods that the custodial manager can convert into numbers of men and types of cleaning equipment. However, the cleaning standards policy statement is only the starting point in solving staffing problems.

Following the establishment of cleaning standards, the building maintenance manager should proceed to develop a custodial task inventory, that should consist of a listing of all the building housekeeping jobs for which the division is responsible during one complete year. The evaluation questionnaire suggested earlier can be of considerable help as a start in developing the custodial task inventory. The task inventory will allow the housekeeping manager to determine what the annual man-hour load for his section should be. With hour deductions for vacations, holidays, and estimated sick leave, etc., the total work force needs cannot be justified in terms of high personnel costs. Therefore, the custodial task inventory must be refined in order to more accurately determine custodial manpower needs.

Three basic approaches to determine proper staffing levels are utilized with no widespread agreement as to which method is the most effective except the general agreement that the more complex methods will probably increase custodial efficiency and will definitely require more time and energy to put into practice.

The following staffing determination methods are presented in order of complexity, from simple to complex.

1. **Staffing by Square Footage**
   This approach simply utilizes a crude rule-of-thumb guide, such as one man-year per 15,000 general square feet (arbitrary figure). The manager simply divides the recreation system's total building floor area by the arbitrarily selected figure to identify the number of persons needed to handle the annual workload. Because of its simplicity, it is probably the most popular staffing method. Because it fails to distinguish among the different kinds of space to be cleaned (i.e., gym floors versus office space), it is definitely the least accurate method unless carefully modified on the basis of experience and results.

2. **Staffing by Typical Area Measurement**
   This system is basically a modification of the traditional time and motion study and requires custodial managers to follow six basic steps.
   - Catalog each building in the system for the different spaces to be cleaned: office, meeting, activity room, etc.
   - Time the work of several custodians in each kind of area and observe the different cleaning methods employed.
   - Average all times for like areas. This number will be important for calculating total work force and for estimating future workload changes resulting from new buildings.
   - Divide each building into floors. Calculate workload for each floor by multiplying the number of each area by its average cleaning time. For example, 6 offices at 10 minutes per office means 60 minutes cleaning time is required.
   - Add all the times together. Divide by the number of minutes each custodian works per day to get the number of men required to perform the duties at the specified cleaning level.

- To establish the budget request, classify the positions and multiply the number of positions by the proposed wage.

3. **Staffing by Time and Motion Study**
This method requires a total inventory of each task the custodial division must perform.

- Supervisors must go into every room of every building in the system and count the number of desks, chairs, file cabinets, trash baskets, light fixtures, air registers, window shades, and blinds, and then record the different types of cleaning surfaces on these fixtures, floors, walls, and ceilings.

- With such an inventory, the supervisor looks up what the average cleaning time should be for each task. His source might be the average cleaning times as estimated and published by the Environmental Management Association, 1710 Drew Street, Clearwater, Florida, or as modified to his experience. (See Figure 4-4, A Sample Inventory of Light Duty Custodial Tasks, and Figure 4-5, A Sample Inventory of Heavy Duty Custodial Tasks.)

- Using the cleaning standards utilized by his organization, the custodial manager then multiplies the frequencies for each job by the average cleaning time.

- By adding the results, the manager will find the total number of man-hours required annually. From this sum he can determine the number of men needed for the custodial staff.

Since these calculations utilize national averages, the important variable to watch for is local differences in worker productivity, which can be significant. Custodial managers can develop a more accurate variant of this method by measuring and averaging actual work times of employees and comparing them with the time standards of the National Sanitation Foundation. This kind of inventory is time-consuming to compile, but it will provide several potential benefits.

1. It will help the manager establish staffing requirements with greater accuracy than the other methods.
2. It will enable the manager to develop realistic and equitable job assignments.
3. It will provide the manager with comprehensive job descriptions.
4. It will allow the manager to exercise daily quality control by use of complete task check lists.
5. It will permit the manager to exercise effective job correction procedures.

SAMPLE INVENTORY OF LIGHT DUTY CUSTODIAL TASKS

Building _____ Room _____ Square Feet _____

Operation	Weekly Fre-quency	Quantity	Unit Measure	Unit Time	Weekly Time
Ash Tray, clean			Each	0.25	
Ash Urn, empty			Each	1.00	
Bookcase, dust			Each	0.36	
Bulletin Boards, change			Each	1.80	
Chairs, Medium, dust			Each	0.58	
Chairs, Small, dust			Each	0.37	
Chalk Boards, clean			100 Lin Ft	17.70	
Desk, Large, dust			Each	0.80	
Desk, Small, dust			Each	0.63	
Doors, clean			Each	0.67	
Drinking Fountain, wash			Each	2.00	
Filing Cabinets, dust			Each	0.37	
Floor, dry clean (Heavily Obstructed)			M Sq Ft	16.00	
Floor, dry clean (Slightly Obstructed)			M Sq Ft	10.00	
Floor, dry clean (Unobstructed)			M Sq Ft	5.00	
Furniture, vacuum			Each	2.16	
Hospital Unit, clean			Each	15.00	
Hospital Unit, Check Out, clean			Each	30.00	
Lamps, dust			Each	0.25	
Lecturn, dust			Each	0.25	
Lockers, dust			100 Lin Ft	5.00	
Mirror, wash and polish			Sq Ft	0.10	
Pencil Sharpener, empty			Each	0.25	
Piano, dust & wash keys			Each	2.50	
Radiator, dust			Each	0.60	
Rugs, vacuum			M Sq Ft	22.20	
Shelves, dust			100 Lin Ft	2.00	
Sink, Soap Dispenser, clean and refill			Each	2.00	
Stairs, dust			Flight	4.00	
Telephone, dust			Each	0.15	
Toilet, clean, private			Each	1.00	
Towel Disp, clean/refill			Each	0.25	
Venetian Blind, dust			Each	3.50	
Waste Basket, empty			Each	0.25	
Window Sill, dust			Each	0.20	
Windows, wash, inside			Sq Ft	0.168	

Reproduced with permission of the Environmental Management Association.

Figure 4-4 A Sample Inventory of Light Duty Custodial Tasks

SAMPLE INVENTORY OF HEAVY DUTY CUSTODIAL TASKS

Building _____ Room _____ Square Feet _____

Operation	Weekly Fre-quency	Quantity	Unit Measure	Unit Time	Weekly Time
Airvents, clean			Each	2.00	
Drapes, remove & replace			Pair	20.00	
Elevator, clean			Each	3.25	
Floor, mop, damp (Heavily Obstructed)			M Sq Ft	32.00	
Floor, mop, damp (Slightly Obstructed)			M Sq Ft	23.00	
Floor, mop, damp (Unobstructed)			M Sq Ft	16.00	
Floor, scrub (Heavily Obstructed)			M Sq Ft	55.00	
Floor, scrub (Slightly Obstructed)			M Sq Ft	45.00	
Floor, scrub (Unobstructed)			M Sq Ft	35.00	
Floors, auto scrub			M Sq Ft	12.00	
Floors, refinish (Heavily Obstructed)			M Sq Ft	180.00	
Floors, spray buff			M Sq Ft	100.00	
Light Fixture, relamp & clean			Ea/Sec/	10.00	
Mats, wash & replace			Each	10.00	
Rugs, shampoo			M Sq Ft	210.00	
Stairs, mop			Flight	10.00	
Toilet & Partition, clean			Each	3.00	
Urinal, clean			Each	2.00	
Venetian Blind, wash			Each	20.00	
Walls, wash			Sq Ft	0.30	
Windows, wash, outside			Sq Ft	0.168	

Figure 4–5 A Sample Inventory of Heavy Duty Custodial Tasks

Following the selection and use of one of the aforementioned methods to determine annual workload, the custodial manager should proceed with several additional calculations before completing his work. The number of hours per work week (assuming 40) are multiplied by the number of weeks per year (52), which results in 2,080 potential work hours per year. However, the custodial manager must correct the 2,080 hours to allow for vacation time, holidays, average sick leave, etc., which usually reduces the number of productive work hours to approximately 1,800. By utilizing this latter figure, the manager can divide his annual man-hour workload to get the number of custodial personnel needed. He can then estimate the number of supervisors necessary to provide a proper span of control over the custodians. The proper span of control is the number of subordinates a particular supervisor can supervise effectively, and is influenced by such factors as the managerial skill of the supervisor, the level of competence of the subordinates being supervised, availability of training, etc. The number of supervisors added to the number of custodians should give the total work force needed.

Custodial Work Assignments

Two basic methods are widely used for assigning regularly scheduled custodial work. The first involves assigning one individual the responsibility for all custodial work in a designated area such as one floor of a large building. The second method requires assigning a group of custodians to handle all the cleaning jobs in a larger area such as a whole building. The following are potential advantages of each of the two basic methods of scheduling custodial work.

Individual Cleaning (1) Pride of achievement is generally stronger when an employee knows he has sole responsibility for an area. (2) Less monotony results when an employee has a variety of different tasks to handle each working day. (3) The improved morale due to pride of achievement and less monotony helps reduce turnover, which is always a problem with custodial workers. (4) Responsibility for poor work, breakage, and even petty thievery is established when each area is assigned to one employee. (5) It is relatively easy for one man to arrange his work sequence around the use needs of the occupants.

Crew Cleaning (1) The primary advantage is greater specialization. Instead of one man performing all the tasks in a certain area, crews specialize in a limited number of tasks and, theoretically at least, complete them more efficiently. Because of specialization, proponents claim that more work is accomplished by fewer men. (2) Morale is improved because employees have company while working. (3) Less custodial equipment is needed than with area assignments. (4) Custodial workloads are more equitably distributed. (5) Unexpected absences cause less disruption, since several workers cover every area and can fill in.

Many organizations have found it advantageous to combine individual and crew cleaning. For many simple, daily tasks, individual area assignments would seem to be most efficient. For many of the heavier, more complicated, and less frequent jobs, crew assignments are more appropriate. Damp-mopping, dusting, trash collecting, and similar simple jobs require only one man; two or more would be wasteful.

On the other hand, refinishing floors, cleaning high areas with scaffolds, and cleaning and reinstalling venetian blinds inevitably require more than one person. Such infrequent jobs could be assigned to specialized crews that would perform them in all buildings according to a regular schedule. This approach eliminates the problem of teaching every individual specialized skills that he would only use occasionally.

Labor-Saving Designs and Practices

Building Design and Cleanability

The custodial manager who "inherits" a building that is over-costly to clean is more to be pitied than censured but the reverse is true when he stands idly by and accepts the architect's dream building without questioning its cleanability. Cleaning requirements seem to be low on the totem pole of architectural and engineering priorities in building design. Few architects seem to have a reasonable conception of how the cleaning will be accomplished in the building they design and build for an unsuspecting client.

Building cleanability is enormously important because custodial labor costs have more than doubled in the last twenty years while numerous innovations in methods, equipment, building design, and materials have occurred. Few of these changes are reflected in design for greater cleanability, without the vigorous prompting of alert custodial managers during the design stage of building development.

If the custodial manager is to succeed in his mission toward greater building cleanability, he must follow a two-step program. First, he must interpret to the architect the necessity of certain essential custodial facilities and design features that will help to guarantee economical cleaning service. This is best accomplished by providing the architect with a check list. Second, the custodial manager must insist on the opportunity for plan review at every important phase of the design process. When developing a checklist of materials, design features, and custodial facilities, the custodial manager should take into systematic consideration the following possibilities.

Floors
- Avoid floors requiring hand maintenance or care by other than average custodians.
- Along corridors, avoid recesses and projections.
- Insist that concrete subfloors be machine trowelled and properly cured with all depressions and high points corrected before the application of resilient tile. Such irregularities wear more quickly and increase maintenance costs.
- Install floor drains in all washrooms.
- Avoid floors that meet at different levels. Flush joints are preferred; if a difference of elevations is unavoidable, then choose ramps with nonskid surfaces instead of steps.
- For wall bases, use scrub-free material, cove design and rounded joints.

Walls
- Use glazed materials on walls of abuse-prone hallways, stairways, washrooms, kitchens, and custodial closets.
- Require paints that are durable, washable, light reflective, and light in color. Where decorative effects are needed, try plastic wall coverings with proper flame-spread ratings.
- In general, select materials that can be dusted as well as wet-cleaned.

Ceilings
- Gypsum base acoustical tile is better than softer materials. Hard plastered ceilings covered by high quality enamel are best for

food service and washroom areas. Health departments usually prohibit acoustical treatments for these ceilings.

Openings

- Walkways leading to doors should be of hard material and properly drained to prevent tracking.
- Use matting or walk-off rugs at entrances to trap soil.
- Choose flush rather than panelled doors to prevent collection of dust.
- Remember that translucent or tinted glass is easier to maintain than transparent glass.
- Caulking should be smooth and continuous.
- To eliminate painting, select aluminum window framing instead of wood or steel.
- In multi-story structures, consider a permanent device for window washing. At the very least, provide lugs for window washers' safety belts.
- For minimum maintenance, use marble or slate window sills.

Furnishings and Equipment

- Dispensers and cabinets should be large enough to provide at least a full day's requirements; double dispensers for holding a reserve supply are most effective and reduce waste.
- To permit rapid cleaning and prevent damage to equipment, hang fixtures such as urinals, ash trays, and water fountains, on the wall.
- Use soap dispensers with metal or plastic containers that may be refilled without spilling.
- Metal, plastic and composition materials are more easily cleaned than wood furniture.
- Lockers should be placed on concrete or ceramic base so soil cannot be trapped underneath, and their tops should be slanted for easy cleaning.
- Place waste receptacles immediately adjacent to areas where waste is created, using liners and covers for odorous or edible material.

Custodial Facilities

- Provide adequate sources of both hot and cold water throughout the building as well as sufficient electrical outlets in halls and stairways for custodial use.
- Be sure custodial closets and lockers are adequate in number and size and are properly located.

- Devise a standard layout to provide storage for all reserve supplies and to facilitate laundering, treating and hanging tools such as dust cloths, dust mops, and wet mops.

Figure 4-6 enumerates and illustrates criteria for custodian closets as recommended by the University of New Mexico Physical Plant Department.

Contract Cleaning

Most custodial managers consider contractual cleaning at some point—often when faced with a major expansion or revamping of their operations. Private firms are sometimes able to provide better service than an in-house operation and at a lower cost. Through extensive studies, specialized cleaning firms are able to engineer carefully planned housekeeping programs that eliminate much of the waste that can develop in an in-house cleaning operation. However, before deciding whether or not to employ a contractor, the manager should analyze existing operations and evaluate the following advantages and disadvantages.

A primary advantage to be enjoyed is that a contractor will take over administrative tasks such as staffing, scheduling, supervision, and training. A good firm can manage these tasks more efficiently than can a small park/recreation organization with a cleaning staff of less than ten employees. Such a service can also prove economical for the large recreation/park system with widely scattered buildings and for those systems that have difficulty finding enough employees.

A distinct disadvantage, under certain conditions, can be a deterioration in cleaning quality. The inescapable fact about contract cleaning is that making a profit is the primary goal of all commercial firms. Maintaining the best environment for recreation will always be secondary to this end. In order to maximize profits, such firms face a constant temptation to cut services as much as they possibly can and still hold the job.

Additional disadvantages of contract cleaning include less flexibility, delays in service for unusual or emergency jobs, charges for "extras," less control over the type of individuals hired for the work, and additional security problems.

LOCATION OF CUSTODIAN CLOSETS

IS *VERY IMPORTANT!*

- Custodian closets should be centrally located.
- There should be no area in a building more than 150 feet in walking distance from a "wet" closet.
- In a school building each custodian closet should not serve in excess of 15,000 square feet.
- Well-planned buildings should have custodian closets on every floor.
- Good locations for secondary custodian closets are: close to elevators . . . . close to main pedestrian areas . . . . between two restrooms.

  - CRITERIA FOR VERTICAL TRANSPORTION

  1. There should be an elevator in every multi-storied building.
  2. The elevator should land on every floor including the basement.
  3. This elevator should be available to custodian and maintenance personnel.

A PROPER WORK ROOM IS INDISPENSABLE TO THE MORALE AND EFFICIENCY OF THE CUSTODIAN.

WE CONSIDER IT POOR PLANNING TO LOCATE A CUSTODIAN CLOSET:

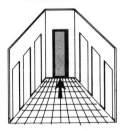

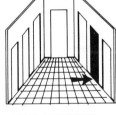

LEAST EFFICIENT   MOST EFFICIENT

AT THE DEAD END OF A CORRIDOR. A situation such as this results in many unnecessary steps for the custodian.

ON A STAIR LANDING. A stair landing closet would cause the custodian to always carry utensils and equipment up and down stairs.

INSIDE ANOTHER ROOM (unless that closet serves only that room).

UNDER STAIRWAYS. Low ceilings and narrow dimensions are hard to ventilate.

IN NARROW SPACES. The custodian must move his equipment into the hall to utilize a narrow room.

TELEPHONE SWITCHING GEAR, ELEVATOR CONTROLS, ELECTRIC PANELS, OR OTHER SERVICE FUNCTIONS ARE NOT COMPATIBLE WITH CUSTODIAN OPERATIONS, AND SHOULD NOT BE LOCATED INSIDE CUSTODIAN CLOSETS. . . . OPENINGS TO PIPE CHASES OR MECHANICAL EQUIPMENT AREAS SHOULD NOT BE LOCATED INSIDE CUSTODIAN CLOSETS.

NO!

Reproduced with permission of the University of New Mexico Physical Plant Department.

Figure 4–6 Criteria for Custodian Closets

CUSTODIAN SERVICES are inherent to the operations of buildings, and proper service areas must be considered WITH ALL OTHER AREAS DURING THE PROGRAMMING AND PLANNING STAGES of each building.

Universally accepted standards have yet to be set for custodian closets and storerooms. However, certain criteria for size, shape, location, and special appurtenances have been developed which are compatible with present cleaning procedures and today's cleaning equipment.

CUSTODIAN CLOSETS should be planned to function primarily as the WORK ROOMS of the men and women responsible for cleaning the interior surfaces of the building. We, at the University of New Mexico, have developed the following criteria for our custodian closets:

CUSTODIAN CLOSETS SHOULD HAVE:

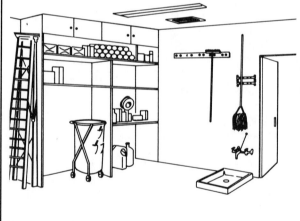

RECESSED LIGHT FIXTURES (to allow for clearance of long broom and mop handles) providing 75 F.C. of light.

ADEQUATE VENTILATION FACILITIES.

SLOT FOR A LADDER.

PEGS for storage of rotary brushes.

HANGERS for wet mops over the sink.

HANGERS and WALL SPACE for dust mops and brooms.

HARD SURFACE WALLS—impervious to water.

SHELVES in closet to accommodate supplies in case lots, and to allow for storage of liquids in original 5- or 6-gallon containers.

A 36" DOOR that swings OUT, not into the room.

HOT and COLD WATER OUTLETS not less than 24" above a FLOOR TYPE BASIN. Basin curb should be 6" minimum above the floor.

A grounded duplex OUTLET in "open" wall; not behind shelves. FLOOR SPACE for large machines.

Figure 4-6 (Continued)

Large recreation systems are less likely to benefit from contract services than small systems, but even they may find it profitable to supplement their on-going, in-house service with some contract work. Many systems contract out dangerous jobs such as washing upper story windows as well as the more specialized tasks of tree trimming and athletic field lumenaire replacement. This kind of arrangement allows the system to bring highly trained personnel to their location for difficult projects and simultaneously retain an in-house staff for regular and emergency cleaning.

The most important precaution prior to employing a contractor is the preparation of a set of detailed specifications covering all facets of the job, including how, when, and by whom the work is to be done. To prepare these specifications, the custodial manager should first compile a complete inventory of areas to be cleaned and specify cleaning standards to be achieved for each. Such a survey can also provide a realistic price estimate to use in evaluating all bids submitted. See the Specifications for Contract Janitorial Services in the appendix to this chapter.

Contract Cleaning Specifications

The maintenance manager should also evaluate the contractor's integrity and competence as carefully as the price. This can be accomplished by investigating the contractor's references, previous work, personnel, and working methods and financial status. Any bid that is considerably lower than all others should be investigated. If the low bid cannot be traced to some economy in methods, do not award the contract to that bidder. Otherwise, the contractor will probably be forced to cut services in order to make a profit. It would be wiser, then, to hire a firm with a reputation for responsible performance. After the contract is awarded, some member of the maintenance division staff should be assigned the task of systematically inspecting the contractor's work to insure that it is in compliance with all provisions of the contract.

Review Questions

1. Describe the basic corps of tradesmen necessary for structural and system building maintenance.

2. Indicate the basic elements involved in a preventive building maintenance program.

3. Describe a satisfactory method for scheduling the infrequent but routine preventive maintenance jobs.

4. What criteria should be considered when determining the feasibility of purchasing various building maintenance equipment items?

5. Describe building custodial cleaning standards and how they are developed.

6. Outline the three basic methods of determining building custodian staffing requirements.

7. Discuss the advantages and disadvantages of individual and crew custodial cleaning.

8. In what ways does building design relate to building "cleanability"?

9. Describe the recommended features that should be included in a building custodian closet.

10. Cite the advantages and disadvantages of contract building cleaning.

11. What investigative steps should the maintenance manager take in the event that an unusually low bid for janitorial work is received from an unfamiliar contractor?

12. What should be included in written contract specifications for contract janitorial services?

Bibliography

Books and Manuals

District Heating Handbook. National District Heating Association.

The Economy of Energy Conservation in Educational Facilities. Educational Facilities Laboratories. 477 Madison Avenue, New York, New York 10022.

Environmental Management Association. "Sample Inventory of Light and Heavy Duty Custodial Tasks." 1710 Drew Street, Clearwater, Florida 33515.

Feldman, Edwin B. *Housekeeping Handbook for Institutions, Business and Industry.* New York: Frederick Fell, 1969.

Guide and Data Book. American Society of Heating, Refrigerating and Air Conditioning Engineers, 1972.

Haines, John E. *Automatic Control of Heating and Air Conditioning,* 2nd ed. New York: McGraw-Hill, 1961.

Maintenance Guide for Commercial Buildings. Cedar Rapids, Iowa: Stamats Publishing Company, 1970.

Morrow, L. C., ed. *Maintenance and Engineering Handbook.* New York: McGraw-Hill, 1957.

1970 Manual of Practice. The Construction Specifications Institute, Washington, D.C.

Price, Seymour G. *Air Conditioning for Building Engineers and Managers, Operation and Maintenance.* New York: Industrial Press, 1970.

———. A Guide to Monitoring and Controlling Utility Costs. BNA Books, 1231 25 Street, N.W., Washington, D.C. 20037.

Slack, Thomas F. *A Complete Guide to Buildings and Plant Maintenance.* New Jersey: Prentice-Hall, 1965.

Standard Handbook for Electrical Engineers. New York: McGraw-Hill, 1971.

Terry, Harry. *Mechanical-Electrical Equipment Handbook for School Buildings: Installation, Maintenance and Use.* New York: John Wiley & Sons, 1960.

Urquhart, Leonard Church. *Civil Engineering Handbook.* New York: McGraw-Hill, 1950.

Weber, George O., ed., and Fincham, Michael W. *A Basic Manual for Physical Plant Administration.* Washington, D.C.: The Association of Physical Plant Administrators of Universities and Colleges, 1974.

Monographs

Hopkins, William J. "Building and Structure Maintenance—Equipment, Materials and Supplies." A monograph prepared for the Park and Recreation Maintenance Management School, North Carolina State University. Raleigh, 1975.

——. "Building and Structure Maintenance—Doors, Windows, Walls and Roofs." A monograph prepared for the Park and Recreation Maintenance Management School, North Carolina State University. Raleigh, 1975.

Otten, Robert J. "Building and Structure Maintenance—Floors and Floor Coverings." A monograph prepared for the Park and Recreation Maintenance Management School, North Carolina State University. Raleigh, 1975.

Young, Charles A. Jr. "Building and Structure Maintenance—Mechanical Systems." A monograph prepared for the Park and Recreation Maintenance Management School, North Carolina State University. Raleigh, 1975.

Magazines

American School and University. *The Buildings Magazine.* Educational Communications Division of North American Publishing Company, 134 North 13 Street, Philadelphia, Pennsylvania 19107.

Building Operating Management. Trade Press Publishing Company, 470 E. Michigan Street, Milwaukee, Wisconsin 53202.

Building Research, Journal of the BRAB. Building Research Institute, BRAB Building, National Research Council, 2101 Constitution Avenue, N.W., Washington, D.C. 20418.

Buildings, The Construction and Building Management Journal. Stamats Publishing Company, 427 Sixth Avenue, S.E., Cedar Rapids, Iowa 52406.

Plant Engineering. Technical Publishing Company. 1301 S. Grove Avenue, Barrington, Illinois 60010.

Appendix

Multiple Level
*Maintenance Standards for Buildings**

Foundations

1. No termites or insect infestations.   **Level I**

2. Concrete free of spalling, leaks, cracks, and exposed reinforcing.

3. No warping, checking, splitting, broken, and damp wooden members.

4. Exposed masonry units have no cracked or open joints, leaks, cracked, or spalling elements.

5. Bolts and fasteners in place and secure.

6. Vents free from rust and corrosion, holes or rotten fabric, clogged or blocked openings, loose or missing hardware, and securely attached.

7. Ground surfaces free of debris and trash and graded.

8. Quarterly inspection to insure conformance.

*Reproduced with permission of the National Park Service of the U.S. Department of the Interior.   **199**

Level II   1. No termites or insect infestations.

2. Concrete and masonry free of leaks and cracks.

3. No broken or damp wood members.

4. Bolt fasteners secure.

5. Vents free from rust, holes, loose hardware.

6. Ground surface free of debris and trash.

7. Semi-annual inspection to insure conformance.

Level III   1. No termites or insect infestations.

2. Concrete, masonry and wooden units free of leaks and dampness.

3. Bolts and fasteners secure.

4. Vents free from holes.

5. Annual inspection to insure conformance.

Exterior Walls

Level I   1. Masonry units free of cracks and spalling, eroded or sandy joints, cracked units, stains, leaks.

2. Wood has no warping and cracking, rot and termites, stains, loose and missing fastenings, leaks.

3. Metal free of rust and pittings, loose, missing or broken fastenings, holes and punctures. Repaint when film is less than 3 mils in thickness.

4. Repainting scheduled on a three-to-five year cyclic basis or as required by climatic conditions.

5. Quarterly inspection to insure conformance.

Level II   1. Masonry units free of cracks, stains and leaks.

2. Wood free of leaks, termites and insect infestations, missing fastenings.

3. Metal has no rust and pitting. Repaint when film is less than 2 mils in thickness. Replace missing or broken fastenings.

4. Repainting scheduled on a five-to-seven year cyclic basis.

5. Semi-annual inspection to insure conformance.

1. Masonry units free from leaks.   **Level III**

2. No termites and insects.

3. Metal painted for protection.

4. Repainting scheduled on a seven-to-ten year cyclic basis.

5. Annual inspection to insure conformance.

Interior Walls and Ceilings

1. Free from leaks, cracks, decay and insect infestations, stains,   **Level I**
   and scuff marks, loose fastenings.

2. Paints and coverings free from abrasions, punctures, tears,
   fading and stains, and adhesive failures.

3. Repainting on a one-to-three year cyclic basis.

4. Metal surfaces polished.

5. Horizontal and vertical surfaces dust and grime free.

6. Quarterly inspection to insure conformance.

1. Free from leaks, decay and insect infestations, stains.   **Level II**

2. Paints and coverings free from abrasions, punctures, and tears.

3. Repainting on a two-to-four year cyclic basis.

4. Surfaces dust free.

5. Semi-annual inspection to insure conformance.

1. No leaks, termites and insect infestations.   **Level III**

2. Repaint on a three-to-five year cyclic basis.

3. Annual inspection to insure conformance.

Doors and Windows

Level I   1. Wood sash, doors, and trim have no splits, rot, cracks, loose or tight fits.

2. Metal sash and doors free from rust and corrosion, warping, and loose or tight fits.

3. Screens free from loose, broken or missing hardware; no rust or corrosion; no holes in fabric or wire; no wood rot, stain, or cracks and breaks.

4. No loose, broken or missing hardware; free from rust and corrosion; movement free and unhampered.

5. Glass clean and free of broken or cracked elements. Glazing compound secure, none missing.

6. Venetian blinds, draperies, etc., clean; free of spots and tears; no broken or loose fastenings; cords free of frayed or broken strands.

7. Daily inspection to insure conformance.

Level II   1. No cracks, rust, or corrosion in wood and metal elements.

2. No holes in screens; no broken or missing hardware; loose or tight fits.

3. Hardware secure; no broken or missing elements.

4. Glass clean and no more than 10 percent broken elements.

5. Venetian blinds, draperies, etc., clean and no tears or broken fastenings.

6. Bi-weekly inspection to insure conformance.

Level III   1. No cracks in wood and metal sash, doors, and trim.

2. Screens free of holes and hardware secure.

3. No more than 20 percent broken glass.

4. Venetian blinds, draperies, etc. clean.

5. Quarterly inspection to insure conformance.

Floors

1. Carpet and rugs free of ravelling, cuts and tears, fading and discoloration, loose anchorage, insect damage; vacuumed free of dust and dirt.

2. Resilient floors show no evidence of cracking, chipping, breaking, scratches, tears, uneven and loose bonding; free of moisture; waxed and buffed.

3. Wood free from sagging, splintering, loose, warped, rotten or scratched elements, stains, discoloration, and moisture; waxed and buffed. No termites or insect infestations.

4. All areas free of loose, damaged or missing bases, binding strips and thresholds, projecting nails, bolts or screws, slippery surfaces, loose or missing nosings or treads.

5. Daily inspection to insure conformance.

1. Carpets and rugs free of cuts and tears, loose anchorage, insects, dust and dirt.

2. Resilient floors show no evidence of cracking, chipping, breaking, scratches, tears, uneven and loose bonding; free of moisture; buffed.

3. Wood free from sagging, splintering, loose, warped, rotten, or scratched elements, stains, discoloration, and moisture; waxed and buffed. No termites or insect infestations.

4. All areas free of loose, damaged or missing bases; binding strips; and thresholds; projecting nails; bolts or screws; slippery surfaces; loose or missing nosings or treads.

5. Semi-weekly inspection to insure conformance.

1. Carpets and rugs free of cuts and tears, loose anchorage, dirt and dust.

2. Resilient floors free of uneven and loose bonding; no moisture; buffed.

3. Wood free from rotten and loose elements, moisture, termites. No dirt and dust; buffed.

4. No loose base strips, projecting nails or fastenings; loose nosings or treads.

5. Weekly inspection to insure conformance.

Gutters, Downspouts, and Roof Drains

Level I
1. Free of rust and corrosion, breaks or leaks.
2. Aligned and fastened.
3. Open and clear of leaves and dust, dirt accumulation.
4. Wire guards provided and in place.
5. Splash blocks in place, connection to storm sewer secure.
6. Repainting scheduled on a three-to-five year cyclic basis.
7. Quarterly inspection to insure conformance.

Level II
1. Free of rust and corrosion, breaks or leaks.
2. Securely fastened.
3. Clear of obstructions.
4. Splash blocks in place.
5. Repainted on a five-to-seven year cyclic basis.
6. Semi-annual inspection to insure conformance.

Level III
1. Free of breaks and leaks.
2. Securely fastened.
3. Clear of obstructions.
4. Repainted on a seven-to-ten year cyclic basis.
5. Annual inspection to insure conformance.

Roofs

Level I
1. Metal free of broken seams, rust or corrosion, holes and open joints, loose, broken, or missing fastenings.
2. Wood shingles, tile, or slate free from warped, broken, split, curled, and loose or missing elements.

3. Built-up roofs free from cracks, exposed coatings, blistered, curled, or buckled felts.

4. Watertight and free or water ponding.

5. Flashing free from rust, corrosion, open joints, loose, and missing fastenings.

6. Quarterly inspection to insure conformance.

1. Metal free of broken seams, rust or corrosion, holes and open joints, loose, broken, or missing fastenings.   **Level II**

2. Wood shingles, tile, or slate free from warped, broken, split, curled, and loose or missing elements.

3. Built-up roofs free from cracks, exposed coatings, blistered, curled, or buckled felts.

4. Watertight and free of water ponding.

5. Flashing free from rust, corrosion, open joints, loose, and missing fastenings.

6. Semi-annual inspection to insure conformance.

1. Metal free of broken seams, rust or corrosion, holes and open joints, loose, broken or missing fastenings.   **Level III**

2. Wood shingles, tile, or slate free from warped, broken, split, curled, and loose or missing elements.

3. Built-up roofs free from cracks, exposed coatings, blistered, curled, or buckled felts.

4. Watertight and free of water ponding.

5. Flashing free from rust, corrosion, open joints, loose, and missing fastenings.

6. Annual inspection to insure conformance.

Heating, Ventilating, and Air Conditioning

1. Air filter clear of dust, grease, and lint deposits or cleaned and replaced as necessary to maintain maximum efficiency of unit.   **Level I**

2. System mechanical elements free of dust, dirt, soot, grease deposits, lubricant drippings, rust and corrosion, chemical fumes, and loose, broken, or missing parts.

3. Wiring and electrical free of loose connections, frayed or worn braid, improperly sized or defective fuses.

4. Exposed piping has no clogged, rusted, or corroded, leaking parts. Valves, traps, and strainers clear of scale and leaks.

5. Ducts free from soot, dirt, grease, loose connections, joints, and seams.

6. Boiler standards according to *Heating, Ventilating and Air Conditioning Guide,* American Society of Heating and Ventilating Engineers. Annual inspections made by state inspector.

7. Monthly inspection to insure conformance.

Level II

1. Air filter clear of dust, grease, and lint deposits or cleaned and replaced as necessary to maintain maximum efficiency of unit.

2. System mechanical elements free of dust, dirt, soot, grease deposits, lubricant drippings, rust and corrosion, chemical fumes, and loose, broken, or missing parts.

3. Wiring and electrical free of loose connections, frayed or worn braid, improperly sized or defective fuses.

4. Exposed piping has no clogged, rusted, or corroded, leaking parts. Valves, traps, and strainers clear of scale and leaks.

5. Ducts free from soot, dirt, grease, loose connections, joints, and seams.

6. Boiler standards according to *Heating, Ventilating and Air Conditioning Guide,* American Society of Heating and Ventilating Engineers. Annual inspections made by state inspector.

7. Semi-annual inspection to insure conformance, except for Item #1.

Level III

1. Air filter clear of dust, grease, and lint deposits or cleaned and replaced as necessary to maintain maximum efficiency of unit.

2. System mechanical elements free of dust, dirt, soot, grease deposits, lubricant drippings, rust and corrosion, chemical fumes, and loose, broken, or missing parts.

3. Wiring and electrical free of loose connections, frayed or worn braid, improperly sized or defective fuses.

4. Exposed piping has no clogged, rusted, or corroded, leaking parts. Valves, traps, and strainers clear of scale and leaks.

5. Ducts free from soot, dirt, grease, loose connections, joints, and seams.

6. Boiler standards according to *Heating, Ventilating and Air Conditioning Guide,* American Society of Heating and Ventilating Engineers. Annual inspections made by state inspector.

7. Annual inspection to insure conformance, except for Item #1.

Interior Plumbing

1. Free of leaks, breaks, corrosion, stoppages, odors, and gases.   **Level I**

2. Insulation sealed and free of moisture.

3. Valves, checks, traps, operational, free of leaks, corrosion, incrustation, and obstructions.

4. Fixtures free of cracks in china, chips in porcelain, odors, stains.

5. Daily inspection to insure conformance.

1. Free of leaks, breaks, corrosion, stoppages, odors, and gases.   **Level II**

2. Insulation free of moisture.

3. Valves, checks, traps, operational, free of leaks, corrosion, incrustation, and obstructions.

4. Fixtures free of cracks in china, chips in porcelain, odors, stains.

5. Semi-weekly inspection to insure conformance.

1. Free of leaks, breaks, corrosion, stoppages, odors, and gases.   **Level III**

2. Valves, checks, traps, operational, free of leaks, corrosion, incrustation, and obstructions.

3. Fixtures free of cracks in china, chips in porcelain, odors, stains.

4. Weekly inspection to insure conformance.

Interior Electrical

Level I   1. According to National Electrical Code 1965, NFPA No. 70, ASA C1-1965 as adopted by the National Park Service.

2. Quarterly inspection to insure conformance.

3. Breaker boxes and fuse panels labeled and identified by circuit.

Level II   1. According to National Electrical Code 1965, NFPA No. 70, ASA C1-1965 as adopted by the National Park Service.

2. Semi-annual inspection to insure conformance.

3. Breaker boxes and fuse panels labeled and identified by circuit.

Level III   1. According to National Electrical Code 1965, NFPA No. 70, ASA C1-1965 as adopted by the National Park Service.

2. Annual inspection to insure conformance.

3. Breaker boxes and fuse panels labeled and indentified by circuit.

Lighting

Level I   1. Illumination units free of dirt and dust and secure. No cracked or broken luminaries and fixture parts, exposed wiring, broken or missing pullcords, loose socket connections.

2. Fluorescent units free of flickering and loud humming lamps.

3. No burned out lamps.

4. Daily inspection to insure conformance.

Level II   1. Illumination units free of dirt and dust and secure. No cracked or broken luminaries and fixture parts, exposed wiring, broken or missing pullcords, loose socket connections.

2. Fluorescent units free of flickering and loud humming lamps.

3. No burned out lamps.

4. Semi-weekly inspection to insure conformance.

1. Illumination units free of exposed wiring, loose socket connec-   **Level III**
   tions; no broken luminaries or fixture parts.
2. No burned out lamps.
3. Weekly inspection to insure conformance.

Housekeeping

1. Furnishings, tools, and equipment located not to hamper circu-   **Level I**
   lation and as per design.
2. Free from protrusions from cabinets, desks, racks, bins,
   benches, aisles, and work areas. Free of boxes, baskets, and
   clutter. Boxes, containers, supplies, materials in storage bins,
   shelves.
3. Wastebaskets and ash trays empty and clean. Radiators, desks,
   cabinets, louvers, exhibit cases, panels and displays clean and
   dusted.
4. Metal surfaces polished.
5. Restroom and washroom areas free of odors and clean. Soap,
   paper, and towel racks filled. Mirrors clear of fingerprints and
   shelves clean, polished, and free of debris.
6. No clothing, boxes, packages hung or lying on benches, desks,
   tables, counters, machines.
7. Drinking fountains clean and clear of debris and leaks. Trash
   receptacles when paper cups provided. Free of spots and water
   marks. Fully operational.
8. Stock storage areas clean and cleaning equipment near and in
   place.
9. Washbasins, toilet bowls, and porcelain clean and bright, free of
   spots and smears.
10. Daily inspection to insure conformance.

1. Furnishings, tools, and equipment located not to hamper circu-   **Level II**
   lation and as per design.
2. Free from protrusions from cabinets, desks, racks, bins,
   benches, aisles, and work areas. Free of boxes, baskets, and

clutter. Boxes, containers, supplies, materials in storage bins, shelves.

3. Wastebaskets and ash trays empty and clean. Exhibit cases, panels and displays dusted.

4. Metal surfaces clean.

5. Restroom and washroom areas free of odors and clean. Soap, paper, and towel racks filled. Mirrors clear of fingerprints and shelves clean, polished, and free of debris.

6. No clothing, boxes, packages hung or lying on benches, desks, tables, counters, machines.

7. Drinking fountains clean, clear of debris and leaks. Fully operational.

8. Stock storage areas clean.

9. Washbasins, toilet bowls, and porcelain clean and bright, free of spots and smears.

10. Semi-weekly inspection to insure conformance.

Level III

1. Furnishings, tools, and equipment arranged neatly.

2. Free from protrusions from cabinets, desks, racks, bins, benches, aisles, and work areas. Free of boxes, baskets, and clutter. Boxes, containers, supplies, materials in storage bins, shelves.

3. Wastebaskets and ash trays empty and clean.

4. Metal surfaces clean.

5. Restrooms and washrooms clean and supplies furnished.

6. No clothing, boxes, packages hung or lying on benches, desks, tables, counters, machines.

7. Drinking fountains clear of debris and leaks.

8. Washbasins, toilet bowls and porcelain free of spots and smears.

9. Weekly inspection to insure conformance.

Sample Specifications for Contract Janitorial Services

Metropolitan Recreation District

Maintenance Division   Date _____

Section I   Information for Bidders

The Janitorial Services Contractor shall furnish all labor and equip-   **1-01**
ment necessary to perform the janitorial services, including cleaning, dusting, wicking, mopping, stripping, waxing, polishing, washing, removal of trash and waste materials, refilling of dispensers,
plus "As Required" services described herein such as minimal access snow removal in the buildings listed, and to be included in any
buildings which might be added in an extension of this contract.

A general map is attached showing the location of each of the   **1-02**
above buildings. The contractor must physically inspect each building before submitting his bid. *Space diagrams of each building are
attached as part of these specifications.* These show the area to be
cleaned in each building and approximate net area of each room.
Floor areas may be verified if desired.

BUILDINGS TO BE CLEANED	GROSS SQ. FT.	NET SQ. FT. TO BE CLEANED	**1-03**

Source: *A Basic Manual for Physical Plant Administration* (Washington, D.C.: The Association, 1974), pp. 191–199. Reproduced
with the permission of The Association of Physical Plant Administrators of Universities and Colleges.

1-04 Bids are requested in two ways, (1) a monthly Lump Sum charge for each of these buildings, (2) a bid based upon a "Time and Material" basis. The system reserves the right to award the contract for any one or any combination of buildings, whichever is in the best interest of the recreation system, on either the "Lump Sum" or "Time and Material" basis.

1-05 The Standard General Conditions of Contract attached hereto shall apply to this work.

1-06 Contractors are required to submit a bid bond for the sum of items in the lump sum prices based on the *total* lump sum contractual cost for a six-month period; or in lieu thereof a certified check in the amount of 5% of the total lump sum bid. Bond or check are forfeitable if bidder is awarded the contract and fails to perform.

1-07 The Contractor should clarify any questions he may have prior to his submission of a bid by contacting the Buildings Custodial Services Supervisor, located in the _____ Building, phone number_____ . The submission of a bid shall indicate that the Contractor thoroughly understands the scope of the work and the services to be performed.

1-08 While this initial contract is to be awarded for a six (6) month period, it can be extended for an additional six (6) month period, after periodic reviews and mutually agreed upon amendments up to a total of at least three (3) years.

1-09 It shall be the Contractor's responsibility for compliance with all local, county, state, and federal laws.

Section II General Conditions

2-01 The right is reserved by the Recreation District to reject any or all proposals, and to waive any formal requirements as the interest of the District may require. No Bidder may withdraw his bid within thirty (30) days after the formal opening thereof. Acceptance of any proposal will be subject to approval of submittal data and engineering equipment.

Bidders must allow sufficient time for all bids, either mailed or hand-carried, to reach this office by the date and time indicated for the bid opening. Late bids, including those postmarked prior to the bid opening date, will not be considered.   **2-02**

Forms for Bid Proposals are included in this specification. Bids are requested in triplicate. If you are not in a position to bid on the work at this time, please so state in writing on the Bid Proposal Form in order that the District may retain your name on its listing of preferred bidders for future work.   **2-03**

Contractors and Subcontractors should include the applicable Sales and Use Tax on all purchases. Contractors will be required to pay the tax on all purchases and can recover it only as a part of his price.   **2-04**

This contract is to be in force for a period of six months commencing _____ and terminating on _____ .   **2-05**

The District and the Contractor shall each have the right to terminate the Contract upon thirty days written notice to the other party.   **2-06**

In view of the policy of the District with respect to endorsement of products, materials or equipment of any manufacturer, the Contractor shall not permit endorsements by photographs or written statements involving the District without prior written approval of the District through the Building Custodial Services Section.   **2-07**

All work under this contract shall be inspected by the Supervisor   **2-08** of Building Custodial Services Section, or his representative, to insure strict compliance with the specifications.

2-09   Because of the acute shortage of parking space, the Contractor's personnel will be required to park in those parking areas where assigned. Failure of the Contractor's employees to park their personal automobiles where assigned may result in a parking violation citation, with accompanying monetary penalties or in violations of safety regulations the vehicles may be towed away and held until towing charge is paid.

2-10   Since the District cannot be responsible for losses of Contractor's supplies, tools, or equipment, Contractors are hereby notified of their responsibility for providing proper identification and security for such items at their own expense.

2-11   The Contractor will be responsible for all damages to District property caused by his employees. Such damage shall be repaired promptly by the Contractor to the satisfaction of the District, at no expense to the District.

2-12   The Contractor shall be responsible for payment of all of his payrolls including withholding taxes, social security, unemployment compensation insurance, and for payment of his public liability insurance and employee bonds. Particular attention is called to records required if the contract is awarded on the "Time and Material" basis.

2-13   Payment for services shall be made to the Contractor once a month upon submission of an invoice consisting of an original and two copies, properly certified.

2-14   The District reserves the right to increase or decrease the cleaning of certain areas as circumstances may require. In the event of increased or decreased cleaning requirements, the Contractor shall submit in writing to the Building Custodial Services Section the change in man-hours of time and the additional cost or credit to the District. The cost or credit will be expected to be reasonably proportionate to the initial bid price compared with square footage of cleaning area. When the proposal is accepted by the District it shall be confirmed in writing.

2-15 The Contractor shall provide all necessary machines, equipment, tools and labor, etc., as may be necessary to perform the work outlined herein. The District Building Custodial Services Section, Maintenance Division, shall approve all cleaning material or supplies, such as roll paper towels, toilet tissue, cleaners, liquid wax, liquid floor soap, seals, detergents, disinfectants, and liquid or bar hand soap for the use by the Contractor. The Contractor shall deposit trash in the refuse containers adjacent to the building.

Section III   Personnel Requirements and Work Procedures

3-01 The Contractor shall present on the job at all times during the working hours, a competent Superintendent and any necessary assistants. Prior to the commencement of work, the Contractor shall submit in writing to the Building Custodial Services Section, for prior approval the name of the person intended to be employed as Superintendent for the execution of this contract, along with his qualifications and past experience. The Superintendent shall be required to report to the Building Custodial Services Section, Maintenance Division, as necessary to review cleaning requirements and deficiencies with the District Supervisor of Building Custodial Services.

3-02 The District reserves the right to execute a background investigation of any employee of this Contractor and to require the Contractor to remove any employee from the campus whose actions are considered detrimental to the best interest of the District. The Contractor shall at all times enforce strict discipline and good order among his employees and shall not employ or permit to remain on the work, any person he considers unfit. He shall enforce all regulations relative to the use of water, heat, power, smoking, and the control and use of fires as required by law. Employees shall not be allowed to loiter on the premises either before or after their working hours.

3-03   Due to the existence of valuable equipment and property, strict supervision shall be maintained to prevent petty larcenies and thefts. The District shall reserve the right to search the Contractor's employees prior to their leaving the premises, without any prior notice of such action.

3-04   Contractor's employees may use janitor's closets in each building where they may change clothing and wash up. The Contractor shall insure orderliness and cleanliness of such areas at all times.

3-05   The successful Contractor shall properly identify each employee engaged for this work. Also, the Contractor shall provide each employee with an identification card, approved in form by the Building Custodial Services Section, for entrance and exit from the building. Additionally, the employee shall be required to punch a time clock each working night upon arrival and departure. Contractor shall submit weekly tabulations of all employees who have worked with accrued time, which form must be signed by Contractor's Superintendent and the Building Custodial Services Supervisor assigned.

3-06   The District will periodically inspect all work performed by the Contractor. Normally, at least a weekly joint inspection shall be conducted by Contractor or his representative and a representative of the Building Services Section.

3-07   Keys for buildings are controlled by the District Night Supervisor, Buildings Custodial Services Section, or his assigned assistant at all times. The Night Supervisor or his assistant will unlock all doors after cleaning has been accomplished and see that the building has been secured after quitting time and keys returned to the Building Custodial Services Section Office. Every effort shall be exercised by Contractor's employees to conserve electricity by only lighting areas in which work is currently being performed.

Contractor's employees shall report on forms furnished by the Dis-   **3-08**
trict to the Supervisor, Building Custodial Services, any conditions of leaky faucets, stopped toilets and drains, broken fixtures, etc., and any unusual happenings in the building.

Contractor's employees shall close and lock windows and turn off   **3-09**
all lights when night cleaning is finished, except as may be desig-nated to remain lighted for security lighting.

Contractor's employees shall not disturb papers on desks, open   **3-10**
drawers or cabinets, use telephones, televisions, radios, or drink or gamble while on duty on the campus. Violations will be grounds for dismissal.

Contractor shall not hire any personnel employed by the District   **3-11**
regardless of their classification since work beyond forty (40) hours weekly at the same place of employment entitles workers to OVERTIME RATES.

For the purposes of coordination and control the Contractor must   **3-12**
so arrange his employees' HOLIDAYS, SICK LEAVE, AND VA-CATIONS to conform to District schedules. These specifications are not intended to dictate to the Contractor what his leave poli-cies will be. However, the Contractor must make proper allowance for the employees' fringe benefits in this building. The District will not pay for any time away from the job.

Complete cleaning services will be required daily in all buildings,   **3-13**
fifty-two (52) weeks per year.

Section IV   Workmanship and Hours

4-01   All work shall be performed Monday through Saturday, inclusive, between the hours of midnight and 4:00 AM except as described in paragraph 4-02. Also, the Contractor shall schedule and arrange his work so he will not interfere with operational functions of the building. At indeterminate times, some areas of the building will be occupied and used by employees for after-hours work, and such circumstances shall not alleviate responsibility of required cleaning at a later time.

4-02   Special Personnel Requirements: Contractor shall be required to provide the following personnel as indicated in specified buildings.
LIST HERE ANY SPECIAL COVERAGE BY BUILDING AND TIME:

Section V   Work Standards

5-01   Definition of various operations:

Cleaning: To free from dirt or impurities, removing stains, either by hand or with tools such as urinals, water closets, sinks, drinking fountains, light fixtures, mirrors, etc.

Buffing: To clean or shine with a floor machine, surfaces such as resilient tiles, terrazzo, wood, slate, etc.

Dusting: To remove surface dust or dirt as from furniture, files, sills, blinds, telephones, vents, grills, lighting fixtures, with properly treated cloths.

Emptying: To remove accumulation of trash or residue

from waste containers, ash trays, receptacles, etc., and deposit in designated containers on outside of buildings.

Mopping, Damp and Wet: To wash, wipe and remove from floor and stair surfaces to leave acceptably clean.

Polishing: To smooth and brighten as by rubbing with polishing cloth using proper pastes, etc., as surfaces may require, such as brass, furniture, counters, mirrors, etc.

Refill: To replace the contents of a container such as soap, toilet tissue, towel dispensers, etc.

Stripping: This is a colloquial term for removing built-up waxes, seals and other floor dressings, the original natural surface before applying a fresh coat of protective cover to surfaces such as resilient tile, wood, terrazzo, etc.

Sweeping: To remove or clear away dirt or debris with a broom or brush. Normally all horizontal surfaces subject to foot or wheel usage.

Vacuum: To clean with a vacuum cleaner. Regular emptying of collector device is important and proper setting of height above surface will improve effectiveness.

Washing: The act or process of making thoroughly clean by moistening, wetting, scrubbing, rinsing, with water plus proper quantities of soap, detergents and disinfectants as furnished for various objects and equipment.

Waxing: To cover or treat with liquid wax or other floor finish in proper quantities over properly prepared surfaces to protect and beautify.

Wicking: This is a trade term to describe the process of sweeping, dusting and cleaning floor surfaces with a treated yarn mop.

5-02   Frequency of Operations—The Contractor shall be required to schedule his work to insure that the following frequency of operations are adhered to or exceeded in order to insure the District of the cleaning standard it deserves.

5-03   **Daily:**
1. Clean ash trays.
2. Clean elevator tracks and interiors.
3. Clean mirrors and glass surfaces.
4. Clean toilets, urinals, sinks, fixtures, partitions, paper holders.
5. Clean coatracks, etc.
6. Clean erasers—chalk board type.

Dust: Bookcases; Desks; Filing cabinets; also pianos if present; Lamps; Floors; Tables; Telephones; Window sills; Radiators; Convertors and unit; Ventilator cabinets; Refrigerators and Vending Machines.

Empty: Pencil sharpeners; Waste baskets.

Refill: Soap dispensers; Toilet tissue holders; Paper towel dispensers.

Sweep: Stairs; Floors.

Vacuum: Carpeting and rugs (particularly walk-off rugs in entrances).

Wash: Chalkboards and chalk trays; Drinking fountains and sanitize; Hand rails.

Damp Mop: Lobbies; Hallways; Restrooms; Laboratories, if necessary.

Buff: Lobbies; Hallways.

Weekly: 5-04
1. Damp mop floors.
2. Dust shelving, including books, library stacks.
3. Damp mop stairs.
4. Dust lockers.
5. Sweep exterior entrances to adjoining sidewalk.

Monthly: 5-05
1. Clean air vents and interior doors.
2. Dust tab arm chairs and venetian blinds.
3. Wax and buff floors (resilient).
4. Vacuum upholstered furniture and draperies.

Quarterly: 5-06
1. Scrub uncarpeted floors.
2. Wax resilient floors.

Semi-Annually: 5-07
1. Strip and wax resilient tile floors.
2. Wash exterior doors.

Annually: 5-08
1. Clean lighting fixtures.
2. Shampoo carpeting.
3. Wash venetian blinds and wash windows interior and exterior.

As Required: Snow removal off porticos and steps down   5-09
to juncture with grade or sidewalks. Sprinkle sand when necessary.
This type of special service is required *at the expense* of interior
cleaning to insure safe access by students to class and to avoid hard
packing and freezing on steps. This is a judgment decision which
must be made depending on type and severity of snow. Optimum is
clearing of entire steps in light snowfall to a 5' wide access path in
heavy snowfall.

Chapter 5

General

Outdoor Maintenance

Introduction

Major efforts of most park and recreation maintenance departments are centered on outdoor maintenance. This chapter is concerned with outdoor maintenance problems and will focus attention on vital issues—solid waste and sanitation, outdoor lighting, fencing, signs, artificial outdoor recreation surfaces, and maintenance of parking lots, roads, and trails. Grounds maintenance, another major outdoor maintenance topic, dealing with lawn, shrubbery and tree care, is considered to be important enough to devote an entire chapter (Chapter 6) to this subject.

Solid Waste

The solid waste problem is one of the most serious facing America today. While accounting for only seven percent of the world's population, Americans consume nearly one-half of the earth's industrial raw materials. Only recently have Americans become concerned with the environmental problems associated with the collection of trash, garbage, and other solid wastes. Environmental Protection Agency statistics indicate that the household, municipal, and industrial waste being produced in the United States today totals 360 million tons. Of this annual total, over one-half (190 million tons), or some 5.3 pounds per person per day, are being picked up by some collection agency for disposal. The annual cost of this disposal is more than 4.5 million dollars per year. It is estimated that our solid waste production is increasing at twice the rate of our population increase. The annual disposal of solid waste includes 48 billion cans, 26 billion bottles and jars, 4 million tons of plastic, 7.6 million television sets, 7 million cars and trucks, and 30 million tons of paper. Packaging in disposable containers has aggravated the problem. Many of these containers compound the problem because they are non-biodegradable and will not burn.

The problems of solid waste in park and recreation areas mirror the general problems facing the nation. In park and recreation areas, the problem focuses primarily on litter control. The National Park Service spends an estimated $1.5 million annually on litter pick-up and removal, the U.S. Forest Service spends an estimated $2.5 million on sanitation and litter. The city of Los Angeles spends $1.4 million on beach clean-up and an additional $1.7 million on park clean-up. Litter clean-up on all public lands cost an estimated $22 million in 1971, an increase of 12 percent over 1970. This figure represented more than the entire budget of the Bureau of Sport Fisheries and Wildlife.

Demonstrating that a serious problem exists is not difficult to substantiate. The more important question is, what can the park

Litter is unsightly and costly to pick up.

and recreation administrator do to help solve the problem? The following methods of attacking the problem are suggested.

Educate the public. The littering problem is not restricted to a small percentage of the American population and therefore widespread educational efforts are needed to make people aware of the problem. It is also believed that most littering is not intentional but rather a thoughtless act and by repeating the anti-littering message over and over, a conditioned response not to litter can be developed. Keep America Beautiful, a non-profit organization, has pioneered nationwide litter education efforts, and they have a variety of materials available including an excellent series of films that can be used in efforts to reach school and civic groups. Johnny Horizon, Woodsy Owl, and Pitch In! are all recognizable symbols of efforts to educate the public regarding the litter problem in the United States. These programs have also developed materials that can be used and/or adapted by the park and recreation administrator.

Techniques that can be used by the park and recreation administrator to help educate the public include educational displays, encouraging staff members to make themselves available for talks to civic groups about the solid waste problem in general and in their parks specifically, and by displaying anti-litter posters and signs at park and recreation facilities. Caution must be urged in displaying posters and signs. A park covered with anti-litter posters and signs is as aesthetically unattractive as the litter itself.

Keep park and recreation areas clean. This may well be the single most important suggestion given. Park administrators agree that patrons are more careful with trash and litter when the area is kept as immaculately clean as possible. Theme parks in the U.S. are an excellent example of how effective cleaning can make their facilities more attractive to the public.

The entire park and recreation staff should become litter conscious. If all staff members accept the responsibility for keeping litter picked-up in park and recreation areas, the problem is greatly reduced. In addition, their efforts are contagious and will encourage the public to do the same. All park and recreation vehicles should be equipped with a litter container to ease the disposal problem.

Provide adequate trash receptacles. As educational efforts become effective and as the park and recreation patron becomes more litter conscious, the public will make a greater effort to properly dispose of trash and litter. Park and recreation agencies should make litter disposal as easy and convenient as possible by providing an adequate number of properly distributed trash receptacles.

Trash receptacles that blend into their surroundings are pleasing to the eye.

Selection of an appropriate trash receptacle is an important consideration. Criteria for the selection of trash receptacles should include the following:

1. Function—the kind of litter and trash expected to be deposited is an important consideration. In picnic and camping areas where a mixture of organic material and paper products can be anticipated, a traditional type garbage can is an appropriate container. In a refreshment stand area where candy wrappers, paper cups, and other paper products can be anticipated, a wire mesh container may be appropriate.
2. Aesthetics—receptacles should be attractive and blend with the environment, but at the same time, they must be conspicuous enough to discourage littering.

3. The receptacle must be durable.

4. Easy to handle—a number of smaller trash receptacles are better than a few large ones because they are easier to handle by the maintenance personnel who must empty them and because better distribution is possible. The 30- to 35-gallon container has proved to be a reasonable size. For example, a 32-gallon container holds about .15 cubic yards or about 25 pounds of typical solid waste.

5. Securely fitting lid—the trash receptacle should be provided with a tight fitting lid to protect waste from rodents, insects, and other disease-carrying vectors. Unless securely fastened, lids are a popular target for vandalism. Chaining the lid to a permanent post should be considered if a potential vandalism problem exists.

6. The receptacle must be easy to clean.

Metal trash receptacles placed on the ground rust very quickly. This problem can be solved by attaching the receptacle to a permanent post or by setting the receptacle on a concrete pad. In some locations, animals (dogs, racoons, bears) present a serious problem. Tight-fitting lids, attachment to permanent posts, and specially designed animal-proof tops are possible solutions to this problem.

Trash containers should be protected by a concrete base, and covers should have retaining chains.

Keeping trash receptacles clean is a vital maintenance consideration. A dirty, smelly garbage can may ruin an individual's recreation experience. Trash receptacles must be cleaned on a regular basis. Steam cleaning is an economical and efficient method. In recent years the use of plastic liners has become widespread. General acceptance of plastic liners has come because they improve sanitation by keeping trash receptacles from accumulating encrusted waste, and they speed up collection by eliminating the need to lift each container to empty it into the collection vehicle. Generally bags of at least 2.00 mil thickness are used because thinner bags often tear, spilling waste.

Automated litter pick-up saves maintenance labor.

In areas of intensive use where large volumes of solid waste can be anticipated, bulk containers should be considered. Bulk containers vary in capacity from 1 to 50 cubic yards. They have their best application when used as a secondary container (smaller trash receptacles are emptied into the bulk container for storage). The obvious advantage is less frequent collection. A number of campgrounds are successfully using a system whereby each family is given plastic bags and several large bulk containers are spaced throughout the campground. Campers deposit their daily accumulation of solid waste. In this application the collections are generally made daily but the individual trash receptacle is eliminated and collection is simplified.

Support and encourage anti-litter legislation and enforcement. Park and recreation agencies, first of all, should be certain that adequate legal measures have been taken to prohibit littering and dumping solid waste in areas under their jurisdiction. Then they should be certain these laws are enforced. This suggestion is particularly applicable to dumping solid waste in remote park areas, a very serious and vexing problem for many park and recreation agencies.

Consider special programs and ideas to combat the litter problem. Trash receptacles using animal heads and vacuum systems are attractive to children and have been successfully used by many park and recreation agencies. The occasional use of a public display of trash and litter collected for a period of time can be an effective educational tool. Many agencies have successfully designed and carried out extensive clean-up campaigns and programs using voluntary service agencies in the community. These programs have been particularly successful on large lakes where shoreline accumulations of trash are particularly difficult for an agency with a limited maintenance staff to handle and in areas where extensive trail systems are maintained.

The solid waste problem is a difficult and expensive one to handle. A well conceived and coordinated effort by the park and recreation agency can help ease the burden. The only incorrect approach is for the agency to throw up its hands and say the problem is too big to handle and to be satisfied with a park that is clean only at the beginning of the season.

Collection and Disposal

Even if park and recreation patrons and employees properly dispose of litter the problem of solid waste is not completely solved, because the problems of collection and disposal remain. Frequency of collection depends on the amount of use a particular area or facility receives and the number and capacity of trash receptacles used. Normally collections will be made daily; however, three or four times a week may be sufficient for a lightly used facility or one that receives predominantly weekend use. With heavily used facilities, particularly on weekends and holidays, collection on a two- or three-times-a-day basis may be indicated.

Several different types of vehicles can be used appropriately for trash and garbage collection. Volume rather than weight usually determines vehicle selection. Where large amounts of trash and garbage must be collected, a conventional compacting garbage truck should be used. Several companies are manufacturing small garbage trucks designed for, among other uses, park and recreation agency use. Where the amount of trash and garbage is relatively light, jeep or tractor drawn trailers, pick-up trucks, or stake body trucks can be used more appropriately. One of the problem areas faced by the maintenance department is picking up trash and garbage in areas where no conveniently established service roads exist, e.g., some picnic areas or athletic fields. In these areas the jeep or tractor drawn trailer may be the only practical solution to the collection problem.

Another method of trash collection that should be considered in heavily used areas where trash is concentrated in relatively small areas is a bulk collection system. In this system large in-place units are used for collection at strategically located points, and the entire unit is moved to the disposal point. There are several factors that should be considered when selecting the type of vehicle to be used for trash and garbage collection. These factors include—

1. amount of material to be collected. Many trips with small vehicles or the use of a large vehicle for a small amount of material is not economically feasible.
2. loading height of the vehicle. Ease of loading the vehicle by the maintenance workers should be considered. For this reason a pick-up truck with a high bed is not particularly desirable for collection.
3. the trash compartment of the vehicle should be covered to prevent trash from being blown out of the vehicle as it moves from place to place. Another advantage of the use of plastic liners is that you eliminate the hazard of wind-blown loose trash.
4. the vehicle should be durable. Trash and garbage collection vehicles are subject to rough treatment and must be constructed durably. Trailers, when used, should have metal rather than wood bed and side construction.
5. ease of unloading.

Loading height is an important feature to consider when selecting a vehicle for trash collection.

Historically, the most common method of solid waste disposal in park and recreation areas has been an open pit that is periodically burned off. With increased emphasis on environmental awareness and more stringent government regulation of all types of waste disposal, this method is no longer satisfactory. Two acceptable disposal methods for park and recreation areas are the sanitary landfill and incineration. Another method which should be considered by the park and recreation administrator is recycling. In most areas this method is not now practical. However, as recycling technology improves, this method has potential for future use in park and recreation areas.

Sanitary landfill is an engineering method of disposing of solid waste on land by spreading it in thin layers, compacting it to the smallest possible volume, and covering it with soil each working day. Soil cover material should be a minimum of six inches per day. During off-season use when the landfill is infrequently used, a one-foot cover should be provided. The final cover should be a minimum of two feet.

Sanitary Landfill

Three methods are commonly used for sanitary landfill: the area, ramp, and trench methods. The trench method is generally the most practical for park and recreation areas. In this method, a trench is excavated as deeply as soil and ground water conditions allow. The trench should be twice as wide as the equipment used for compaction and covering. Solid waste is dumped into the trench, compacted and covered. The soil excavated from the trench is used as cover material. The landfill should be convenient to the recreation facilities it serves to reduce the transportation factor, but at the same time it should be located away from public use areas.

Incineration

Incineration has not been used as widely in park and recreation areas as sanitary landfill. Where land is not available for landfill, incineration is an acceptable alternative. The incinerators that have been used in park and recreation areas in the past have not met air quality standards. There are currently available a number of relatively small incinerator units that are completely acceptable for use in park and recreation areas. One of these is a "starved-air" combustion unit. This unit recirculates hot combustion gases to sustain high temperatures, and reduces the total amount of air used in combustion. Units are available that can burn from 200 to 1200 pounds of solid waste per hour, a capacity sufficient to handle the solid waste from almost any park and recreation development. Operational costs are low because auxiliary fuel is used only to start combustion, and one man can operate these units.

Sewage Disposal

The primary purposes of sewage disposal systems are the sanitary disposal of human waste from recreation areas and protection from diseases transmitted through sewage. Problems associated with the selection and design of adequate sewage disposal systems are compounded by recreation areas and facilities that are often in remote locations, have a wide fluctuation in the quantity of sewage being generated because of peak load use on weekends, and the seasonal nature of many of these operations. Urban park and recreation facilities can usually tie into municipal or county sewerage systems, while facilities located in rural areas must have self-contained sewage disposal systems.

A basic knowledge of the characteristics of sewage is necessary to understand the methods of treating sewage. Sewage is approximately 99.95% water and 0.05% solids. Chemically, sewage consists of a wide variety of organic and inorganic materials. Oxygen dissolved in water is required to convert these complex materials into simpler compounds. Fish and other living organisms use this same dissolved oxygen. Therefore, if untreated or improperly treated sewage is discharged into a water course (lake, river, or pond) the dissolved oxygen may be depleted resulting in the killing of fish and other organisms. The amount of oxygen-using material in sewage is referred to as the Biochemical Oxygen Demand (BOD). The efficiency of treatment of a sewage disposal system can be measured by determining the BOD level before and after treatment.[1]

Decomposition of organic matter is biological in character and is dependent upon the action of aerobic and anaerobic bacteria. Aerobic bacteria depend upon the presence of free oxygen for their metabolism. Anaerobic bacteria also depend on oxygen; however, they obtain their oxygen from substances such as sulphates, phosphates, and other organic compounds found in sewage. The action of both types of bacteria is dependent upon warm temperatures above 40 degrees Fahrenheit.

Determining factors in selecting an appropriate sewage disposal system include—

1. public health requirements. All systems require the approval of the appropriate public health agency.
2. quantity of sewage to be treated.
3. initial construction or installation cost.
4. operating cost.
5. amount of maintenance required.
6. land area available consistent with future development plans.
7. absorption qualities of soil.
8. water table level.
9. presence or absence of a water course to handle treated effluent.

Sewage Disposal Systems

Pit and Chemical Toilets

Pit and chemical toilets are an unattractive and inefficient disposal method. However, they do have a legitimate application in remote areas where water is not available. These methods are unsuitable for heavily used permanent facilities under any conditions. Because of the low developmental cost, the pit toilet has been badly over-used by park and recreation agencies, and in many instances another more suitable sewage disposal system should have been used. Where pit and chemical toilets have to be used, they should be made as attractive as possible through the use of high quality building materials and the design of well lighted and well ventilated structures.

Septic Tanks   The septic tank and absorption field is the most widely used sew-age disposal system for park and recreation facilities. The primary reason for its use is that the system can handle the limited volume of sewage generated by many recreation developments. As recreation developments are designed to handle larger and larger numbers of people, more complex systems must be considered. A limiting factor in the use of septic tanks is the lack of soil percolation in some locations.

The septic tank system generally consists of an underground waterproof concrete tank of varying size depending on the volume of sewage anticipated, a distribution box, and a tile drainfield. The drainfield consists of tile placed loosely end-to-end on a bed of gravel. Sludge settles to the bottom of the septic tank where it is digested and liquified by anaerobic bacterial action. This conversion to a liquid is never complete and the sludge level should be checked annually and pumped out when necessary. The liquid effluent from the tank dissipates into the ground through the absorption field. A percolation test is necessary before an absorption field is installed. This test measures how fast the liquid effluent will filter into various soils, and the size of the absorption field needed can be determined.

The Imhoff tank system is similar to the septic tank. The Imhoff tank is a two-compartment tank, an upper and lower tank. Sedimentation takes place in the upper tank and the sludge falls into the lower tank where digestion takes place. The Imhoff tank system is used where capacity greater than the septic tank provides is needed. This system requires almost daily maintenance to break up the scum layer and push sludge into the digestion chamber. The sludge level in the digestion chamber must be checked at regular intervals and pumped out as needed.

In areas where soil percolation is very poor, a sand filter normally about three feet thick can be substituted for the normal absorption field. The liquid effluent is distributed over the surface and filters through the sand. This treatment when combined with disinfection normally produces a high quality effluent. Trickling filters are also used as an effective secondary treatment method. In a trickling filter, sewage is sprayed over a rock filled tank. BOD producing material is removed by living organisms such as bacteria, algae, and protozoa growing on the rock surfaces.

The Lagoon

The lagoon (also commonly called a stabilization pond or oxidation pond) system consists of a pond or basin which, when properly designed and maintained, will provide an environment for the natural reduction of sewage to its stable form through the action of aerobic bacteria. Effluent from the lagoon must generally be chlorinated. However, no other maintenance of the system is needed. The lagoon should have a water depth of about 3 to 5 feet. When operating properly, the lagoon will be odorless. Odor is a sign of overloading, and when it occurs frequently, artificial aeration may be necessary. The lagoon system will handle relatively large amounts of sewage and can be used for a complex of park and recreation facilities. When adequate land area is available this is the most inexpensive method of treatment of large amounts of sewage.

Aerobic Digestion

Aerobic digestion (also called extended aeration) is technically an activated sludge process. This system is one of the most effective methods for treating sewage with some systems getting 95-percent BOD removal. The system consists of two or three components, an aeration tank, a settling tank, and in some instances local health officials require a sludge holding tank. The system utilizes aeration of sewage by mechanical means and provides high quality treatment. Raw sewage and activated sludge are mixed together in the aeration tank. Sewage is normally held in the aeration tank with air added for 24 hours. Aerobic bacteria break down the organic matter into stable or inorganic material. Solids are then allowed to settle in the settling tank. The liquid effluent from the aerobic digestion system is generally chlorinated before it is discharged into a water course. This system can handle large quantities of sewage and is generally used for a complex of recreation facilities. The system requires careful attention by trained personnel and the initial cost is high. For efficient operation of this system a reasonably steady flow of sewage is needed.

Except for pit and chemical toilets, professional engineering help is a requisite in planning any sewage disposal system. The park and recreation professional must be able to project the volume of sewage anticipated from recreation facilities. Once this has been determined, sanitary engineers can design an appropriate system to serve the proposed facilities.

Water Systems

Potable drinking water is an essential element for any park or recreation facility development. In addition to drinking water, a water supply may be needed for the development of specialized recreation facilities. For example, large quantities of water are essential for golf course irrigation, a swimming pool, a ski slope where artificial snow making equipment is to be used, etc. In this discussion, the primary concern is with the development of potable drinking water for public use.

Sources of potable water include—

1. natural water supply. A stream or pond within a protected watershed may provide a natural supply of water that can be used without treatment. Such occurrences are rare but should be mentioned.
2. wells. The capacity of a water supply system utilizing wells can be increased substantially by adding storage tanks.
3. an impure water supply generally from lake or river and an adequate treatment system.

Water treatment is necessary to remove dirt and bacteria and consists of three steps, sedimentation, filtration, and chlorination. In a sedimentation tank or reservoir, suspended dirt particles slowly settle out of the water. Chemicals can be added to speed up this process. In the second step, filtration, the water passes through a sand bed or a mechanical filter. Chlorination is necessary to remove potentially harmful bacteria.

Once an adequate source of water has been found or developed, it is necessary to develop a distribution system. Distribution systems are of two basic types. The first is a gravity system whereby the water supply is stored in a holding tank higher than all facilities to be fed. The second requires the use of a pump or pumps. These systems can be designed to use either a submersible well pump and pressure tank or an above ground pump, also utilizing a pressure tank. Distribution systems for other than potable water for irrigation or other purposes operate on these same principles.

Properly designed and constructed water systems do not require a great deal of maintenance. Good preventive maintenance practices must be perfomed to keep pumps and filtration systems in good working condition, and leaks caused by broken or damaged water lines must be repaired when they occur. The maintenance department must maintain a file of blueprints and drawings accurately locating all water lines serving park and recreation facilities.

Food Service Areas

Sanitation in food service areas is particularly important and all areas under direct or indirect (as in the case of concessionaire use) control should be carefully scrutinized. All states exhibit relatively strict control over public food service facilities through public health agencies. These agencies should be consulted during the planning and developmental stages of any food service facility ranging from a simple snack bar to a first class restaurant operation. In addition, public health recommendations concerning sanitation should be followed in the operation of all food service facilities.

Night Lighting

There is an application for night lighting at almost all outdoor recreation activities. Baseball and softball fields, football fields, tennis courts, swimming pools, par-3 golf courses, and multiple-use games courts are all examples of outdoor recreation facilities that are commonly lighted.

There are several advantages to lighting recreation areas and facilities. It allows families to participate together. It allows activities at a time when adults who work during the day can participate. Night lighting may, in some instances, attract people to recreation areas. Conversely, there are also some disadvantages to night light-

Lighting for all types of recreation areas and facilities is important.

ing recreation facilities. Lighting in urban areas can be disturbing to residents located too close to lighted facilities. The high cost of energy to light facilities greatly increases operational cost. Maintenance also becomes a problem where facilities are used for long periods of time. This occurs both from the standpoint of finding time when the facility is not in use and maintenance can be performed and also from the overuse of the facility, especially the compaction of turf areas. Lighting 18-hole golf courses in particular has created many maintenance problems not associated with normal golf course maintenance.

Technical Lighting Data   The degree of illumination is measured in footcandles. Thus the footcandle indicates the amount of light available in a recreation area where the activity takes place. The output of a light source is measured in terms of lumens. Almost all lighting standards are in the form of footcandles.

Another term commonly used is "luminaire." A luminaire is a complete lighting unit consisting of a lamp; components designed to distribute light, to postion, and protect the lamp; and to connect the lamp to the necessary power supply. Three different floodlighting luminaires are designed to produce long, medium, and wide beams. This allows flexibility in the design of a lighting system. For example, with a battery of three tennis courts, luminaires with wide beams would be used to light the courts near the light source and medium beams to light the middle courts. In a par-3 golf course or driving range, installation of all three (wide, medium, and long) beams would be logical.

The least expensive lighting systems use luminaires affixed to wooded cross arms on wooden poles with overhead wiring. Underground wiring allows the removal of unsightly, and often dangerous guy wires notwithstanding the obvious aesthetic advantage. Although generally more costly, underground wiring should be seriously considered for all recreation night-lighting applications. Steel poles and cross arms also add quality to the lighting installation. (Steel poles must be used for heights over 70 feet.)

Types of Outdoor Lighting Systems

Incandescent

The incandescent lighting system is the oldest system and still is used widely for outdoor recreation lighting. Advantages of the incandescent system include low initial cost—the system turns on and off instantly, and produces a very high quality light—and good color (although poor in blue range). Disadvantages of the system include short lamp life when compared with other available lamps, lamps subject to change in life and output by voltage changes, subject to shock and vibration changes, and high energy usage. The last disadvantage listed, high energy usage, is an extremely critical factor when considering an incandescent system. The increasing cost of energy will generally discourage the use of this system when long hours of operation are anticipated. The system may still have a good application when short operating hours can be anticipated, e.g. a football field used for five or six games a season. The requirement of short operating hours is rare in most recreation installations, and thus, the incandescent system has limited usefulness.

The Quartz Lamp

Technically the quartz lamp is an incandescent type that uses a halogen, usually iodine or bromine. In the halogen cycle, evaporated tungsten returns to the filament and as a result, the inside walls of the lamp do not blacken. The clean-up action of the halogen is so effective that even after extensive use, the lamp appears to be as clean as when new. The average life of the quartz lamp is about twice the life of a regular incandescent lamp. Other advantages of the quartz lamp system include lower operating cost and lamps, over the entire life of the bulb, give more light per luminaire. Disadvantages of the quartz system include more expensive initial installation and the rectangular fixture allows limited use patterns. Quartz lighting is good for applications requiring a wide horizontal and relatively narrow beam spread.

High Intensity Discharge Systems   The two most frequently used high intensity discharge systems found in outdoor recreation lighting are mercury and multi-vapor. In high intensity discharge lamps, light is produced by a continuous electric arc. Inside a discharge lamp there are two electrodes and some form of metal that can be vaporized and broken down into electric particles to conduct current in an electric arc from one electrode to the other. The arc has a negative resistance characteristic in which the resistance drops as current increases. Thus, a ballast must be used to limit the current.

Because of the ballast circuit, the high intensity discharge system is generally more expensive in initial installation cost. However, this is balanced by much lower operating cost and very long lamp life. The quality of light from the high intensity discharge system is not as good as the incandescent systems. However, great improvements have been made in light quality of these systems in recent years.

Maintenance of Lighting Systems

All electric lamps have a rated lamp life. The rated lamp life is an average figure. Thus, some lamps will burn out before and some after the rated lamp life. At the end of rated life, 50 percent of the lamps remain burning. The remaining lamps produce only about seven percent more light before they burn out. This is an important consideration when considering a relamping maintenance schedule. It is often more economical to replace lamps in a group if the high labor cost of replacing single or a few lamps at a time is considered as an alternative. Another important consideration is the efficiency of the lamp after use over a considerable period of time. Decrease in lighting efficiency varies with type of lamp used and can be determined from data supplied by the manufacturer.

Another important maintenance consideration is the dirt that accumulates on the reflective surfaces of the luminaire. The luminaire dirt depreciation can be determined only by experience. Field tests on actual installations are the best guide. Luminaire dirt depreciation can vary widely depending on environmental conditions. There are two primary methods of minimizing luminaire dirt depreciation: first, by installing hermetically sealed and filtered luminaires, and second, by regular cleaning of the luminaire. For economy of maintenance, luminaire cleaning and relamping should be scheduled at the same time.

A consideration that will provide for considerable operational cost savings is to design a flexible lighting system at the outset. For example, a driving range system should be designed so that one-half of the lights can be used at any one time to provide for times when the range is lightly used. An 18-hole par-3 golf course should be lighted in sections so that the lights can be turned off as players complete playing portions of the course at closing or so that only nine holes can be used during periods of very light use. By use of these and other techniques, substantial savings in operating costs can be made.

The park and recreation administrator must seek professional engineering help when developing night lighting for recreation facilities. Many power companies employ recreation lighting specialists and manufacturers of lighting equipment provide excellent technical advice. Consulting electrical engineers are also available. The wise administrator will take advantage of several of these sources to insure the best possible quality lighting system.

Fencing

The appearance of park and recreation areas should be as natural as possible. Fences of any type tend to destroy the natural quality of the environment and should be avoided whenever possible. Before fencing is used several alternatives should be considered. One of the most practical alternatives is the use of shrubbery. By careful choice of plant materials such as barberry, privet, yew, and ornamental and native trees, plantings can be used to control pedestrian traffic or screen unsightly areas—in short, to serve the same function as a fence. One of the problems arising from the use of plant materials is the time required to establish them. This drawback can be overcome by planting mature plant materials, which is extremely expensive, or by erecting an inexpensive type of fencing until the plantings have matured, and then remove the fence. In many instances fence removal is not necessary because the shrubbery has overgrown the fence.

Plant screens are a natural alternative to fencing.

Other alternatives include the use of water as a barrier. Boulders or rock outcroppings can also be used effectively in combination with other treatments. Grade separations can be used; however, care must be taken not to create untenable maintenance problems.

Despite attempts to keep areas completely natural and to use natural alternatives, the use of fencing is many times the only practical alternative. Factors to be considered in determining the type of fencing to be used include the following:

1. function is a primary consideration. Function determines the height, shape, form, and strength of a particular installation of fencing. Fencing may be used to control access to an area, to

direct pedestrian traffic flow, to control payment of an admission fee among other functions.

2. initial cost of installation.
3. durability.
4. maintenance cost.
5. aesthetic considerations—how well the fencing blends into the natural setting.

Many different types of fencing can be used. Local conditions and availability of materials will often dictate the best fencing for a particular application. No attempt will be made to discuss all types of fencing. However, several of the most commonly used types and their advantages and disadvantages are worthy of discussion.

The major advantages of split rail fencing are its natural appearance and long life when locust posts and chesnut, spruce, or sassafras rails are used. It is also easy to mow under the rail fence, and the initial cost is relatively inexpensive. The disadvantages are that it does not provide a very formidable barrier and is climbed easily. It is also relatively weak and easily damaged. This disadvantage is balanced somewhat by it being easy to repair.

Split Rail Fencing

The advantages of chain link fencing (galvanized or aluminum) are that it provides a good barrier because it is difficult to climb. It is also very strong, durable and will last a long time when 9- or 11-gauge wire is specified. The disadvantages are a high initial cost and unattractive appearance. The chain link fence also creates a mowing problem when installed on turf areas. Despite its aesthetic unattractiveness, chain link is widely used in park and recreation areas because of the excellent control and durability factors. Chain link fence can be improved aesthetically by using wood slatting or woven plastic strips in the fence.

Chain Link Fencing

The only major advantage of a woven wire fence is its low cost. On the debit side, it is not durable, it is easy to climb, it will not last as long as other types of fencing, and it presents the same mowing problem as chain link. Locust or treated posts are a must with a woven wire fence installation.

Woven Wire Fencing

Rail fencing can be attractive when used appropriately, and it is easy to install.

Post and Board Fencing   Although when painted post and board fencing does not give a natural appearance, its aesthetic qualities are very good in some applications. For example, when used around a riding stable it can be very attractive fencing material. The major disadvantages are that it is easy to climb and very expensive to maintain.

Solid Board Fence Fencing   This type of fence is generally used where visual screening is desired. When natural materials such as cedar or redwood are used, very little maintenance is required. It is good from the standpoint of presenting a solid barrier to prevent access to an area. The disadvantages of the solid wood fence is that compared with other alternatives it will not last as long, and the initial cost is quite high.

Brick, stone and ornamental iron are other types of fencing that may be used in special applications. Where stone is readily available, it can be used to blend beautifully into the park setting.

Care of vegetative growth under and immediately adjacent to all fencing presents a serious maintenance problem. Ways of easing this problem include chemical sterilization of soil under and six inches on either side of the fence, use of growth retardants, and incasing the fence in an asphalt or concrete strip level with the ground to allow easy mowing. Fencing around tennis courts or multiple-use courts should be inset six inches to eliminate hand mowing.

Signs

Signs are used for a variety of purposes in park and recreation areas. Signs can be used to inform, direct, describe, name, beckon, and prohibit. They can be used to inform the park and recreation visitor of the facilities and recreation opportunities available. They can be helpful to direct the visitor over an unfamiliar route to a destination point. They can make the visitor's experience more enjoyable by describing more fully the environment. They may be used to simply name a tree, a trail, a road, a building, or a room. By their attractiveness, they can beckon a visitor and lead him or her to a popular park feature or attraction. Finally, they can be used to prohibit, to caution, and to help guide the visitor's actions while they are in the area.

A good sign system does all the things mentioned with an air of hospitality, welcome, and dignity. Signs reflect the management philosophy of the agency. If the sign system is done poorly, it can be irritating to the visitor. A primary concern in developing a sign system should be how *few* signs are needed to achieve the agency's full purpose, not how *many*. A second vital consideration should be to make the sign system do an adequate job without unwarranted intrusion upon the natural environment of the area. So, the first question that must be asked is, "Is this sign really needed?"

There are also a number of practical considerations which must be taken into account when designing a sign. Signs must be easily and clearly understood. A National Park Service sign, FEE INFORMATION, has caused park visitors to stop and request the "free" information. Messages on signs are important. They should be brief but not abrupt, simple to comprehend but not insulting to the intelligence of the visitor, informative but not wordy, and they should be accurate, particularly when interpreting some feature or story.

Signs must be legible. The style, height, and width of lettering and color contrast used are all extremely important considerations. The National Recreation and Park Association Management Aids Bulletin, *Signs and Symbols,* is an excellent source and lists standards related to a variety of problems related to legibility.

Additional factors that must be considered when selecting sign materials are initial cost, ease of maintenance, and maintenance cost.

One of the most important considerations in wording signs, particularly prohibitive ones, is to word them positively rather than negatively. The "no" and "do not" signs should be avoided wherever possible. Instead of DO NOT PICK THE FLOWERS, a sign saying PLEASE LEAVE FLOWERS FOR OTHERS TO ENJOY, conveys a positive message. PICNIC IN DESIGNATED AREAS ONLY is an improvement over the traditional NO PICNICKING. Rather than a sign on a restroom, CLOSED FOR THE SEASON, the message RESTROOMS AVAILABLE AT VISITOR CENTER conveys the management intent. At Coot Bay, a bird sanctuary in Everglades National Park the sign FISHING IS STRICTLY FOR THE BIRDS has elicited a much more favorable public response than the alternative NO FISHING could have.

The use of symbols on park and recreation area signs can also be effective. The National Park Service arrowhead is easily identified by Park Service visitors nationwide. Many municipal park and recreation departments also make use of symbols such as pine trees, oak leaves and shamrocks to serve as a quick identification for their park and recreation areas and facilities. In addition, symbols are being used to replace words on signs. Many federal, state and local recreation and park agencies have adopted the use of the Federal Recreation Symbols to identify recreation areas along roads and highways.

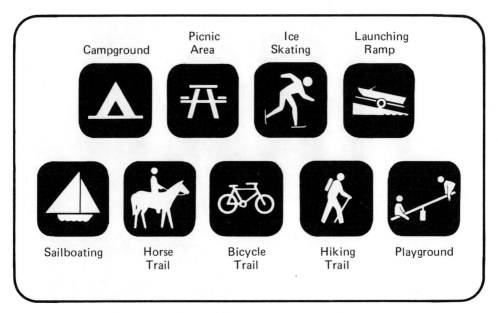

Campground   Picnic Area   Ice Skating   Launching Ramp

Sailboating   Horse Trail   Bicycle Trail   Hiking Trail   Playground

Federal recreation symbols are being used more widely.

Many types of signs are used in park and recreation areas and these signs can be made or purchased commercially. A variety of materials are used. Many park and recreation departments manufacture or fabricate a large percentage of their own signs.

Types of Signs

One of the most commonly used types of signs is the routed wood sign. A variety of woods including cedar, redwood, poplar, white pine, and cypress can be used. Signs can be hand routed or commercial sign-making machines are available at relatively low cost. The basic sign is painted or stained and the routed letters are painted a contrasting color. The routed sign gives a somewhat rustic appearance when appropriate colors are used, and it blends well into most park environments.

The raised letter sign made from wood or metal gives the same general appearance as the routed sign. Letters are cut out and attached to the painted or stained sign board. Some park administrators believe the raised letter sign is easier to maintain than the routed sign. A number of park and recreation agencies utilize wooden signs with painted letters or letters and drawings applied by a silkscreen process. These signs can be very attractive but require much maintenance. Annodized aluminium is another material

Routed signs can be made by the park and recreation agency.

that is being used more and more frequently. Its major advantage is permanence and little maintenance. These signs must be purchased commercially, and the initial cost is quite high.

For small permanent informational signs, plastic is quite commonly used. Attractive commercial plastic signs can be used for a variety of purposes, particularly for interpretive uses. Routed plastic signs can also be used effectively for a variety of applications. They have an effective application for labeling plant materials in formal gardens, botanical gardens, and arboretums. A number of relatively inexpensive sign-making devices are available for temporary and semi-permanent signs used in connection with bulletin boards and as a means of notifying people of recreation program opportunities.

One of the most important signs a park and recreation agency develops is the entrance sign. The initial impression the visitor receives from an entrance sign is important. Entrance signs should be simple and they should complement rather than detract from the park environment. Entrance signs with commercial advertising displays are poor and should be avoided regardless of the obvious cost benefit.

Above, signs made of anodized aluminum require little maintenance. They are practical for use in remote or unsupervised areas because they are more difficult to vandalize. Below, an attractive sign welcomes visitors to a neighborhood park.

The entrance sign to a park and recreation area can convey an important first impression to visitors.

Traffic control signs present a minor dilemma. Should these signs be made to blend with other signs in the park and recreation system by using a similar style, or should standard highway traffic signs be used? Most park and recreation administrators use standard highway signs because of safety considerations.

Sign Maintenance   A good sign system can be impaired by poor maintenance. Signs must be repainted and replaced when necessary. In most instances, signs that need to be repainted are taken down during the off-season and repainted in the maintenance service center shops, although in some instances repainting in the field is more practical. Duplicates of key signs for areas used on a year-round basis should be considered. A sign maintenance schedule should be developed so that one-third to one-half of all signs are repainted each season.

Signs are a popular target for vandalism. Vandalism can be deterred through the use of high quality materials that are difficult to vandalize. Setting sign posts in concrete or using a "T" or "X" brace underground to prevent removal or turning is a worthwhile precaution to take. This is particularly important in areas with sandy or loose soil.

Outdoor Recreation Surfaces

As the demand for outdoor recreation space grows, the park and recreation administrators must make every effort to obtain optimum utilization of areas under their jurisdiction. One of the ways this can be accomplished is to provide adequate recreation surfaces to maximize their usefulness.

There is no one surface which is satisfactory for all recreation activities. If it were possible to design the perfect outdoor recreation surface, it would have the following qualities:

1. It must be a multiple-use surface.
2. It must be dustless and stainless.
3. It must have good durability with good wearing quality despite continued heavy use.
4. The initial cost must be reasonable.
5. It must be easy to maintain. Ease of maintenance implies little "down time" when the surface cannot be used because of maintenance being performed.
6. It must have low maintenance cost.
7. It must have a pleasing appearance.
8. It must be nonabrasive.
9. It must be resilient.
10. It must be available for year-round use.
11. It must not be slippery.

Although a single surface does not exist that meets these specifications, this list does form a reasonable set of factors to consider when evaluating outdoor recreation surfaces.

Types of Outdoor Surface Materials

Earth Surfaces

The basic earth surface is undoubtedly the oldest and probably the most frequently used of all outdoor recreation surfaces. The advantages are its ready availability and extremely low initial cost (even when a high quality earth surface is developed). Disadvantages include high maintenance cost and appearance. However, the greatest disadvantage is that the surface is unbearably dusty in dry weather and unusable for most activity because of mud in wet weather. Long drying time often makes the surface unusable for long periods after a heavy rain.

Turf Surfaces When appearance and resilience are considered, turf is a very attractive recreation surface. For certain activities it is a rather ideal
surface. The major disadvantages of turf are its high maintenance
cost, and it is not a durable surface under intensive use. For example, turf would be an ideal material to use under all types of
playground apparatus; however, even under relatively light use conditions it is impossible to maintain an adequate turf surface.

Concrete and Both of these surface materials are widely used as outdoor recrea-
Bituminous Surfaces tion surfaces because of their excellent durability and the fact that
the surfaces are virtually maintenance free. If constructed properly
they are excellent year-round surfaces and can be used under any
weather conditions. Concrete is an excellent surface material where
a smooth, level surface is required, such as for shuffleboard courts.
The major problems with these two surfaces lie in their complete
lack of resiliency (although bituminous surfaces can be "softened"
sufficiently to be attractive surfaces for some types of activity, e.g.,
tennis) and their abrasiveness. These two important qualities discourage the use of these materials for many types of recreation
activities.

Synthetic Surfaces As our technology and experience increases, synthetic materials
may be the answer to many future outdoor recreation surface
problem areas. The use of materials such as astro-turf, poly-turf
and tartan have been well accepted under certain conditions. Except for the initial cost and abrasiveness (in the case of synthetic
turfs), these two surfaces meet most of the criteria established for
an ideal outdoor recreation surface. When the maintenance cost
factor is considered over a period of time, even the high initial cost
becomes less frightening. Applications of various types of synthetic
materials are still in the experimental stage, but they hold great
promise for the future. Synthetics are being used successfully for
surfaces under playground apparatus, athletic fields, driving range
and golf tees, golf putting greens, running tracks, and for areas
around recreation buildings and facilities that are difficult to maintain with any other surface material.

   The artificial appearance of even the high quality synthetics
will preclude their widespread use as a universal recreation surface
of the future. However, they will play a major role in meeting
many present and future outdoor recreation surfacing needs.

Other types of synthetic surfaces that should be mentioned are efforts to develop artificial ice and snow surfaces. Artificial surfaces have been developed on an experimental basis for both skiing and ice skating. It remains to be seen whether user acceptance will allow their widespread use.

What does the future hold? The U.S. Open Golf Tournament is played on a synthetic turf course, The Stanley Cup Hockey Tournament is contested on a plastic rink, professional champions ski on mountainous artificial slopes during the summer. An impossible dream! Who would have predicted in 1960 that the Orange Bowl football game would be played on a mat of artificial grass?

Roads, Parking Lots, and Trails

Park and recreation agencies are responsible for the maintenance of many miles of roads and many acres of parking lots. When the agency has the financial responsibility for maintaining these surfaces, a major budget item is incurred. Adequate maintenance of these roads and parking areas is essential if long-term costs are to be held to a minimum.

Access roads, service roads, and parking lots serving park and recreation facilities are of two primary types, bituminous and gravel. Proper maintenance of these surfaces should consist primarily of preventive measures. The two surfaces need different maintenance and must be considered separately.

Exposure to sunlight, water, heat, and cold causes deterioration of bituminous road and parking lot surfaces. Failure of surfaces, indicated by checking and cracking, can be traced generally to improper or poor construction. Checking and cracking is most frequently caused by improper drainage of subgrade and base course, inadequate thickness or lack of structural strength of the base course material, inadequate thickness of the surface course, or poor subgrade soil conditions.

Bituminous Surfaces

Even when the road surface or parking lot is adequately constructed, drying out of the surface causes serious problems. Oxidation of the asphalt binder is caused from the combination of infrared and ultra-violet rays from sunlight. This causes the binder to lose its adhesive and cohesive qualities, and it becomes hard and brittle. The stone aggregates that were held together by the binder become looser from erosion and abrasion. As cracks appear in the pavement, water enters and causes them to increase in size and number during freezing and thawing cycles. Parking lots are subject to additional deteriorating effects from dripping oil, fuel, and grease from parked cars. These substances are solvents and soften the paved surface. For this reason, parking lots should be covered with a good quality sealcoating soon after construction. Roads should also be sealed, but only after they begin to show signs of deterioration.

The durability of a bituminous surface, whether on a road or parking lot, depends largely on the base course. It must be of sufficient thickness, laid on hard subbase soil, sufficiently compacted and adequately drained. A good drainage system will prevent water from reaching the paved surface and collecting under it. Good drainage must be provided during the initial construction but it must also be maintained during the life of the paved surface by keeping all drainage ditches and culverts open. When drainage problems appear, new drainage ditches, culverts, or diversion ditches may be needed to reduce damage to paved areas. Concrete, vitrified clay, and corregated galvanized metal are the materials most frequently used for culverts.

Gravel Surfaces   Maintenance of gravel surfaced roads differs from maintenance of a bituminous surface in two important respects. The gravel road must be bladed periodically, and some dust control method must be instituted. Blading the road surface is necessary to maintain the road's crown and insure adequate drainage, and to reduce the wash boarding effect as a result of heavy traffic. Blading may be accomplished with a farm-type tractor and blade or with larger motorized grading equipment. The blading should always be done after a rain when more than average moisture content is present. Potholes must be filled as soon as they occur.

Dust can normally be controlled by one of two methods. Calcium chloride may be used to help retain moisture already present in the road surface. Calcium chloride should be applied when the surface is damp; best results are obtained by mixing the salt with the surface layer of gravel. This can be accomplished by applying the material to the road surface prior to blading. Since calcium chloride is subject to leaching action, it must be replenished periodically.

A second method for controlling dust is the use of a light asphaltic oil. The oil has an added advantage of partially water-proofing the surface, reducing evaporation and aiding in stabilizing the road surface. The asphaltic oil can be applied with a sprinkling wagon. Vehicles should be kept off the road until the oil has had a chance to soak into the surface. A freshly oiled road will make a mess of an auto or camping vehicle.

Trails

The most serious problem in designing and maintaining an adequate trail system comes in attempting to accommodate (or failing to accommodate) the variety of trail users who desire and demand trails to meet the specifications of their particular activity. The park and recreation administrator is easily overwhelmed when he surveys potential trail uses—hiking, horseback riding, mini-bikes, interpretation, off-road motorized vehicles, bicycles, and handicapped persons. Few of these uses are compatible with each other. Bikes, horseback riders, and hikers can stand some mixing, but when use by any one group becomes heavy, the recreation experience for the others is greatly diminished. In many instances separate trails for each group is the only realistic answer to the problem.

Because of the variety of uses, traditional trail engineering standards must be carefully examined. Construction standards calling for a particular trail width (generally four feet), maximum grades (generally 15 percent up to 20 percent in very severe areas), water bars, clearing specifications, drainage, etc., still have value and should be considered in trail construction. However, strict adherence to these standards, with no regard for the function of the trail and its users, is a mistake. Despite the problems encountered in multiple-use of trails, there are some general principles which are applicable to any type of trail.

Whenever possible trails should be one-way loops. This principle holds for a one-quarter-mile nature trail, a five-mile bike trail through an urban park, or a ten-mile wilderness hiking trail. Returning over the same route decreases visitor enjoyment and doubles the traffic load. The loop trail is a relatively simple method for increasing the user's enjoyment of his recreation experience. Multiple loops add the flexibility of providing for the user who is not physically able to walk or ride the entire trail distance, and the user who is operating under a time constraint.

Normally the trail should be wide enough to accommodate motorized maintenance vehicles (jeep, electric cart, etc.). Maintaining miles of trails on foot is either very expensive or the time and effort necessary is not expended and trails become badly littered and eroded as a result of neglect. An exception to this principle might be long hiking trails where rough terrain is encountered. Many hikers enjoy an occasional steep climb or descent, climbing over fallen trees or through tight places in a rock outcropping. To destroy all of these opportunities for the sake of easy of maintenance is a mistake.

This well designed trail leads to a popular overlook.

The trail surface should protect the environment. Other than natural cover, the materials used most frequently to stabilize and protect the trail surface are wood chips, gravel and, in heavily used areas, blacktop paving. Again, care must be used depending on trail function. A coarse aggregate gravel is a completely unacceptable surface for bike trails. Trails using wood chips must have excellent drainage or the surface material will be lost. For the same reason, loose surface material should not be used on portions of trails where the percent grade exceeds nine percent.

Heavily used trails often require paving.

Erosion due to water movement is one of the greatest deterrents to good trail maintenance. Good drainange must be maintained through the use of breaks in grade, water bars, and dips. Water should never be allowed to run unchecked over more than fifty feet of a trail. Check dams, diversion ditches, and culverts must be constructed and maintained where needed to minimize erosion problems on trails.

Exposed tree roots indicate a serious trail erosion problem.

Review Questions

1. *How serious is the solid waste problem in America?*

2. *What can the park administrator do to help solve litter problems in areas under his jurisdiction?*

3. *How do you determine what type of trash receptacle is best for use in park and recreation areas?*

4. *What type of vehicle should be used to pick up trash and litter?*

5. *What are the acceptable methods of solid waste disposal?*

6. *How do you determine which is the best sewage disposal system for a park?*

7. *How can a water system for a rural park be provided?*

8. *Describe the characteristics of an ideal recreation surface.*

9. *What surfaces can be used for tennis courts? What are the advantages and disadvantages of each of these surfaces?*

10. *What types of lighting systems can be used to light a football or baseball field?*

11. *What factors determine the best type of fencing to be used in park and recreation areas?*

12. *What is the purpose of signs in park and recreation areas?*

13. *What factors must be considered when developing a good sign system for park and recreation areas?*

14. *What factors should be considered when developing a good trail system?*

Note to Chapter 5

1. Ronald C. Speedy, "Sewage Disposal," A monograph prepared
    for the Park and Recreation Maintenance Management School,
    North Carolina State University. (Raleigh: 1975), p. 1.

Bibliography

Bachman, Donald G. "Outdoor Recreation Surfaces." A monograph
    prepared for the Park and Recreation Maintenance Management
    School, North Carolina State University, Raleigh, 1974.

Bolton, R. L., and Klein, L. *Sewage Treatment.* Ann Arbor: Ann
    Arbor Science Publishers, Inc., 1971.

Bureau of Outdoor Recreation. *Proceedings: National Symposium
    on Trails.* Washington, D.C., 1971.

Cottrell, Richard L. "Trails—Pathways for People." A monograph
    prepared for the Park and Recreation Maintenance Manage-
    ment School, North Carolina State University, Raleigh, 1974.

Douglass, Robert W. *Forest Recreation.* Oxford: Pergamon Press,
    1975.

Hagerty, D. Joseph; Pavoni, Joseph L.; and Heer, John E., Jr. *Solid
    Waste Management.* New York: Van Nostrand Reinhold Co.,
    1973.

Henry, Jay E. "Maintenance of Roads, Parking Areas, and Barri-
    ers." A monograph prepared for the Park and Recreation Main-
    tenance Management School, North Carolina State University,
    Raleigh, 1974.

Moody, J. R. "Lighting Maintenance." A monograph prepared for
    the Park and Recreation Maintenance Management School,
    North Carolina State University, Raleigh, 1974.

Speedy, Ronald R. "Sewage Disposal." A monograph prepared for
    the Park and Recreation Maintenance Management School,
    North Carolina State University, Raleigh, 1975.

U.S. Environmental Protection Agency. *Design Criteria for Solid
    Waste Management in Recreation Areas.* Washington, D.C., 1972.

——. *Sanitary Landfill Design and Construction.* Washington,
    D.C., 1972.

——. *Toward a New Environmental Ethic.* Washington, D.C., 1971.

U.S. Public Health Service. *Environmental Health Practice in Rec-
    reation Areas.* Publication 1195. Washington, D.C., 1965.

Water and Sewage Equipment. Davco Manufacturing Company.
    Thomasville, Ga.

Chapter 6

Grounds Maintenance

Introduction

One of the most important elements for maintaining park and recreation areas is grounds maintenance, a term which generally applies to the maintenance of turf areas, shrubbery, and trees—anything that grows. The maintenance problems involved in growing plant materials are compounded considerably by the intensity of recreation use of an area. The mechanics of planting and growing grass, trees, and shrubs in a neighborhood park are not a difficult task to accomplish. However, when a playground is heavily used or when a softball diamond is used for three or four games a day, the maintenance problems become considerably more complex. Natural environmental conditions can generally be overcome by growing a specialized hybrid grass on a golf course green; however, with 300 golfers a day playing the course, ball marks and turf compaction are problems that must be dealt with successfully if the green is to be maintained in top quality condition.

Thus, the grounds maintenance manager deals with a variety of areas, each of which must be treated slightly differently. In areas that are lightly used for non-specific recreation activities, general principles of grounds maintenance prevail. Heavily used areas and areas that need specialized playing surfaces, require highly specialized maintenance. The grounds maintenance manager should be professionally trained in horticulture, turf management, or forestry.

265

This chapter will deal with the problems of general turf care, specialized turf care, irrigation systems, the use and care of shrubbery, shade trees, the park nursery, and erosion control as it relates to grounds maintenance in park and recreation areas.

Turf Management

A park, whether it be a 5,000-acre state park or a 15-acre neighborhood park in a city, usually consists of many acres of open land covered with grass. This may include road shoulders and banks, grassed areas around picnic areas, areas around lakes and ponds, open play areas for a variety of non-specified recreation activities such as flying kites, throwing frisbees, neighborhood pick-up touch football games, etc. Some of these areas are completely open, others are partially wooded for shade and aesthetics.

What is needed to maintain good general turf areas? Basically, the five essential elements of good turf care are (1) soil, (2) grass, (3) water, (4) air, and (5) sunlight. To some degree each of these five elements can be manipulated or modified to produce better turf. Soil can be modified by adding nutrient elements, soil conditioners and controlling pH. Grass control comes in the selection of the proper grass to meet existing environmental conditions. Water is manipulated by providing good drainage and irrigation. Air can be manipulated through aeration of the soil. Control of sunlight is perhaps the most difficult of all, but the elimination of obstacles such as trees so grass can receive adequate sunlight is often possible.

The grounds maintenance supervisor needs to exhibit the greatest control over the first three elements—soil, grass and water. The basic principles related to these three elements need to be understood in some depth.

Soil

Soil Composition   Soil is an important element because it supplies nutrients, water, and oxygen to the roots of the grass. Soil consists of two basic layers, topsoil and subsoil. Topsoil can be broken down into five ingredients: (1) mineral particles (sand, silt, and clay), (2) organic matter (also called humus) formed from dead plants and animals, (3) living plants and animals, (4) air, and (5) water.

Soil texture refers to the proportion of sand, silt, and clay present in the soil. Heavy textured soils have a high percentage of clay; these soils are more likely to become compacted. Compacted soils are said to have poor soil structure, that is, there is very little air space between soil particles. Compacted soils have poor water holding capacity, limited ability to supply nutrient elements to grass roots, and limited aeration. Light textured soils have a high percentage of sand and also have poor water holding capacity. The quality of soil can be improved by adding sand to heavy textured soils and calcined clay or peat to light textured soils.

Good topsoil has an abundance of organic material or humus present. The color of the soil is a good indication of the presence of organic matter—the darker the soil, the more organic matter present. Organic matter provides three major benefits to the soil: (1) it acts as a buffer for materials that are toxic to the grass, including acidic or alkaline conditions; (2) it increases the soil's holding capacity for plant nutrients and water; (3) it provides a healthy environment for the growth of microorganisms. Microorganisms are essential in the nitrogen cycle supplying needed nutrients for the growth of grass.

Another extremely important consideration in growing good turf is soil pH, an expression of the concentration of hydrogen ions in soil solutions. A soil's pH factor is measured on a scale of 0 to 14. Zero is the acidic side and 14 the alkaline. A pH of 7.0 is neutral. Most turfgrasses do well with a pH condition between 6.0 and 8.0. A pH factor below 5.5 has an adverse effect on grass. Both nitrogen and phosphorous in fertilizer are affected by low pH, and fertilizer loses its effectiveness with a low pH condition. In addition, acidic soil is relatively impermeable to moisture, and dead grass roots decay very slowly. The pH factor of soil can be raised with the addition of lime. Lime tends to move downward in the soil with very little lateral movement; thus, when spreading lime very thorough coverage is important. Soil pH can be lowered by adding sulphur, although under certain soil conditions (high organic content) the addition of sulphur is not as effective in lowering the pH factor of soil.

Soil pH

Soil Preparation   One of the best ways to ensure good turf stands is through adequate initial soil preparation. Problems arising from inadequate soil preparation can be extremely difficult to correct after a recreation facility has been developed. Steps to follow in preparing soil for seeding turfgrass are as follows—

1. Test the soil. A soil test measures the pH and nutrient content of the soil in the area to be planted. Soil testing is done in most states by their department of agriculture. Soil testing is extremely important, and it is a step that should not be overlooked. Guessing at the correct application of lime or fertilizer is foolish. At best it may be a waste of money, at worst, it may create a soil condition that is not conducive to the growth of turfgrass. The soil test should be repeated for general turf areas every two years. For specialized turf areas, such as a golf course green, the soil should be tested annually.

2. Grade area to desired slope to ensure adequate drainage and remove any gross materials such as rocks, stumps, etc. For ease of mowing, slopes greater than 1 to 4 should be avoided.

3. Remove undesirable plant materials by sterilization if necessary. If the final grade of an area to be established in turf is severely altered by grading, the topsoil from the area should be stripped and stockpiled until the proper grade of the subsoil has been established. While it is stockpiled, sterilization can take place. Methyl bromide is generally used for sterilization. The soil to be treated is covered with plastic and should be treated for 24 hours. After treatment it is best to wait three to four weeks before planting grass. Methyl bromide will do an effective job of killing most weed seeds in the soil. It will also kill nematodes and control some diseases. The weather should be warm (above 50 degrees) for the methyl bromide application.

4. Add one-half of the lime as indicated by soil test. Do not apply a total of more than 50 lbs. of limestone per 1000 sq. ft. of turf area. If more lime is needed to raise the soil pH to the acceptable level, additional limestone should be added in six months or one year.

5. Plow the entire area to be seeded. Plowing will normally turn up soil to a depth of 4 to 6 inches. Where heavy topsoil or subsoil conditions exist, subsoiling to a depth of 12 to 18 inches will ultimately produce a healthier turf. Grass roots normally grow to a depth of 8 to 12 inches.

6. Add the second half of the lime, soil conditioners, and nutrients as indicated by soil test.

7. Rototill or plow lightly in two directions to thoroughly mix added materials.

8. Smooth surface with cultipacker or rake.

9. Plant grass by broadcasting seed on the prepared area.

10. Roll with light roller or rake.

11. Mulch with a seed free material.

12. Water to a depth of four inches.

13. When grass has grown about two inches, lightly topdress with a high nitrogen fertilizer.

14. Mow by setting mower higher than normal (2½ to 3 inches) for first few mowings.

There are three major nutrient elements needed for healthy turf-grass.

Nutrient Elements

1. Nitrogen   This is the most important element of the three because it promotes leaf or blade growth of the grass. With a nitrogen deficiency the blade of the grass turns a light green or greenish-yellow color. When nitrogen is not properly balanced with phosphorous, potassium and lime, a succulent, tender growth is produced. Principle sources of nitrate used in fertilizer are from urea, ammonium nitrate, calcium nitrate, and sodium nitrate.

2. Phosphorous   The chief value of phosphorous as a grass nutrient is to produce healthy root growth. An inadequate supply of phosphorous will retard or even halt growth of grass roots.

3. Potassium (also commonly called potash)   The chief value of potassium is that it is an important ingredient in the manufacture of sugars, starches, and proteins. Potassium gives the grass general vigor, strengthens the plant stems, and provides resistance to disease. Potassium deficiency is indicated by browning of grass tips and blade margins.

In addition to the three major nutrient elements there are other elements, often referred to as trace elements, that are necessary for high quality turf. These elements include calcium, magnesium, sulphur, iron, zinc, manganese, copper, molybdenum, and boron.

Nutrient elements are provided naturally in the soil and by the use of fertilizers. There are two general classes of fertilizer, organic and inorganic.

Organic fertilizer can be subdivided further into two groups, natural and synthetic. Natural organic fertilizers include animal manures, sewage sludges, fish meal, composts, cotton seed meal, tobacco stems, and others. Compared with inorganic fertilizer, the natural organic fertilizers are relatively low in nutrient value. The natural organic fertilizers have an advantage of slow release of nutrient elements. Inorganic fertilizer, by contrast, is used up much more quickly. Because of the obvious problem of people coming in contact with animal manures and sludges, these two forms of natural organic fertilizer are seldom appropriate for intensively used park and recreation areas.

Synthetic organic fertilizers are manufactured by treating urea with formaldehyde. Untreated urea is highly soluble in water, and the nitrogen is used up by the grass blade or passes through the soil too quickly. By adding formaldehyde, the release of nutrients is slowed considerably. This type of fertilizer is often called ureaform. A good formulation of ureaform fertilizer will provide for quick and slow release of nitrogen. When buying it is important to know the percentage of quick and slow release fertilizer contained. Ideally, a bag of ureaform fertilizer should contain 35 percent W.I.N. (Water Insoluble Nitrogen).

Inorganic fertilizers are manufactured from chemical salts. Commercially packaged fertilizers must show, by law, the guaranteed percentage of each nutrient element. These are shown in percentage by weight of nitrogen, phosphorous, and potassium, in that order. Thus, a bag of fertilizer labeled 5-10-10 will contain five pounds of nitrogen, ten pounds of phosphorous, and ten pounds of potassium per 100 pounds.

How and When to Fertilize

Cool season grasses are normally fertilized in fall and/or spring. Some turf experts are now recommending one heavy fall fertilization and none in the spring. Warm season grasses are also generally fertilized in the fall and spring with supplemental fertilization during the late spring and summer with a high nitrogen fertilizer. Fertilizer must be spread uniformly only when grass is dry. There is a danger of fertilizer burn if too much fertilizer is applied at one time or if fertilizer is applied to wet grass. The problem of burning wet grass can be avoided by watering after it has been applied.

Grass Selection

Selection of the proper grass variety is the first step toward developing a high quality turf. The grounds superintendent must choose from an ever widening variety of grasses depending upon environmental conditions and the anticipated use or activity. The first consideration in selecting the best turfgrass must be the general environmental conditions—temperature, soil condition, humidity, disease resistance, and drought tolerance where the turf area is not irrigated. Some grasses are more shade tolerant than others. Some grasses bear traffic better than others. Resistance to wear is an important consideration in virtually all recreation areas. The days of keep-off-the-grass signs no longer exist in parks; even areas planted as general lawns can expect a moderate amount of traffic from people using the park facilities. Wearability is an especially important consideration in the selection of grasses for playgrounds and athletic fields where intensive use can be anticipated. Another important consideration in grass selection is the amount of maintenance required. Frequency of mowing, fertilization requirements, and other special care that may be required to maintain some grasses in top condition is costly. Planting a high budget grass without the fiscal resources to maintain it is poor management.

All grasses can be classified into two basic types—warm and cool season grasses. Warm season grasses have their period of greatest growth during the summer months of June, July and August. These grasses are dormant during the winter and turn brown from October to early May. The warm season grasses have their best application in the Southern states. The cool season grasses have their period of most active growth in the spring and fall and are relatively dormant during the summer months of July and August.

Some of the more common families of warm and cool season grasses will be described indicating their advantages, disadvantages, and applications.

Fescue The fescues can be divided into two groups—tall and fine. Both are drought tolerant, grow well in moderate shade, do well in poor soil, and are disease resistant. Because of low maintenance requirements, the fescues are commonly planted in general

Cool Season Grasses

lawn areas. All fescues can be grown from seed. Common varieties are—

- Kentucky 31 and Alta (tall fescue)
- Pennlawn and Chewings (fine fescue)

Bluegrass This grass gets its name from its bluish color. There are two common types of bluegrass, Kentucky Bluegrass and Rough Stalked Bluegrass. Kentucky Bluegrass does well in full sunlight and in well drained soils. It spreads rapidly with creeping underground stems (rhizomes). It does not wear particularly well. Common varieties are—

- Merion (low growing and disease resistant)
- Newport and Windsor

Rough Stalked Bluegrass is well adapted to moderate shade and is generally used in grass mixtures.

Bentgrass The fine texture of the bentgrass family produces very high quality turf. At the same time, bentgrass requires more maintenance than any other grass. The common types of bentgrass are creeping bent, colonial bent, and redtop. Bentgrass spreads by above ground stems (stolons) and if not properly maintained produces a mat and/or thatch condition. Where very high quality playing surfaces are desired such as golf course greens and tees, tennis courts, and bowling greens, bentgrass is commonly used. Creeping bentgrass must be frequently watered and requires almost full sunlight. Common varieties are—

- Seaside and Penncross

Because of its consistent texture and disease resistance Penncross has become widely used on golf courses.

Colonial bentgrass is used for general lawn areas and is often mixed with bluegrass and fescue. Astoria is a common variety. Redtop is also commonly used in grass mixtures because of its quick growth characteristic. It seldom lives more than three years making it undesirable as a permanent grass.

Ryegrass Ryegrass is a fine textured grass during its first year of growth. It is not drought or shade tolerant and does not do well in wet or acidic soils. It germinates more quickly than other grass and for this reason is commonly used as a cover grass while slower growing grasses become established. It is also used to over-seed warm season grasses to give color during their dormant season. Common varieties are—

• Perennial and Italian

Bermuda Common bermudagrass is a very hardy grass. It bears traffic well, and for this reason is often used on playgrounds and athletic fields. It is a fast growing grass and spreads by rhizomes and stolons. Common bermuda can be planted from seed. The hybrid bermudagrasses are finer textured than common bermuda and are produced principally at the Coastal Plain Experimental Station at Tifton, Ga. In recent years a number of excellent varieties of hybrid bermudagrass have been developed for golf course tees, greens, and fairways and are widely used throughout the South. Hybrid bermudagrass is also commonly used for high quality athletic fields such as football stadiums in the South. In addition to the problem of all warm season grasses of turning brown in the fall, bermudagrass is not shade tolerant and requires heavy fertilization. Common varieties are—

Warm Season Grasses

• Tifgreen, Tifway, Tifdwarf and Common.

Zoysia Zoysia is also a very hardy warm season grass. Some varieties do well in northern climates because it is more cold-tolerant than other warm season grasses. This grass has good wear-resistance and does well in moderate shade. It also has moderate fertility and moisture requirements. Like bermuda, it spreads by rhizomes and stolons but is considerably slower growing and takes longer to establish.
Common varieties are—

• Meyer, Matrella, and Emerald.

Carpetgrass Carpetgrass is a relatively coarse textured grass that does well in moist places and adapts well to sandy soils. It has moderate shade tolerance and has low fertility requirements. Carpetgrass is much less cold tolerant than bermuda.

St. Augustine   St. Augustine is a coarse textured grass found widely in coastal areas of the South. This grass has good shade tolerance but is especially vunerable to insects and leaf diseases. It is a low growing grass that spreads by rhizomes and stolons.

Centipedegrass   The major advantage of centipedegrass is that it grows well on soils of low fertility and requires little maintenance. It does well in moderate shade. It is less drought and cold tolerant than bermuda. It has very poor wear-resistance.

Bahiagrass   Bahia is not a particularly desirable lawn grass because of its coarse texture; however, it is widely used on road shoulders because it requires little maintenance and grows under poor soil conditions. It is relatively shade tolerant. The major problem with bahiagrass is that it produces a seedhead that makes the grass unattractive.

Planting Turfgrass   There are four methods that can be used to establish turfgrass, (1) seeding, (2) vegetative propagation, (3) plugging, and (4) sodding.

Seeding   Seeding is the most commonly used method of establishing turfgrass and generally the least expensive. All of the cool season grasses in addition to common bermuda and carpetgrass, are commonly established by seeding. Soil preparation for seeding was discussed earlier in this chapter. Different varieties of grass have different germination times. Fescue and rye seed germinate rather quickly, generally in about eight days. The bluegrasses are considerably slower and require 14 to 21 days to germinate. When buying grass seed it is important to recognize that seed is bought by weight rather than by seed count. The number of seeds per pound varies greatly depending upon the variety. Rye and tall fescue seed is large with about 227,000 seeds per pound. Kentucky Bluegrass seed is much smaller with slightly over two million seeds per pound. Bentgrass seed is even smaller with 5 to 9 million seeds per pound depending on the variety. The seedrate per 1000 sq. ft. depends on the number of seeds per pound. Cool season grasses are generally planted in the fall although spring planting is possible. Warm season grasses are planted when the temperature is high enough to germinate seed promptly (generally about 55 degrees).

Vegetative Propagation   Vegetative propagation is also commonly called sprigging. As mentioned in the discussion of types of grasses, creeping stems are a typical growth pattern of some varieties of grass. These grasses spread by underground stems called rhizomes and above ground stems called stolons. These creeping stems are used in vegetative propagation. Vegetative propagation is accomplished by taking sod from the grass to be planted, running it through a soil shredder and broadcasting or spreading it over the area to be established. The chopped up grass is then lightly topdressed, rolled and watered. It is extremely important for the grass to be kept moist until it has taken root and the new turf is well established.

Plugging   A third method of establishing new turf is by plugging. Using this method a plug of turf generally 1½ to 3 inches in diameter is placed in the ground 12 to 18 inches apart. The lateral growth pattern of the turfgrass then covers the entire area. This method is slower than vegetative propagation but requires less material and can be used effectively where coverage time is not critical. This method is used to establish athletic fields and to repair spots of golf greens where grass has died.

Sodding   Sodding is by far the most expensive method of establishing turf. Any type of turfgrass can be established by sodding. This method is used where mature turf is needed in a hurry or where traffic will not allow the use of one of the other methods. Sod is cut at about 1½-inch thick in lengths and widths that can be easily handled. The entire area is covered with sod, rolled with a light (150 to 200 lb.) roller and watered.

Sodding is a good solution to the problem of establishing turf on difficult areas.

Irrigation Systems

As mentioned earlier in this chapter, water is an essential ingredient in maintaining high quality turfgrass. The only way to assure an adequate amount of moisture in the soil is through the installation and use of a permanent, underground irrigation system. Permanent irrigation systems can be classified into three types, (1) spray, (2) rotary, and (3) snap valve. All three of these systems can be controlled manually or automatically. The manual system requires the operator to physically operate the system. The automatic systems are electronically controlled and can be operated by a clock.

The spray system utilizes pop up sprinkler heads that discharge a fine uniform spray. Sprinkler heads are spaced 15 to 25 feet apart. This system has a good application for highly manicured lawn areas but is not appropriate for sports fields and other recreation areas because the large number of sprinkler heads provide a hazard for activity. The major advantage of this system is excellent control of the pattern or area being watered providing optimum use of water.

The rotary system also utilizes pop up sprinkler heads. Water is distributed by two orifices within the nozzle which slowly rotate so that a high velocity stream sweeps over a large circular area. This system will throw a stream of water 30 to 60 feet. Part circle heads are also available. This system is used extensively on golf courses and park facilities.

The snap valve system utilizes a long arm rotating sprinkler head. It has the greatest range and will throw water 80 to 200 feet. This system is also widely used on golf courses and large park areas. The initial cost of this system is the lowest of the three discussed; however, the operator must physically put the sprinkler arms in place and labor cost to maintain the system is extremely high when compared with the other two systems. When the high cost of labor is considered over time, the rotary system has proved to be more economical.

A portable irrigation system operates the same way as the snap valve system except the pipe is located above ground rather than underground. This system is very expensive to operate because of the high labor cost to move the system from one location to another. The system, however, has a good application for park and recreation facilities. The system can be used effectively when establishing new turf areas, in times of extreme drought, and to prepare turf areas for special events. The flexibility of the system allows its use in many areas throughout the park and recreation system rather than in one specific area as with the permanent underground systems.

Regardless of the type of irrigation system used, the park grounds superintendent should use a hydrometer to measure the moisture content of the soil. In many instances soil that appears to be dry will be dry on the surface only, and 2 to 3 inches underground sufficient water may be present so that irrigation is not needed.

Aeration

The purpose of aeration is to provide air to the roots of the grass. In normal turf aeration should be performed once a year (in the spring) when the soil is soft but not muddy. Where compaction is a problem aeration should be performed more frequently. The aerifier should remove a soil core to a depth of 6 to 10 inches. These soil cores should be broken up and spread over the surface. This can be accomplished by dragging the area with a flexible steel mat. Aeration should be accomplished before fertilizing and liming.

Mowing   Grass would be healthier if it was allowed to grow to its normal height. Cutting turf areas too closely reduces the depth of the root system. Grass should be cut so that not more than one-third of the blade of the grass is cut during the mowing. Height of cut depends on the type of grass. General turf areas should be cut at 1¼ to 1½ inches. Some varieties can be cut from 3/4 to 1 inch, or even shorter. It is important to vary the pattern of cut of a lawn area and turf should be mowed with a sharp mower. A dull mower tears the grass blade and exposes it to disease attack.

Turf Pests   Turfgrass is susceptible to attack from insects, disease, and weeds. Maintaining good healthy turf will reduce, but not eliminate, the danger from each of these three pests. Healthy turf can be maintained by proper aeration, fertilization, and watering; by maintaining sharp mowing equipment; and by thatch removal when needed. Turf pests can be controlled in one of four ways, (1) biological control utilizing beneficial predators, (2) cultural controls, (3) mechanical controls, and (4) chemical controls. The choice of control method should be predicated on safety, both to the operator and to the general environment, effectiveness and economy. State agricultural universities can be very helpful with these problems.

When insecticides are used they should be applied in late summer or early fall when insects are young and easily killed. Some examples of common insect problems on lawn areas include: grubworms, cutworms, sod webworms, mole crickets, and clinchbugs.

Diseases are the most difficult of the pests to control. Some diseases can destroy turf in a matter of several hours. Fungicides should be used to control turf diseases and should be applied after mowing. Some examples of common disease problems include: Leaf spot, root rot, brownpatch, dollar spot, powdery mildew, and snow mold.

Herbicides are used to chemically control weeds. Two types are used, (1) pre-emergence, applied a couple of weeks before weeds appear, and (2) post-emergence, applied when weeds are beginning to grow. Weeds can also be controlled by using high quality weed-free grass seed. Some examples of common weeds include:

crabgrass, chickweed, dandelion, clinquefoil, nutgrass, white clover, and wild onion.

Although the principles already discussed in this chapter apply to specialized turf areas as well as general lawn areas, specialized turf areas such as golf courses, tennis courts, bowling greens and stadiums do present some unique problems that make the maintenance job more complex. Some of the problems related to golf course maintenance will be used to illustrate the complexity of specialized turf care.

Specialized Turf Areas

Maintaining good turf on a golf course is a complex and time-consuming job.

First of all, different grasses are used on different parts of the golf course. Golf greens are generally planted with either a hybrid bermuda or a creeping bent, the grass on tees may be hybrid bermuda, creeping bent, or Kentucky Bluegrass. Fairways may be planted with Kentucky Bluegrass, common or hybrid bermuda, or zoysia. On courses using warm season grass greens, they are commonly overseeded in the fall with a combination of bent, fescue, and rye. Rye is also used to overseed fairways.

The height of cut of grass will vary with different parts of the course. Greens are generally cut to 3/8 to 1/4 inch, tees 1/2 inch, fairways 3/4 inch and rough areas 2 to 3 inches. On public golf courses, rough areas should be kept relatively short to speed up play.

Compaction can present a serious problem on a golf course. Compaction is most often caused by foot traffic on greens and by golf carts beside tees and greens. These problems can be solved by moving cup positions on greens every two to three days, by aerating and fertilizing more frequently and by constructing cart paths in areas that are heavily used.

The problem of matting and thatching has been discussed earlier. A heavily matted or thatched golf green will produce a surface where the putted golf ball will bounce unless perfectly struck. Golfers dislike the inconsistency of such a putting surface. This problem can be solved by verticutting 2 or 3 times per year or by using mowing equipment that straightens the grass as it is cut.

Because of ball marks and scuff marks from clubs and shoes, indentations gradually develop on golf greens. In order to assure the golfer a smooth putting surface, the green must be topdressed periodically. Topdressing is accomplished by spreading about ¼ inch of soil of the same texture of the basic soil used to construct the green. This material is worked into the surface by dragging with a flexible steel mat. Topdressing is done 2 to 5 times per year.

Because of the short cut of greens, tees, and fairways, golf course grass is not as healthy as normal turf unless special care is given. These areas require more fertilization, particularly with high nitrogen fertilizer and special attention to insect, disease, and weed control problems.

Mowing presents special problems. In order to maintain healthy tees and greens, grass clippings must be removed. On a well maintained course, greens must be cut daily. On a heavily used course it is important that the mowing be done before the course is open for play.

Turf on a golf tee takes a tremendous amount of use and abuse by the golfer. This is particularly true on a par-3 hole where irons are used for tee shots. Good design of tees will provide large tee areas so that tee markers can be moved daily if necessary to allow the turf to recover. Additional fertilization will also help

Turf cannot be maintained properly on areas that must bear heavy traffic, however, paved paths are but one solution to help solve soil compaction problems created by golf carts.

speed the growth of grass and will cover damaged areas more quickly.

A well-maintained golf course requires a tremendous amount of water under normal environmental conditions. Most greenskeepers agree that early morning is the best time to regularly water the course. This is true because there is less wind, less water demand where a municipal system is being used and thus better water pressure, and less danger of turf disease from a green or tee staying wet all night from a late evening watering. Bentgrass greens must be syringed early each morning to remove dew accumulations and also during the day when the weather is hot.

A final critical problem involves making the decision as to when a golf course should be closed to play. In very wet weather golfers and golf carts may do irreparable damage to the course. In cold weather turf may be seriously damaged by golfers walking on lightly frozen greens. The decision of when to allow play should be left up to the course greens superintendent because he is responsible for the condition of the course.

Baseball and Softball Diamonds

Another area of specialized maintenance that is very common with municipal and county park and recreation departments is the maintenance of softball and baseball diamonds. These facilities, when used for competitive league play, require a great deal of care and attention. Maintenance work on a ball diamond can be considered in terms of daily, weekly, and seasonal maintenance needed.

Daily maintenance would include routine items such as litter pick-up, trash collection, restroom and locker room maintenance. The infield must be dragged every day. Many park and recreation departments use a variety of drags made from flexible steel mats, landscaping rakes, and boards covered with carpet. In addition, there are several commercially made drags on the market. Holes in the pitcher's mound, batter's boxes, and areas around the bases should be filled and raked smooth. Baselines and batter's boxes must also be lined each day. Quite frequently, park and recreation departments with a large number of ball diamonds to maintain will employ one or more specialized crews that maintain all diamonds in the system by traveling from one location to another. Game bases are generally put out by a field supervisor or umpire rather than the maintenance crew to assure that the field will not be used until the scheduled teams are ready to play.

Weekly maintenance should include mowing grass in the infield, outfield, and borders of the field. Checks for safety and needed repairs to dugouts or player's benches, stands, fences, backstops, restrooms and locker rooms should be made weekly. Dust from a dry field can make playing on such a surface unpleasant. Wetting the infield daily can help solve this problem; however, broadcasting calcium chloride on the dirt portion of the infield every week or two is a more practical solution. Calcium chloride increases the water holding capacity of the soil and does a good job reducing dust.

Ball diamonds that do not dry quickly after a rain present another maintenance headache. The best solution to this problem is good initial construction of the diamond with enough slope on the infield and outfield to allow adequate drainage from the playing surfaces. Proper soil composition is also an important factor. Most departments construct their infields from a sand-clay mixture. A mixture of 60 percent clay and 40 percent sand has proved to be satisfactory, although this will vary somewhat in different sections of the country.

Seasonal maintenance should include good turf maintenance as discussed earlier in this chapter. In the spring about 10 yards of soil should be added to the infield to replenish soil lost during the previous season. Major repair work such as replacing bleacher seats, repainting, and replacing fencing, should take place during the off season so that all facilities are in excellent condition by the beginning of the baseball season.

Shrubbery and Trees

The use of landscape plant materials in park and recreation areas has gradually changed over the years. Traditionally, many municipal park departments maintained many beds of annual plant materials that were changed with the season. A bed might contain pansies in the spring, dalias in the summer, and chrysanthemums in the fall. Although this planting concept is still used for selected areas, the gradual shift has been toward the use of permanent plantings that are just as attractive and much less costly to maintain.

Formal gardens are attractive but expensive to maintain.

There are several values that accrue when landscaping is accomplished in park and recreation areas. The first value is an aesthetic one. Generally, park and recreation areas should be as natural as possible, and developed facilities should blend into this natural environment. Through the use of native plant materials, park and recreation areas can be enhanced by good landscape design. Also, the use of landscaping can create areas of beauty where none now exist. Restoration of blighted landscapes calls for creation of beauty rather than preservation of natural beauty. In addition to the aesthetic value of landscaping, plant materials can be used for functional purposes such as controlling pedestrian traffic flow and screening unattractive areas from public view in intensively used recreation areas. Plant materials also provide food for birds and animals.

The park and recreation administrator must realize that the use of landscaping is a liability as well as an asset. The use of landscape plantings will generally be costly. There is an initial cost of the plant materials, the cost to maintain these materials once they have been planted, and landscaping will generally increase mowing time by creating islands and uneven borders that require careful trimming and mowing with smaller mowing equipment.

Interior landscaping enhances the work environment at this park headquarters.

The planning of landscaped areas should be done by a competent landscape architect. Many large park and recreation agencies employ landscape architects as part of their permanent planning staff. Other departments use consultants on a job-to-job basis.

When selecting plant materials for park and recreation areas, the landscape designer must first consider environmental conditions—temperature, soil type, moisture and sunlight requirements, and wind resistance. He should select plant materials that are disease and insect resistant. An ideal shrub or ornamental tree is one that has an attractive flower, attractive foliage, attractive fruit (unattractive fruit may eliminate the plant), and good fall color. Few plant materials meet all of these criteria. Flowering Dogwood (Cornus florida) is one that does.

Shade Trees

Many municipal park and recreation departments have the responsibility for trees and shrubbery plantings on city rights-of-way as well as on park and recreation property. Responsibility for these trees includes planting, pruning, removing dead trees, and disease and insect control. Well designed shade tree plantings create an attractive environment in any community. However, improper use and design can create problems. One problem involves the creation of blind intersections by planting trees and shrubs that block the driver's sight line from oncoming traffic creating a safety hazard. This problem can be avoided by proper selection and placement of trees and shrubs. Some tall growing trees, if not properly placed, tend to block out street lights and stop lights. This problem should be corrected by proper placement of trees and street lights rather than creating a situation where trees must be constantly pruned. Root damage from shade trees to both sidewalks and sewer lines can cause costly repairs. The trend in recent years has been to avoid planting in the strip between the street and sidewalk. Also careful attention to the pattern of root growth of trees planted in areas where these problems are likely to occur is an acceptable solution. Trees growing into utility lines are another maintenance nightmare. Underground utilities in many communities have eliminated this problem. Where overhead utility lines exist, planting low growing varieties of trees is a much better solution than constant pruning which results in misshapen trees. When trees die, tree and stump removal is a costly process. Trees must often be removed limb by limb to avoid damage to surrounding property. Stumps are generally removed with a mechanical stump remover. Chemicals can be used to speed the decay process for stumps in non-critical areas.

Trends in shade tree plantings in recent years include using landscape architects to fit plantings to street locations. A downtown area, an area of light commercial use and residential areas call for different landscape treatments. There has been a trend toward the use of a larger variety of shade trees. The traditional shade tree of the 1920s and 30s was the American elm. The Dutch elm disease denuded many American cities of almost all of their shade trees. In Columbus, Ohio alone, 70,000 trees were destroyed by the disease. Planting a variety of trees will prevent this kind of catastrophe in the future. There has also been a trend toward planting ornamental trees. Plantings of dogwood, redbud, flowering crabs, and flowering cherries have become common. One final trend has been to encourage private property owners to plant trees on their property rather than on city rights-of-way. This has been accomplished through giving property owners advice on what trees to plant, how to plant, and in some instances providing small trees free of charge or at very low cost.

Proper care in planting trees and shrubs is essential if a high survival rate is to be expected. Trees and shrubs may be planted bare-root or balled and burlapped. The balled and burlapped shrub or tree will have a better chance of surviving because there is less disturbance of the root system. However, some varieties of plant materials do very well when planted from bare-root stock, and shipping charges from nurseries are greatly reduced.

There is an old park maxim that says, "Plant a 10¢ plant in a $1.00 hole but never, never plant a $1.00 plant in a 10¢ hole." The economics may be outdated, but the message is still a valid one. A rule of thumb is that the hole should be 6 to 12 inches wider on each side and 6 inches deeper than the ball of the plant. Holes for trees and shrubs are generally dug with an auger, either hand held or operated from the power-takeoff of a tractor. Augers up to 36 inches in diameter are available. Adequate drainage around the hole and through the bottom and sides of the hole is essential. The plant should be watered thoroughly at the time of planting. However, fertilization is not generally recommended until the plant has become established. Fertilization at planting tends to burn exposed roots. Care must be taken not to plant the tree or shrub too deep. Some settling of the plant must be anticipated. After settling, the root collar of the plant must be level with the surrounding terrain. Approximately one-third of the plant should be pruned after planting. With bare-root stock, the pruning may need to be even more severe.

Small trees and shrubs generally do not need to be supported after planting. Larger trees (7 to 10 feet or more) should be supported by staking or using guy wires. In areas where heavy use can be anticipated, such as a playground, smaller trees may also need protection. Under these circumstances guy wires present a safety hazard and staking is recommended. In some areas young trees should be protected from climate, insects, and rodents. This is accomplished by using tree-wrap paper or burlap.

When a large number of small shrubs are to be planted in the same bed, it is often more practical to rototill the entire plant bed rather than dig individual holes for each plant. Where drainage is poor, and with plant materials like azaleas that require excellent drainage, raising the entire bed may be indicated.

After planting, mulching is essential. The mulches can be organic or inorganic. Organic mulches commonly used include pine

Planting and Care

straw, wood chips, bark, and coarse peat. Inorganic mulch generally consists of gravel or small rocks. Mulch is important in shrubbery beds because it holds moisture and slows runoff of water. A
heavy mulch will reduce weed growth. Organic mulches add some
organic matter to the soil, and they have considerable aesthetic
value.

After planting, the essentials of caring for trees and shrubs
include mulching, weeding, watering, pruning, fertilizing, and controlling insects and disease. Mulching simply involves replacing
mulch as it is needed. Organic mulches, depending upon the type
used, will generally last 2 to 3 years. If a good mulch is maintained,
very little weeding of shrubbery beds should be necessary. Labor to
weed shrubbery beds is considerably more costly than the cost of
maintaining an adequate mulch. Even with a good mulch, some
weeding will be necessary in most beds. Watering is especially important during the first two years after trees and shrubs have been
planted. Slow, deep watering is much more effective than frequent
shallow watering.

Pruning trees and shrubs is more time consuming than any
other maintenance task. Pruning may have three purposes: shaping
the tree or shrub, rejuvenation, and removal of dead wood. Pruning
for shaping may be necessary in some instances. However, trees and
shrubs in parks should be allowed to grow into their natural shape.
Topiary, the art of pruning trees and shrubs in various shapes and
designs, may have a place in specialized areas, but should not be
used in parks. Severe pruning of any shrub or tree gives it an
artificial, synthetic appearance and detracts from rather than com-
pliments the park environment. Pruning for rejuvenation varies
with different plant materials. Some shrubs require only periodic
light pruning, others do best with a severe cutback each year. Pruning dead limbs from trees in intensively used areas of parks is
critical from a safety standpoint. This work should be done by an
experienced in-house crew or by contract. Tree limbs should be
removed with a jump cut to avoid splitting the bark. All wounds
should be painted with a commercial tree paint to prevent insect
and disease damage.

Fertilization of trees and shrubs should be based on a soil
test. Most trees and shrubs do best in slightly acidic soils. However,
the preference range varies with different plant materials. Trees and
shrubs should be fertilized in the late fall or early spring. Fertilizer

is generally applied to trees by the punch-bar method, drilled holes, or surface application. When using either the punch-bar or drilled holes methods, holes should be about two feet apart and 12 to 18 inches deep. Shrubbery beds are fertilized by broadcasting, or in small plantings, plants may be treated individually. Shrubbery should be fertilized annually; every three to five years is generally sufficient for trees.

The most important factor in disease and insect control is correct diagnosis. Few park and recreation departments will have a staff person who is knowledgeable about all insect and disease problems. Help can be secured through the local U.S.D.A. Cooperative Extension Service office. Application of pesticides requires specialized equipment. Large departments will have enough use to justify purchase of this equipment. Smaller park and recreation agencies handle their spray program by contract.

The Park Nursery

Many park and recreation departments maintain their own plant nurseries. In many instances, the nursery may be economically feasible, that is, the department may save money by propagating and growing its own nursery stock. For the most part, the nursery is maintained because the desired variety of plant materials is not available from commercial nurseries. Another valid reason for establishing a nursery is to test and evaluate new plant materials before they are used extensively in park plantings. When deciding whether or not the park and recreation department should establish its own plant nursery, the following factors should be considered—

1. volume of plant materials needed. The agency must use enough plant materials to make it economically feasible to invest in the equipment, facilities and personnel needed to justify operating their own nursery. A park and recreation agency with extensive tree and shrubbery plantings, a large formal garden or gardens, and responsibility for shade tree plantings and landscaping streets and highways may be able to save substantial amounts of money each year by operating its own nursery. A small department with a relatively low demand for trees and shrubs will have difficulty justifying the nursery on the basis of economic feasibility.

2. investigate commercial sources. There are many excellent commercial nurseries in the United States and they may be able to supply higher quality materials at lower cost. By communicating anticipated needs to the local nurserymen, the commercial grower may be willing to grow the variety of plant materials needed by the park and recreation agency. The possibility of having plant materials supplied by commercial nurseries should not be overlooked. The commercial nursery can supply a highly professional service that need not be duplicated by the park and recreation agency.
3. land availability for developing needed facilities.
4. capital financing available to develop needed facilities.
5. availability of qualified personnel to operate the nursery. A professional staff person trained in ornamental horticulture is needed.

The facilities necessary to maintain a high quality park nursery are expensive. If an agency is going to do its own propagation, a greenhouse is necessary. Cold frames can be substituted but these are not entirely satisfactory. Considering the high cost of energy, the operating cost of a greenhouse is extremely expensive. After plants have been propagated in the greenhouse or cold frames, they are generally moved to a shade house where small material is grown until it is of sufficient size to be moved to the nursery beds. The park and recreation agency can eliminate the need for a greenhouse by purchasing rooted cuttings (lining-out stock) from commercial sources. This eliminates a costly facility from the operation. However, securing the desired variety of rooted cuttings is difficult without the close cooperation of commercial nurserymen. An irrigation system for watering plant materials is essential to the successful nursery operation. With adequate facilities and staff, the park nursery can be a valuable addition to the park and recreation system.

Soil Erosion

When the natural soil cover is disturbed during the construction of park and recreation facilities, erosion is likely to occur. Precautions must be taken during the construction phase to minimize the effect of soil erosion. The deteriorative effect is considerably more evident when large areas are effected, such as during the construction of a golf course or athletic field. The soil loss from these large acreages can cause severe siltation problems to streams, rivers, ponds, and lakes downstream, in addition to the loss of valuable topsoil from the area. Even in small construction sites, efforts to control loss of soil are an important consideration. The use of temporary check dams and early soil stabilization will greatly reduce the soil erosion hazard.

Soil erosion is a serious problem.

Soil erosion can be classified as two basic types, (1) sheet erosion and (2) gully erosion. Sheet erosion occurs by a gradual wearing away of entire layers of topsoil. Sheet erosion can be caused either by wind or water. In the eastern United States, most erosion is caused by water; however, wind erosion of sandy soils is a problem in many coastal areas. The process of sheet erosion is often scarcely discernible, because it occurs over a period of many years. Gully erosion is often the second stage in the erosion process. As small depressions and channels are formed in the sheet erosion process, they gradually deepen into gullies that cut through the surface structure of the soil.

The secret to solving both types of soil erosion is to slow the movement of water and protect fragile surfaces. Sheet erosion can generally be controlled by establishing a good vegetative cover of grass, shrubs, ground cover, or trees. On long gentle slopes contour plowing and terracing will slow the flow of water and allow greater absorption. On steep slopes, stabilized mulch and brush strips along the contour of the slope are effective. In either case, control of the watershed above the slope is essential. When large amounts of water are involved, diversion ditches around the slope may be indicated. To control gully erosion it is first necessary to control water flow feeding into the gully by stabilizing the watershed above the gully and by diverting the flow of water perhaps through the use of diversion ditches. The use of concrete, wooden and brush dams can also be successful. Several references listed in the bibliography give good detailed information concerning specific soil erosion control methods.

A good ground cover and rip rap have eliminated soil erosion problems on this lakeshore embankment.

There are a number of problem areas related to erosion control that warrant special mention. Problems related to erosion control on trails were discussed in Chapter 5. Soil erosion is often a serious problem in picnic areas and campgrounds. Heavy use often destroys the natural ground cover and compacts the soil to the point where absorption of moisture is greatly reduced. Aeration of the soil to reduce compaction and replenishing the ground cover with wood chips or other materials can reduce erosion problems.

Runoff from roads, parking lots, roofs of buildings, paved games surfaces, and other artificial surfaces produces, when aggregated, a volume of water that must be handled by planning for adequate drainage during the construction of the facility. After adequate drainage from developed facilities has been assured through good planning and design, proper maintenance of drainage systems is essential. Culverts, drainage ditches, and catch basins must be inspected regularly and cleaned out when needed. Many soil erosion problems are caused by improper maintenance of adequately engineered drainage systems. Water courses that carry away drain water must also be maintained by clearing sand and gravel bars and trash accumulations.

The U.S.D.A. Soil Conservation Service is an excellent source of help with soil erosion problems. The alert park administrator will take advantage of the services of this office.

Review Questions

1. Describe the best soil conditions for growing grass.
2. How do you prepare soil for planting turf areas?
3. Why, how, and when should you aerate soil?
4. Describe the importance of nutrient elements in the care of turfgrass.
5. What kinds of irrigation systems can be used for turf areas?
6. Describe the methods of establishing turfgrasses.
7. How do you determine what variety of turfgrass is best for a particular park and recreation area?
8. What are some of the problems that make care of a golf course more complex than general lawn care?
9. What is the value of landscaping park and recreation areas?
10. How do you determine what plant materials are best for park plantings?
11. What must be done to properly care for shrubbery?
12. Should a park and recreation department develop its own plant nursery?
13. What facilities are needed for a nursery operation?
14. What responsibility does a park and recreation department have for shade trees?
15. What are the current park practices with regard to shade tree selection and planting?
16. Differentiate between sheet and gully erosion.
17. What can be done to control erosion?

Bibliography

Beard, J. B. *Turfgrass, Science and Culture.* Englewood Cliffs, N.J.: Prentice-Hall, 1973.

Black, C. A. *Soil-Plant Relationships.* New York: John Wiley and Sons, 1968.

Carpenter, Philip L.; Walker, Theodore D., and Lanphear, Fredrick O. *Plants in the Landscape.* San Francisco: W. H. Freeman, 1975.

Conover, H. S. *Grounds Maintenance Handbook.* New York: McGraw-Hill, 1958.

Cottrell, Richard L. "Erosion Control and Soil Compaction." A monograph prepared for the Park and Recreation Maintenance-Management School, North Carolina State University, Raleigh, 1974.

Galle, Fred C. "Maintenance of Trees and Shrubs." A monograph prepared for the Park and Recreation Maintenance-Management School, North Carolina State University, Raleigh, 1974.

——. "Maintenance of Trees and Shrubs in the Nursery." A monograph prepared for the Park and Recreation Maintenance-Management School, North Carolina State University, Raleigh, 1974.

Gilbert, William B. "Lawn Care and Special Turf Areas." A monograph prepared for the Park and Recreation Maintenance-Management School, North Carolina State University, Raleigh, 1974.

Hanson, A. A. and Juska, F. V. *Turfgrass Science.* Madison, Wisconsin: American Society of Agronomy, 1969.

Madison, J. H. *Practical Turfgrass Management.* Princeton: Van Nostrand Reinhold, 1972.

Pirone, P. P. *Tree Maintenance.* New York: Oxford University Press, 1972.

——. and Dedge, B. O. *Diseases and Pests of Ornamental Trees.* New York: The Ronald Press, 1970.

Roberts, D. A. and Boothroyd, C. W. *Fundamentals of Plant Pathology.* San Francisco: W. H. Freeman, 1972.

Sprague, Howard B. *Turf Management Handbook.* Danville, Illinois: Interstate Printers and Publishers, 1970.

Chapter 7

Maintenance Equipment

Introduction

Until a few years ago, the majority of park maintenance work was done manually. Ditches were dug by hand. Grass along road shoulders was cut with scythes. Trucks were loaded with shovels. Litter was picked up by hand. Sand in golf course traps was raked by hand. Watering was done with hand-held hoses or with sprinklers that had to be manually put in place and moved to assure even coverage. Edging was done with a hoe, and holes for planting trees and shrubs were dug by hand. Because of the recent technological advances, park and recreation agencies today employ a great variety of mechanized equipment to perform the maintenance functions. Departments are constantly looking for new and more refined equipment to reduce maintenance labor costs.

In this chapter we will attempt—

- to survey some of the most commonly used maintenance equipment;
- to discuss the selection and care of equipment;
- to consider the importance of maintenance records;
- to review the function of the maintenance service center.

Survey of Equipment

Maintenance vehicles including trucks, jeeps or other four-wheel drive vehicles, tractors, etc., are used to transport personnel,

Maintenance Vehicles

The triplex greens mower has reduced greatly the labor force required to maintain a golf course.

supplies, equipment and materials to locations within the park and recreation system where the maintenance function is performed. As with all maintenance equipment, vehicle selection must be based on the function to be performed by a particular maintenance unit.

One vehicle that has a good application in some park and recreation operations is the golf-cart type vehicle. This vehicle can transport one or two people and a small amount of equipment more economically than any other. It may be electrically or gasoline powered. The potential application for the use of this type vehicle for litter pick-up on trails, transporting one- or two-man repair crews, and transporting personnel for facility inspections is very great.

A variety of trucks, from the pick-up to large dump trucks, are useful for park and recreation maintenance departments. When facilities are widely spaced and transportation time is an important factor, these vehicles are extremely practical. There is no substitute for trucks when heavy and bulky supplies, equipment, and materials must be moved from place to place.

The tractor is still one of the most versatile pieces of maintenance equipment; with attachments, it can perform a great variety of maintenance jobs. Both gasoline and diesel powered tractors are commonly used. When many hours of continuous operation are indicated, such as when a tractor is used almost exclusively for mowing operations, the diesel tractor may be the most economical vehicle because of lower operating costs. With appropriate attachments, maintenance jobs that can be performed with a tractor include: mowing; digging trenches and holes for trees, shrubbery, and posts; dragging baseball and softball infields; hauling, light grading, and scraping; snow removal; loading soil, sand, and other materials; sweeping roads and parking lots; spreading fertilizer; sawing wood; plowing; subsoiling and total seedbed preparation; among others. No other piece of equipment can come close to matching such versatility.

Mowing turf areas is the single most expensive item in the typical park and recreation department's maintenance budget. It is important that the grounds maintenance supervisor select equipment that can handle this time consuming job most efficiently. For example, an 18-inch hand-operated power mower will require about five hours to cut one acre, under normal conditions. A 30-inch mower

Mowing Equipment

A chain skirt guard on rotary mowers is a desirable safety feature.

will reduce mowing time to about three hours. A tractor-drawn 80-inch rotary mower can cut this one acre of grass in about 45 minutes.

There are four basic types of mowing equipment: rotary, reel, flail, and sickle bar. All four types of mowers may be pulled by, or mounted on, a tractor or other vehicle, or they may be self-contained with their own power sources. All four types of mowers also can be purchased in a variety of sizes, from small 18- to 21-inch units up to units that cut a 15- to 17-foot swath.

The tractor is a versatile piece of maintenance equipment.

Rotary mowers are used for general purpose cutting. The rotary mower does a good job cutting coarse grass and weeds. A rotary mower can be used where a cutting height of one inch or more is desired. The reel mower gives the best quality cut and is used where low, smooth turf is desired. However, the terrain must be relatively smooth for the reel mower to be effective. Reel mowers have a cutting height range from about ½ to 2½ inches. Specialized units can be purchased for lower or higher cutting. The flail mower has come into more widespread use for general mowing because of the safety features, as compared to the rotary mower. Unlike the rotary mower, the flail mower, because of its design, will not throw foreign objects that may injure persons or damage property. The sickle bar (also called cutterbar) mower is used primarily for very tall grass such as on road shoulders and banks. Smaller sickle bar units are also valuable when trimming under post and board or split rail fences: the slender cutting unit will fit under the low boards of these fences where other mowing units will not.

The size of the area to be mowed, obstacles, terrain, and type of turf to be maintained will determine the size and type of mowing unit best suited for a particular area. Naturally, the

A rotary mower is well suited to areas that are difficult to reach.

grounds maintenance manager wants to use the largest equipment practical to cut a particular turf area. Large expanses of turf can be maintained most economically with large tractor-drawn equipment; very confined areas must be cut with small hand-operated equipment. For intermediate areas too confined for large tractor-drawn equipment, the self-propelled riding mower of 25- to 72-inch width has proved to be an excellent choice.

In addition to mowing equipment, a variety of other types of equipment is needed for proper care of general and specialized turf

Turf Conditioning Equipment

A 60-inch rotary mower is good for intermediate size areas.

areas including aerifiers and spikers used on compacted soil. The aerifier is preferred over the spiker because it removes a plug of earth from the ground while the spiker simply makes a hole, pushing surrounding soil particles closer together. A verticut machine is a unit with vertical knives that cut stolons and alleviates matting and thatch problems. A renovator is a piece of equipment used to prepare existing turf areas for reseeding. The top dresser and fertilizer spreader are similar pieces of equipment used to spread soil mixtures and nutrient elements. Other useful types of turf conditioning equipment include rollers, sod cutters, shredders, seeders, hydroseeders used on road shoulders and banks, mulchers, and edgers. Most of the equipment listed can be purchased to operate behind a tractor or other vehicle, or the equipment can be self-propelled independent units.

Spray Equipment   When selecting spray equipment for chemical sprays, it is extremely important to select equipment that will permit effective use of smaller dosages and will reduce drift of harmful residues. Despite our present technology, the use of chemical sprays for the control of some insect, disease, and weed problems is still indicated. As our knowledge and application of other control methods becomes more sophisticated, we may be able to reduce the use of chemical sprays even further. However, in many instances, the use of chemical sprays is the only effective control measure known.

The spray equipment operator is also important. This person should be extremely well trained in the use of spray equipment. In a number of states, certification for operators is required. This practice will become more widespread in the future.

Generally, a sprayer consists of a storage tank in which the solution to be used is agitated by a mechanical or hydraulic system, a pump, a power source, a pressure regulator, and a distribution system usually consisting of one or more spray nozzles. A spray unit must be able to handle a variety of types of chemical sprays including those with water and oil bases, oil-water emulsions and wettable powders that are insoluble. Many of the chemicals used are quite corrosive; thus, the equipment must be constructed with corrosive-resistant materials and cleaned thoroughly after each use.

Four types of sprayers are commonly used in park and recreation areas.

1. *Fogging units* These are units that generate an atomized aerosol spray by thermal or mechanical means. The fogging unit is commonly used for insect control in picnic areas, campgrounds, and other outdoor recreation areas where a large population of insect pests persists.
2. *Boom-type sprayers* These units operate under relatively low pressure (40–100 psi) and are trailed behind a tractor or other vehicle. This type sprayer is used primarily on turf areas to dispense insect, weed, and disease control chemicals.
3. *High-pressure general purpose sprayers* These units, like the boom-type sprayer, are hydraulic units. As the name suggests, they operate under high pressure (generally 400–800 psi) and are used for general-purpose spraying, such as for smaller turf areas and shrubbery.
4. *Mist sprayers* These units are used primarily for spraying trees. The mist sprayer utilizes an air stream to carry spray droplets and is effective for spraying greater distances with less wind deflection.

Another type of sprayer not included in this discussion is the power duster. Dusts have a greater drift hazard and, generally, are not recommended for use in park and recreation areas. Application of one of the four spray types mentioned previously should handle the needs of park and recreation agency spray programs.

**Hand-held
Power Equipment**

Hand-held power equipment is largely designed for use in remote areas where the use of large mechanized equipment is not practical, for small jobs in areas that are delicate, and where it is difficult to use larger equipment. This type of equipment would include: post hole diggers, chain saws, back pack vacuums and blowers, pruning shears, chemical spray equipment, and paint spray equipment. Improvements are constantly being made to increase the efficiency and ease of operation of such equipment.

A relatively new piece of equipment that can be extremely helpful is the hand-held weed cutter. This unit is powered by a small gasoline or electric motor, and it utilizes a short nylon filament that rotates at high speed to trim weeds in hard to reach places such as around tree trunks and along fences, backstops, walls, and buildings. The unit is very safe to use and does an excellent job on small areas that need to be manicured.

**Miscellaneous
Maintenance
Equipment**

There are several pieces of equipment that do not fit any of the categories discussed. One valuable piece of equipment used by many park and recreation maintenance departments is the hy-

The hydraulic bucket and chipper are invaluable aids in
the maintenance of shade trees.

draulic bucket. Departments that have responsibility for shade trees usually have one or more such units. They are especially valuable for pruning high tree limbs and for tree removal. In addition, they are useful for working on electric lines and for replacing light bulbs and cleaning outdoor lighting fixtures. Another piece of equipment used by departments with shade tree responsibility is the chipper. This is a fast and economical way to dispose of brush and tree limbs. The wood chips produced are good for replacing ground covers in picnic areas, campgrounds, and playgrounds. Blowers and power vacuum units are valuable for leaf and litter removal. In many instances, these two types of units have greatly reduced the need for raking. Blowers are commonly used to pile leaves, litter, and debris into rows; so, it can be picked up easily by vacuum units. A final group of miscellaneous equipment is used in connection with winter sports. The group includes snow removal equipment, ice resurfacing equipment, and equipment needed to maintain ski and toboggan slopes.

Specialized equipment is needed for winter sports areas.

Selecting Maintenance Equipment

The first step for developing a good fleet of maintenance equipment is the selection of proper equipment. The following subjective criteria should be used as a guide when selecting equipment.

The Equipment Should Be Functional Equipment must be capable of doing the job. For example, a riding mower for an area that has many trees and shrubbery plantings may be needed. A prime consideration when selecting a piece of equipment to do this job is maneuverability: a mower with a short turning radius is indicated. When purchasing a hydraulic bucket unit for pruning and maintaining electrical fixtures, it is important to know that the equipment selected will reach the heights needed for the particular application where it will be used. It is a good idea to field test equipment when its capabilities are in question.

Another consideration related to equipment function is versatility. When possible, it is desirable to select equipment that can be used for more than one purpose. Single-purpose equipment has a place when the job demands it; however, purchasing expensive equipment that will be used only two or three times a year is not good economics. In such instances, renting equipment or having the work done by contract may be a more practical answer.

Purchase Quality Equipment Generally, industrial or commercial grade equipment that has a long life span when properly cared for is the best buy. Purchasing a lightweight 21-inch rotary mower when heavy use is anticipated is poor economy. Such equipment needs constant repair and will wear out quickly. When making this decision, experience with the equipment can be extremely helpful—maintenance records are an invaluable aid in this respect. When a maintenance department has experience with the equipment to be purchased, and records to back it up, a better value judgement can be made. Those who will use the equipment you may be purchasing can also be very helpful. The department should benefit from their experience by soliciting their advice.

Availability of Parts and Service The most functional and durable piece of maintenance equipment can be rendered useless when parts and service are not available. It is important to ascertain if the local distributor carries a full line of parts for the equipment you anticipate purchasing. Time spent waiting for parts to be shipped by the manufacturer can be extremely costly.

Safety There are at least two important aspects to safety. First, the safety of the operator using the equipment is important, and the safety of the persons using park and recreation facilities must be considered also. In many instances, equipment must be operated in park and recreation areas that are heavily used. When this is true, the safety of the park patron must be given a high priority.

Consider Standardization of Equipment The advantages of standardization of equipment generally outweigh the disadvantages. One advantage is being able to interchange operators without additional training. A more important advantage can be realized when repairing identical or similar equipment made by the same manufacturer. The mechanic's job is greatly simplified, and the department can stock parts that are frequently used without having to maintain an enormous inventory. A final advantage comes when one piece of equipment is worn out or damaged beyond repair. Under these circumstances, useable parts can be salvaged for other machines.

The major disadvantage of standardization is in selection of equipment. If you standardize with one manufacturer, you become "locked into" their equipment. When another manufacturer develops a better line of equipment, the maintenance department may not be aware of the equipment because of lack of experience with it. Also, it is difficult to find a manufacturer that produces the "best" equipment in all types. One manufacturer may produce excellent reel mowing equipment; yet, their rotary mowers may be inferior to other brands. If a department decides to standardize most of its equipment, it is desirable to take bids on a large quantity of equipment at one time.

Other considerations that are important when selecting equipment include ease of maintenance and operation. In this regard, consultation with the mechanics who must maintain the equipment and with the operators who must use it is important.

Finally, the cost of the equipment must be considered. It is important to think in terms of long-term cost rather than the immediate cost. When the other criteria discussed are considered, saving $75 on a $1500 piece of equipment may be false economy.

Care and Maintenance of Equipment

If the first step, selection of quality equipment, is accomplished; the second, care and maintenance, is equally important. The two important aspects of care and maintenance of equipment are *preventive maintenance* and *repair.* If the park and recreation agency is going to get maximum life from equipment, both aspects must be well handled.

Preventive Maintenance

Preventive maintenance may be defined as the on-going maintenance necessary to keep equipment in optimum working condition. Examples of the kinds of tasks that must be performed in a preventive maintenance program include lubricating, changing oil, washing, checking water level of the battery, checking tire pressure for proper inflation, checking safety equipment, keeping proper adjustments and tuning, replacing expendable items such as air and fuel filters, checking emission control systems, checking metal parts subject to corrosion and repainting where appropriate, inspecting brake linings, and so on. Primary responsibility to see that preventive maintenance is performed is at least twofold. Both the equipment operator and departmental mechanical staff share this responsibility. Perhaps the most important factor in achieving good equipment care and maintenance is the equipment operator. That equipment must be used, not abused is a trite but extremely true aphorism. Most maintenance departments assign the responsibility for a single piece of equipment to one employee. Frequently, merit salary increases are based partially on how well the employee cares for equipment. Some time must be spent in staff training convincing employees of the importance of good preventive maintenance and in developing pride in the way the employees care for equipment assigned to them.

The responsibility for specific preventive maintenance tasks must be clearly delineated between the operator and maintenance service center staff. Normally, the routine daily tasks of greasing, washing, checking water, oil, tire pressure, etc., will be the responsibility of the equipment operator. Items such as oil changes, tune-ups, checking brake linings, etc., are handled by a qualified mechanic. Having an untrained operator do mechanical work is liable to create problems that can be avoided by a precise understanding of who is responsible for what types of preventive maintenance jobs. Key elements in all equipment care are the operational and maintenance manuals that accompany equipment. Both the operator and mechanic should be thoroughly familiar with the instructions prepared by the manufacturer.

Repairing Equipment

The second major aspect of good equipment care and maintenance is repair. The objective of a good preventive maintenance program is to prevent costly repairs and breakdowns; however, parts do wear out and must be replaced. The method of handling routine repair work will vary depending largely on the size of the park and recreation agency and the amount of equipment operated. Many small departments have repair work performed by commercial garages. Larger agencies maintain maintenance center garage facilities. The capital investment to adequately equip and operate a garage is substantial; however, when the agency owns a large fleet of maintenance equipment, it is practical, both in terms of economy and convenience, to develop a garage. The garage must be well equipped and well staffed if the needed service is to be provided. Finding mechanics who are capable of working on the variety of equipment operated by a typical park and recreation agency is difficult. The mechanic must be able to handle repair work on small motors, tractors, automotive vehicles, buses, generators, etc. Many equipment manufacturers operate excellent training programs for mechanics. Local technical institutes also provide valuable training in specific mechanical technology that may be needed to supplement a good mechanic's basic training. Time and money spent by the park and recreation agency for this type of supplementary training is well spent.

If the service center garage is to operate efficiently, a policy must be established related to priority of repair requests. When five equipment items are simultaneously brought to the maintenance service center garage for repair, each operator is convinced that his repair request is the most important. Factors to be considered when making these value judgements include the time required to accomplish needed repair, the effect on the park user of delaying the repair, the economic consequences of putting off the repair, and alternatives such as using another piece of equipment or having the repair done commercially. Such value judgements are not easily made. However, if guidelines for determining priorities are established and understood by equipment operators and supervisory personnel before the controversy stage is reached, chances of disruption of the agency's operation is lessened.

Replacing Equipment

Good fiscal management dictates that a system for equipment replacement be established. In many park and recreation departments, funds for equipment replacement are the most difficult to secure. As a result, much maintenance equipment is used long after its optimum life has been reached. This situation exemplifies poor management for several reasons: (1) the quality of maintenance being performed by worn out equipment may be substandard; (2) the cost of repair to keep the equipment in operating condition is in most instances very expensive; and (3) the safety of the operator and/or park and recreation user may be endangered.

Budgeting for equipment replacement is typically handled in one of three ways: (1) replacement of specific equipment items is included in the regular park and recreation operating budget; (2) replacement of specific equipment items is included in a separate budget, generally designated as the "B" or "C" budget; or (3) a separate maintenance fund is established and a percentage of the operating budget is allocated for non-specific equipment replacement but is used "as needed" during the year. The problem with the first two systems revolves around the time frame in which equipment replacement decisions must be made. Budget preparation generally takes place at least one year and quite often two or three years before the actual replacement is to be made. It is difficult to anticipate equipment replacement needs this far in advance if securing optimum use from a given piece of equipment is the management goal.

In recent years, the maintenance fund concept has become more widely accepted and used. Tanglewood Park in Clemmons,

North Carolina has used a maintenance fund system very effectively for a number of years. In their system, each item of maintenance equipment is depreciated and an equivalent amount of money is set aside each year for the replacement of that piece of equipment. The money for the fund comes from the agency's operating budget, but is set aside in a special maintenance fund to be used for equipment replacement only. At the end of a given fiscal year unspent money is carried over to the next year. Thus, the spend-it-or-lose-it dilemma is eliminated. The fund can be used for non-specific equipment, so that any piece of equipment that is judged to need replacement can be replaced. The maintenance fund concept is a valuable management tool because it allows a park and recreation department to get optimum life from a piece of equipment.

Equipment is not replaced just because it is budgeted for replacement; nor is it used well beyond its useful lifespan because funds are not available for replacement. One of the secrets of any equipment replacement system is establishing realistic depreciation schedules or equipment replacement schedules. With enough experience with a particular type of equipment, the task becomes easier. With new types of equipment and unusual one-of-a-kind equipment (when the experience factor is not available), the judgement becomes considerably more subjective. Consulting the manufacturer and investigating the experience of other departments is a valid means of establishing these schedules.

Equipment Records

The primary requisite for a records system is that the information obtained be usable. In addition, the record-keeping system should be as simple as possible to produce readily available useful information. For some departments, a fairly elaborate computerized system may be needed to produce this result; in small departments, a much simpler system designed by a knowledgeable supervisor or administrator may be just as effective.

Equipment records can generally be classified into two groups: (1) inventory records and (2) operational records. Inventory records should begin with a general list of all equipment owned and operated by the park and recreation agency. Inventory file records for each piece of equipment owned should include details such as, date of purchase, price, serial number, model number, warranty, bid advertisement and specifications, etc. Operational records should include records of performed preventive maintenance (dates of oil changes, tune up, lubrication, for example), fuel consumption, and repair records including cost of parts and labor.

Equipment records are valuable when budgeting operating costs for the coming year. They are extremely valuable when purchasing new equipment. They are useful when assessing the care by the equipment operator. They are valuable when planning and executing preventive maintenance. They are necessary, in case of theft, to determine license number and/or equipment serial number, and they are helpful in determining economy of operation and effectiveness of the maintenance function. To be entirely useful, equipment records must be intelligently analyzed. Analysis can be done manually, using a calculator or other mechanical device, or by computer. Many large departments have developed computerized systems for equipment records. When adequately programmed to produce usable information and when the operational staff is adequately trained to use the computerized results, this technique can be a valuable management tool.

The Maintenance Service Center

Park and recreation agencies have used a variety of names to describe the facilities that service as the hub of their maintenance department function. The terms *maintenance center, service center, central garage* and *park shop* are all terms that are commonly used. We have chosen to use the term *maintenance service center* because it seems to be the most descriptive.

Park and recreation agencies use a number of different methods when establishing the maintenance service center based upon their particular mode of operation. When the area being serviced is relatively small, one center will serve all maintenance functions for the agency. In a large municipality or a state park system where facilities are scattered over a wide area, it is quite common to find district or regional maintenance service centers. In many instances, the district centers are complete facilities handling all of the maintenance service needs, while in other instances the district center provides basic services and another central facility provides

The service center is a hub of maintenance activities.

specialized kinds of maintenance service. Another arrangement used in some state park systems is to have the district or regional maintenance service center provide the specialized function while the basic maintenance services are provided in smaller centers located in individual parks.

In a majority of cases, the maintenance service center is a complete self-contained facility that provides a service function for one intensively developed park, a regionalized group of facilities, or the entire park and recreation system. Normally two or three functions are carried out by the maintenance service center.

It serves as a center for routine maintenance. The maintenance service center serves as a central location for specialized maintenance crews whose job may be garbage and trash collection, janitorial services, general park clean-up, lawn care, or care of trees and shrubs. The specialized crews may provide for some combination of these services. The maintenance service center provides a place for storage of equipment and supplies for these crews. It provides a place where the employees report for work each day to receive work assignments and where supervisory staff for this function is housed.

The center serves as a center for major and minor repair work. A variety of shops are located in the maintenance service center and many items are brought to the center for repair. The same repair personnel will often have to go to specific park and recreation facilities to make repairs. For example, a tractor or mower will generally be brought to the center for repair work while repairs to a broken water line or replacing a broken window in a community center building will be done on site.

Construction crews will be housed in the maintenance service center. When a separate construction crew is maintained, it will often be responsible for major repair work such as re-shingling a roof on a picnic shelter.

In some park and recreation agencies, the maintenance service center may also house non-maintenance but related functions such as the security or park police force.

Site Selection   In considering the site for the maintenance service center, the following factors ought to be considered.

Geographic Location   A site must be selected that is central to the park and recreation facilities to be served by the center. Selecting a remote location requiring extensive travel time would not be wise. Driving time is a more important consideration than lineal distance.

Accessibility to Utilities   The site must have good access to water, sewage, electricity, and telephone.

Good Topography   The site must present no severe grading problems and must be free of rock outcroppings or other environmental conditions that will incur high developmental costs.

Size   The site must be large enough to provide for present facilities and anticipated expansion.

Aesthetic Consideration   Maintenance buildings and facilities need not be architectural gems; but, at the same time, they should not be eyesores. Function is more important than architectural beauty for a maintenance service center. With care in site selection and/or effective screening, this objective can usually be accomplished without great difficulty.

The buildings and facilities needed for a maintenance service center, of course, will depend upon function and how the service center is to be used. A normal, well developed maintenance service center will generally include the following types of buildings and facilities.

Development of Buildings and Facilities

Workshops Again, depending on the function and scope of the department's operation the maintenance service center may include a variety of workshops including carpentry, paint, electrical, plumbing, and metal shops. In a small department, one workshop may be sufficient to house all of these functions, while in a large maintenance service center, workshops for each of the functions may be highly developed with sophisticated equipment for each.

Garage A garage for servicing maintenance equipment is a basic feature of the maintenance service center. Equipment in the garage will depend upon the scope of the operation but will generally include diagnostic equipment, grease rack, welding equipment, and sharpening equipment. Equipment for wheel alignment and body work is generally too specialized for the maintenance service center garage. When needed, this work should be handled by commercial garages.

Storage Buildings A variety of types of storage is necessary in the maintenance service center. Locked storage space must be provided for items such as janitorial supplies, spare parts, small hand equipment and tools, chemicals, fertilizer, etc. Storage for flammable substances such as paint should be separated from other equipment and supplies. Underground storage is a good alternative for dangerous substances. Adequate shed storage is needed for vehicles and larger equipment. Depending upon location and the danger of theft and vandalism, this type of storage area may be open or closed. The entire maintenance service center can be isolated by

The maintenance garage services agency equipment.

fencing or blocking the entrance road. In these instances, open shed storage for equipment is entirely satisfactory.

Outside Storage Space   There are many maintenance items, such as drain tile, bricks, sand and gravel, lumber, galvanized, concrete-asbestos, and plastic pipe, etc., that when adequately protected from vandalism and theft do not need to be stored in a building. An area in the maintenance service center that is easily accessible for maintenance vehicles must be provided.

Fuel Storage   The center will generally have gasoline pumps for maintenance equipment. Underground storage is essential for pumps located away from buildings to reduce fire hazard.

Wash Pits   If equipment is to be kept clean, a well-drained area for washing vehicles and equipment is essential.

Facilities for Employee Comfort   A well developed center should include toilets, showers, locker and lounge facilities for employee comfort and convenience.

When developing a high quality maintenance service center, there are a number of desirable features that should be considered during the planning process. Construction materials used in buildings should require minimal maintenance. Concrete block is such a material used for many maintenance buildings. Traditionally, because of aesthetic considerations, wood has been widely used. Because of the danger of fire associated with many maintenance functions, fire-resistant or retardant walls and roofs should be considered.

The maintenance service center has many potentially dangerous areas and an effective employee safety program is essential. This topic was discussed in Chapter 3. OSHA standards must be incorporated into the planning of maintenance facilities.

All indoor work areas must be well lighted. Lighting engineers recommend 20 footcandles for general workshop lighting and 50 footcandles for areas where delicate or detailed work is performed such as in a sign shop or where bench repair work is done.

Workshops and garages in maintenance service centers must be planned according to function. Functional planning involves such things as installing 12-foot garage doors so that bulky items can be handled easily; sequencing equipment in a carpentry shop so the operator can use a saw, planner, and sander in a logical sequence rather than moving from one part of the shop to another; locating doors directly opposite each other so long pieces of lumber can be handled in the carpentry shop; and providing the garage and wash pit areas with drive-through capability so that equipment with trailers does not have to be driven in reverse. Agricultural engineers and shop equipment manufacturers have studied the problems of functional planning of workshops extensively, and literature from these sources can be helpful for planning workshops and other maintenance facilities.

Buildings should be designed so that expansion is easily possible. This is particularly important for buildings used for equipment storage where future expansion can be anticipated as new park and recreation facilities are developed and new equipment is purchased to maintain these facilities.

Adequate ventilation is essential throughout maintenance center buildings. It is particularly important in areas used for welding and spray painting. Heating and air conditioning engineers recommend that a system be installed capable of handling one cubic foot of air per minute for each square foot of floor space.

Adequate electrical service must be provided. Electrical service should provide 240 volt service so that three-phase power can be utilized. Savings in initial equipment cost and operational cost is well worth the initial cost of developing this power source. When aggregated, the power requirements for the maintenance service center are quite high and every economy in operational cost savings should be carefully considered. In addition, consideration of details such as providing an adequate quantity of electrical outlets for small machinery and equipment will make the maintenance employee's job much easier.

In recent years, the psychological value of color in work areas has been proven through laboratory testing, which indicates that color affects the work performance, health, and safety of employees. Major paint companies can be helpful in selecting a color scheme that will improve the quality of the workshop environment. This should be accomplished as the maintenance buildings are initially constructed; however, it can also be done when repainting becomes necessary in existing buildings.

Communication Systems

The need for good communications between park and recreation units is not limited to the maintenance function although the application to the maintenance function is an important one. The administrative, program, security or police, and maintenance functions all must be linked through a network that provides an effective communications channel. Between fixed locations, such as a community center, swimming pool, golf course, maintenance service center or administrative and supervisory offices, a good telephone system must be developed. Between vehicles and mobile personnel that move frequently from one place to another, a radio communications system must be developed.

Radio communication is particularly valuable and can increase the effectiveness and efficiency of the maintenance operation. Radio communication is needed between the maintenance supervisor and departmental administration, the maintenance supervisor and program supervisor, and between the maintenance supervisor and his staff. The radio system should not be used as a crutch for poor organization and work assignment; however, many instances arise when atypical and emergency situations dictate changes in maintenance work assignments. In these instances a good radio communications system can prevent many wasted man-hours.

The best application of radio communications results when it is available to mobile units for maintenance supervisory personnel, roving work crews, and individuals carrying out repair functions. Normally, it is not necessary to provide radio communications with all maintenance personnel. An individual operating a mowing unit or a building janitor should require little deviation from the work schedule established at the beginning of the day, and communication with these types of personnel is seldom needed.

The two types of radio communication systems most frequently used by park and recreation agencies are:

Two-way Radios

These are mobile units that can be used with or without a base station or stations at a fixed location. Generally, the mobile units are affixed to maintenance vehicles; however, portable hand held units are also available. Communication is possible between the base station and mobile units or between mobile units. Mobile units attached to vehicles are appropriate for maintenance supervisors and roving crews using a vehicle for transportation because much of their work will be done within hearing distance of their vehicle.

A Paging System

This unit is a compact radio receiver that buzzes when the unit is activated. The unit is generally worn on the employee's belt. When the unit is activated, the employee goes to the nearest telephone or two-way radio and contacts the communications center for a message or instructions. These units are appropriate for individuals who frequently move from place to place in their work or frequently are not within hearing distance of the receiver.

The Federal Communications Commission regulates all radio communications in the United States. A license is required to operate transmitting units except low powered walkie-talkies. Some park and recreation agencies use the Citizen's Band wave length; however, range is limited and in most sections of the country traffic is very heavy and its use is not practical. A much better system is an assigned frequency on the Public Service band either in the

VHF or UHF bands. Preference is generally given to the VHF band because it gives a strong signal that does not skip readily and the equipment is less expensive.

When selecting radio communications equipment, it is important to seek the advice of an expert. Salesmen and manufacturers' representatives can be extremely helpful in designing a system to meet agency needs. Consultants are also available; if a large system is involved, they should be considered. Even a small system is relatively complex, and items such as number of units needed, wattage, range, antenna type and height for the base station, etc., should be considered carefully.

Normally, radio communications equipment will be purchased by competitive bidding. If the agency has financial constraints, purchasing used equipment and modifying it is a good alternative. Equipment is also available on lease or lease-purchase basis. Whatever alternative is chosen by the park and recreation agency, it must be sure that the equipment selected will be adequate to do the job.

Once a park and recreation agency acquires a radio communications system, it is vital that concerned personnel be trained to use it. Employees should understand the basic operation of the equipment, they should learn some of the basic code signals commonly used in the 10-code message system, and they should learn basic radio courtesy and appropriate FCC regulations governing radio transmission.

Review Questions

1. Describe the four different types of equipment that can be used for mowing turf areas.

2. What is turf conditioning equipment?

3. What factors must be considered when selecting maintenance equipment?

4. What is involved in caring for the equipment that is owned by a park and recreation department?

5. What records should be kept for maintenance equipment?

6. Why are maintenance equipment records important?

7. Should a park and recreation department maintain its own garage?

8. What is the function of a maintenance service center?

9. What considerations should be given to site selection for a maintenance service center?

10. What buildings and equipment would you expect to find in a well equipped maintenance service center?

11. Under what conditions would a radio communications system be valuable for a park and recreation agency?

Bibliography

Amonett, Leroy. "Operator's Responsibility for Maintenance." A monograph prepared for the Park and Recreation Maintenance-Management School, North Carolina State University, Raleigh, 1974.

Cooper, John. "Communication Systems." A monograph prepared for the Park and Recreation Maintenance-Management School, North Carolina State University, Raleigh, 1974.

Kepner, R. A.; Bainer, Roy; and Barger, E. L. *Principles of Farm Machinery.* Westport, Conn.: The AVI Publishing Company, 1972.

McCormack, John R. "Maintenance of Vehicles and Equipment." A monograph prepared for the Park and Recreation Maintenance-Management School, North Carolina State University, Raleigh, 1974.

Taylor, James W. "The Maintenance Service Center." A monograph prepared for the Park and Recreation Maintenance-Management School, North Carolina State University, Raleigh, 1974.

Chapter 8

Maintenance

and

the Public

Introduction

The business of recreation and park maintenance exists for the sole purpose of serving the public. If we are to serve well it is imperative that we have the enthusiastic understanding and support of the public. Such understanding and support can best be established and maintained by serving in such an unobtrusive manner that the public is hardly aware of our presence and certainly not irritated by it.

This chapter is devoted to several topics related to the topic of maintenance and the public. Specific consideration is given to public relations management, public safety, public liability, and the disturbing problem of vandalism.

Public Relations Management

Lawrence A. Appley writes, "Whatever an organization does that affects the opinions of its various publics toward it is public relations."[1] This definition is remarkable for several reasons. First, it points out that every organization has public relations because it is involved with individuals and groups of people who have opinions about the organization. Consequently, an organization has public relations, good, bad, or indifferent, regardless of whether or not it has a public relations program.

Appley makes the point that a distinction should be made between public relations itself and public relations administration. The point being that an intelligent, conscious effort to influence publics in a positive way constitutes public relations management.

Second, Appley's definition of public relations makes reference to multiple publics not a single public. Certainly the concept of publics applies to recreation maintenance organizations because they·constantly deal with many different groups. This makes public relations management difficult because, in connection with maintenance operations, it is not always possible to comply with all requests for service from each public, because of repair work priorities, scheduling limitations, and other restricting circumstances.

Maintenance is not glamorous in and of itself. Recreation activities, program events, cultural presentations, even innovative administration procedures are capable of capturing the attention of the press and the public much more readily than routine maintenance operations. This simply means that maintenance departments like Avis, *must* try harder.

The essence of good public relations management for maintenance is projecting the image (an honest image) of a unit or agency dedicated to serving the public better. Despite infinite possibilities and varied approaches, this is still the prime goal.

The rather conservative mentality of most maintenance agencies has been a problem over the years. "Who needs that nonsense!" is often the comment of the maintenance chief when he is asked to make a special public relations effort. Unfortunately, this attitude may cost money, manpower, and operational authorization when governing authorities have his overall operating budgets and proposals under consideration.

Sound public relations management is not a gimmick; it is not dishonest. It does not lie or color facts. It consists of communicating ideas, concepts, philosophies in a manner that will enlighten citizens, groups, elected officials, public bodies as to the purposes, goals, and operating techniques of the maintenance organization. It tells a true story, but it tells it well, effectively, in a way that will encourage favorable action by employees, citizens, and authorizing committees.

The Employee and the Multiplier Principle

Alert maintenance managers have long recognized that individual workers are the vital key to good public relations because they create the public image of the recreation system. The suggestion that each employee accentuate the positive follows the powerful voice-and-ear method of influencing others. It capitalizes on the multiplier principle, taking advantage of every contact made by recreation department employees—inside and outside the organization. Surveys indicate that each staff member associates with an average of fifty persons, including members of his or her immediate family, church associates, and members of service clubs or social groups and similar organizations. It is interesting to speculate on what could happen if every member of the staff would make it a point to say just one favorable thing about the recreation system, its staff, its policies, and its services to each of these fifty persons. Everyone who hears the recreation story tends to repeat it to others, and, according to the laws of mathematical progression, a miracle could result for the system. The only thing an individual would have to do is to start this chain of communication. Then, it is a simple suggestion that the maintenance manager encourage employees to accentuate the positive by telling folks what is good about their public recreation program. Therefore, urge employees to make it their business to make friends for themselves and the recreation system. Never underestimate the importance of a single employee's personal influence.

Minimizing User Conflicts

The typical user of recreation areas and facilities generally is not concerned about maintenance problems. Having little knowledge or interest in what is involved, the public's main concern is that the facility is available and in good condition. An unfortunate attitude? Not at all. Haven't we all expressed a similar attitude on occasions when we have wanted a suit altered, driven our cars into a garage for quick repairs, or found the paper towel container empty in a restroom?

One fact often overlooked by those responsible for maintenance procedures is the importance of user-clientele. It would be a
simple task to maintain facilities if people did not use them. We
must constantly bear in mind that these users are the same people
who pay for the facilities and make maintenance jobs possible and
necessary. The following eight considerations are taken from the
concluding portion of public relations manual developed by Oka
Hester, Director of Recreation and Parks, Greensboro, North Carolina.

1. A citizen is not a person with whom to argue or match wits.
   Arguing wastes time and convinces no one of anything but
   your own lack of intelligence.
2. A citizen is the most important person to enter this office, in
   person, by mail, or by telephone.
3. A citizen is not dependent on us. On the contrary, we are
   dependent on him.
4. A citizen is not an interruption to our work; he is the purpose
   of it.
5. A citizen is not an outsider in our work; he is part of it.
6. A citizen is not (and this is most important to remember) a
   cold statistic. He is a flesh and blood human being with feelings
   and emotions like our own.
7. The citizen is the most important person with whom we deal.
8. A citizen is a person who brings us his problems. It is our job to
   handle them in such a way as to be beneficial to him and to
   ourselves.[2]

For these reasons, every effort must be made by the Recreation and Park Maintenance Management team to minimize user
conflict in their combined operations.

The overall problem facing us is how to perform the necessary maintenance and repair tasks with a minimum of conflict?
There is no easy answer to this question because each operation has
conditions peculiar to that particular situation. Factors such as
weather, daily and seasonal operation of programs, preparation of
specialized facilities, hours of operation anticipated by the clien-
tele, types of programs, the abilities and training of maintenance
personnel, available funds, priorities and other restricting circumstances are important factors to be considered.

The task of scheduling maintenance work to minimize user
conflicts requires considerable thought and good judgment. Minimizing conflict with routine maintenance tasks can generally be

handled by the coordination of schedules between the maintenance division and those responsible for programming. Admittedly there are times when an arbitrator is needed. However, the most difficult conflict problems arise when specialized maintenance is needed, when unanticipated major repair, overhaul or reconditioning is required. Or perhaps a special type of programming requires extra attention or preparation by maintenance personnel. The basis of this conflict may be associated with five major elements of management.

• Communications
• Design of Facilities
• Planning
• Scheduling
• Training

All elements are dependent upon one another and all are separately important.

The importance of communications in minimizing user conflict cannot be overstressed. We need good communications in four separate directions:

Communications

1. Between the Maintenance Supervisor and Maintenance Personnel. Maintenance personnel should be aware of regular and special program schedules in order to avoid conflicts.
2. Between the Maintenance Supervisor and the Program Staff. The Maintenance Supervisor should be kept informed of daily activities, schedules of program staff, and when athletic or other program areas need special preparation or attention. Remember the basic justification for the development. Programs should routinely take priority over maintenance functions.
3. Between the Maintenance Supervisors and the Administration. Too often there is a lack of understanding on the part of administrative staff (and program staff) as to the maintenance-user conflicts that are encountered by the maintenance supervisor.
4. Between all Recreation System Personnel and the Users. All users should be treated with courtesy. If major conflicts can be foreseen, good public relations management calls for a news release indicating the work that has to be done and when it is scheduled.

Design of Facilities   One of the more frequent complaints encountered is that the maintenance supervisor is seldom involved in the planning of new facilities or areas or in the redesign of existing facilities. Here is a man who is directly involved in the problems which occur in user-maintenance conflicts. He should be able to offer to the planner empirical information that would result in the reduction of such conflicts.

Very seldom is he asked to provide such information. The management supervisor should offer concrete suggestions. It is suggested that the supervisor make notes on problems throughout the year and periodically present recommended solutions to his manager. He should be able to provide suggestions regarding access and service roads, location of garbage and trash deposits or collection facilities, problems regarding sanitation around restrooms and picnic shelters. He can also be of great assistance when it becomes necessary to redesign or relocate certain facilities by being aware of maintenance-user problems that he encounters.

Planning   An efficient recreation system operation reflects careful planning. Planning is simply a logical approach to an objective, outlining the steps to be accomplished. Every step in the planning process must involve consideration of potential user conflicts. Road patching, tree pruning, turf irrigation, and other similar work items require advance planning and proper scheduling in order to avoid user conflicts.

Scheduling   An important aspect of consideration in minimizing user conflicts is scheduling—setting the time for starting and estimating the completion of a job. Close coordination between those responsible for user scheduling and maintenance scheduling is required. Generally, routine tasks must be performed at non-peak use periods in order to cause a minimum of interference. Refuse collection, mowing, sweeping, and restroom cleaning, in most instances, should be undertaken during periods of minimum use. Such tasks can best be performed early in the morning, late in the evening, and sometimes at night.

A major problem for the supervisor is how to schedule his work force to accomplish their tasks during low use hours. This calls for top communications, proper training, and a clear explanation of duties in job descriptions.

It is sometimes necessary, however, to provide additional maintenance services during periods of peak use. This often involves the very same tasks that ordinarily should be done during low use periods. Routine checks on a regular basis are necessary to determine need. Tasks performed during peak periods of use should be accomplished by your best personnel. Those that project the best image, those that take pride in their tasks, and those capable of dealing effectively with the public.

Training is another factor that can contribute to minimizing user conflict. Maintenance personnel must be trained to perform the varied tasks assigned to them. If a man has a thorough knowledge of his job, and how to do it, in all likelihood, he will perform in a manner that will minimize potential user conflict with maintenance operations.

Maintenance Personnel Training

In any training program for maintenance personnel, the worker must be given not only technical instruction, but also must be trained to recognize the importance of the positive image that he can project through person-to-person contacts while in the field. Conflicts can be lessened considerably if maintenance employees project a good image to the public. Every maintenance employee, either directly or indirectly, consciously or unconsciously, is engaged in public relations work.

Public Safety

Unfortunately overall accident data for park visitors and recreation participants in general is not readily available. However, a 1972 study of visitor accidents occurring in the National Park System[3] revealed the following information.

Of more than 1.3 billion visitors to the national parks in the past decade, 1,135 were killed in accidents. This represents less than one fatality per million visitors. According to John Fleming, Manager of the Public Safety Department of the National Safety Council, more persons were killed on U.S. roads over a ten-day period than were killed in all of the national parks in the past ten years. Motor vehicle accidents, drownings, and falls account for 90 percent of all visitor fatalities. In the last decade, motor vehicle acci-

Fatalities

dents claimed the lives of 508 people—more than fifty people a year. These three causes must be the primary targets in any programs intended to reduce visitor fatalities in national parks.

Injuries   Motor vehicle and non-vehicle associated injuries have decreased moderately since 1968. Given the substantial rise in the number of visitors (from 151 million in 1968 to 201 million in 1971), this would indicate a substantial decrease in the incidence of visitor injuries.

If we accept the premise that the reduction in visitor accidents in national parks holds for parks and recreation areas in general, the respective administrators are to be congratulated. However, there are no guarantees to accompany such an assumption; and, therefore, the intelligent approach suggests the development of an organized program designed to protect the safety of the public when they visit recreation facilities or participate in recreation programs.

The Safety   The first step in an organization safety program is the appointment
Coordinator   of a safety coordinator by the maintenance manager. The safety officer needs reasonable authoritative clout in that he must review safety procedures in all departments and assign responsibility for specific problems. His range of influence includes activities as diverse as employee safety training, purchasing new equipment, revising work practices, and insuring public safety. To accomplish this, he needs unwavering administrative support.

The Safety   A safety committee can also help. It should meet periodically,
Committee   perhaps monthly, to read accident summaries and reports. It can also review the work of the safety coordinator.

Safety Records   Records are most important to help the safety officer answer certain questions such as: What are the most frequent kinds of accidents? Where do they occur? Without such information, the safety officer is operating in a vacuum. Usually, operating and program personnel in the recreation organization provide the needed information. As coordinator, he must arrange a reporting procedure that will channel relevant information to him.

A primary responsibility of the safety officer should be the establishment and maintenance of an accident record system that will identify trouble spots and accident frequencies. Such data will give the safety coordinator an indication of the effectiveness of the existing accident prevention program. If, for example, it is found that the accident frequency rate is rising out of proportion to patron use, the safety officer knows that the program needs redirection. In brief, records of accidents are essential to efficient operations because they are the foundation of any effective accident prevention program.

The American National Standards Institute[4] has published a "Method of Measuring and Recording Patron and Non-Employee Injury Statistics," (ANSI Standard Z 108.1). This system was developed for the purpose of providing an orderly and uniform method of handling patron injury data for comparative purposes.

Patron and Non-Employee Injury Records

Each recreation organization should have a set of standard procedures to follow in case of an injury. These should be reviewed often enough in in-service training programs to keep all staff members (especially seasonal employees) completely familiar with procedures. Although such procedures might necessarily vary according to local conditions and services available, the following suggestions are offered as a guide.

Dealing with Injuries

1. First aid kits should be on hand and readily accessible at each activity area; e.g., centers, playgrounds, athletic contests, etc.
2. Maintain a schedule for checking the contents of the first aid kit.
3. Obtain a list of several physicians who agree to be on call to the department or agency. Having more than one or two will protect you when one is unable to come. Ask them to let you know if they are out of town or otherwise unavailable.
4. Register participants whenever this is feasible, including the name, address, telephone (business and home) numbers of parents or guardians, and the name and telephone number of the family physician.

General Procedures

1. Render first aid immediately *providing you know what to do.* (It is desirable to have maintenance personnel trained in first aid.)

In Case of Serious Injury or Illness

2. Call an ambulance or rescue squad if one is needed. Directions to the person receiving the call should include brief description of injury, first aid administered, and clear, specific directions as to how to get to the injured person. Have someone ready to direct the arriving ambulance to the injured person. In some cities, a central emergency setup exists to which all calls for emergency help are made, then, the appropriate emergency vehicle is sent. This is a great help in most cases. One of the greatest advantages is that one telephone call will bring an emergency vehicle. Under the central emergency control system, the central control knows the whereabouts and availability of all emergency vehicles. Never terminate the telephone call until the person called has finished. Be sure he has said all he is going to say.

3. If the injured is transported to a hospital, call ahead indicating that the injured is enroute, and give name of family physician if available. (Refer to registration card.)

4. Call the parent or guardian indicating action taken.

5. Try to avoid causing anxiety. Care should be exercised when calling a parent about an injury. It is better to understate the seriousness of the injury. If the victim has been sent to a physician or hospital, tell the parent where.

6. If an ambulance is not needed, have parent transport victim.

7. Fill out an accident report. (Be sure to record the names of all witnesses.) See Figure 8-1.

8. Eliminate the cause of the accident. If an area, facility, or piece of equipment is hazardous; its use should be prohibited until the dangerous condition is removed.

9. If the accident is serious, a verbal report should be made to the system manager immediately.

10. The staff should be advised that no admission of fault should be expressed. In some cases, it might be wise to call the agency attorney if there is the least likelihood that negligence will be charged. In any event, the attorney should be informed in writing of all injuries. (A copy of the accident report will suffice.)

11. Show a personal interest in the injured person, even after you have been relieved of all responsibility regarding the accident and injury.

Other Aspects of the Accident Prevention Program In addition to patron injury records and an established policy for dealing with visitors' injuries, there are other important elements to be included in the safety program to protect the visiting public. These

Department of Parks and Recreation, Safetyville, Anywhere

Area or Division Reporting . . . . Injury Report No. . . . .

1. Name of Injured. Sex. . . . . Age. . . . .
    Last,   First,   Initial

2. Address of Injured . . . .

3. Extent of Injury? Burn . . . . . .; Cut . . . . . .; Fracture . . . . .; Sprain . . . . ,
    Other, specify . . . .

4. Part Injured? Arm. .; Face. .; Foot. .; Hand. .; Head. .; Leg. .; Other. . . . . ,
    specify . . . .

5. What Immediate Action was taken?
    a. First Aid Given: . . . .
    b. Injured, seen by physician? Yes. . . . No. . . . If yes, where? . . . .
       . . . . and by whose authority? . . . .
    c. Injured sent to hospital? Yes. . . . No. . . . If yes, how transported. . . . .
       . . . . and by whose authority? . . . .
    d. Parents Notified? Yes. . . . No. . . .
    e. Division Head Notified? Yes. . . . No. . . .

6. What Activity was injured engaged in?. . . . .

7. What physical cause was involved?, for example, equipment, design, playing
    surface, etc. . . . .

8. Has physical cause been corrected? Yes. . . No. . . If not, why . . . .
    . . . .

9. What personal deficiency did injured have that should have kept him from.
    from participating in activity . . . .

10. What unsafe act, on the part of the injured, contributed to the injury? . . . .

11. Was leader present? Yes. . . . No. . . . If no, Why? . . . .
    . . . .

12. Describe events leading to injury? . . . .

13. How could accident have been prevented?. . . . .
    . . . .

14. What follow up preventive action has been taken?. . . . .
    . . . .

15. Names and addresses of witnesses:. . . . .
    . . . .
    . . . .
    . . . .

Signature. . . . .
Person Reporting   Division Head

. . . .
Safety Director

Source: Walter L. Cook, *"Manual for Public Safety for Park and Recreation Departments."* American Institute of Park Executives Management Aid Bulletin No. 20, 1962-1963, p. 41.

Figure 8-1 A Visitor–Participant Injury Report Form

considerations include building plan review, safety hazard inspection, fire protection, building plan review for fire protection, fire hazard survey inspection, fire protection equipment, and the coordination of OSHA-related activities within the park and recreation system. Each of these public safety programs will be discussed in order.

Building Plan Review

This is the first step in the critical accident prevention program. A safety expert can save lives and money by pointing out safety hazards in construction drawings and traffic patterns. Because safety is his specialty, he can find the danger spots that produce fires in buildings and cause injuries to visitors and to employees. By assuring in advance that the planned project complies with building safety and fire protection codes, he can save the recreation/park organization money that might otherwise go into expensive post-completion changes.

To conduct an effective plan review, the safety coordinator must build and maintain a current library of reference materials from the National Safety Council, National Fire Protection Association, and the local OSHA office. In addition, he must keep current with legislation requiring new and remodeled public buildings to be architecturally barrier free by incorporating ramps rather than stairs and curbs, railings, grab bars, and other design features that facilitate access and circulation for handicapped people.[5]

Safety Hazard Inspections

A regular inspection schedule is the heart of any effective safety program. In many cases, the safety coordinator must bring in specialists such as fire marshals and safety engineers to inspect the premises. Periodically, insurance companies also send representatives to determine whether or not the organization is complying with insurance protection requirements. Such experts provide the safety coordinator with information to prepare action lists that detail all important corrections such as remedial remodeling, extra fire doors, and installation of fire dampers in ventilating ducts. On the basis of this same information, the safety coordinator can compile a safety checklist to guide his own inspection tours.

Fire Protection

Most municipal recreation/park organizations rely on local fire departments; however, rural, isolated park systems to a considerable extent depend upon their own personnel and equipment to fight fires on their premises. Yet, the most important initial consideration in fire protection is not a good fire department, but an effective prevention program. This work requires more time than any other safety job. Only very large recreation/park organizations can afford a full-time, well trained fire protection expert. But, every organization must assign at least one part-time, partially trained man to the job. It is his task to coordinate all fire protection activities and to call in specialists to help with complex problems.

Review the Building Plan for Fire Protection. The fire protection expert's job logically begins when a building begins. All basic construction drawings should cross his desk and receive his approval before ground is broken. He checks all plans against codes required by the federal and state agencies as well as the codes recommended by such organizations as the National Fire Protection Association, the American Society for Testing Materials, and the American National Standards Institute. In light of their provisions, he can evaluate the planned building by checking for features such as corridors that provide alternate escape routes, fire doors that retard the spread of flames and smoke, sprinkler systems that adequately cover all areas, and fire extinguishers that are appropriate to the building materials and equipment.

Fire Hazard Survey Inspection Usually, however, the fire protection expert begins with existing buildings, many of which were designed prior to the existence of current fire codes, fire protection features, and fire-fighting methods. His first step, therefore, should be an extensive survey of the recreation system structures. On such a tour he identifies potential fire hazards in structures and housekeeping procedures for handling rubbish, chemicals, and flammable materials. He also examines and evaluates alarms, extinguishers, sprinklers, fire doors, and escape routes. This survey will inevitably produce a list of remedial work for immediate and long-term action.

Additional inspections should follow at regular intervals. For some inspections, the safety director should call in the local fire chief. On such tours the fire chief can learn the layout of recreation system buildings, and the safety supervisor can develop closer working relationships with the department and learn more about the fire chief's specialty—protecting people. From insurance inspectors, who also tour the system periodically, the supervisor can learn more about this inspector's specialty—protecting property.

Fire Protection Equipment

Fire Alarms should be designed into the wiring of a building during its planning stage. Ideally, all systems should connect with the park/recreation security office, and local fire and police departments. With cutoff switches, alarms can be tested periodically without disturbing public agencies. More sophisticated systems have both local alarms, within the buildings, and an annunciator in each main entrance hall to show where in the building the fire originated.

Fire Sprinkler Systems can involve complicated design decisions. Architects and engineers work out basic calculations to determine the number of sprinkler heads, the size area each head should cover, and the size of the water piping required. The safety officer works with these professionals and reviews their efforts for final approval. To adequately protect the recreation system's interests during this critical planning process, the safety supervisor must be as knowledgeable about the technology of sprinklers as he can, asking every question that occurs to him and insisting that designers clearly explain all options. A key choice is between a wet or a dry system. A wet system holds water all the time for instant discharge but risks occasional freezing. A dry system eliminates this risk but does not respond as quickly.

Another major decision centers on how the system should be activated. Most sprinklers are heat-activated but cause considerable water damage when responding to small or localized fires. The supervisor, therefore, must decide how to shut off the system and who should have this authority. Testing sprinklers, of course, is another question that he must research before making any recommendations.

Fire Extinguishers are needed even though a building may be well equipped with alarms, sprinklers, and other sophisticated fire protection devices. With a good portable extinguisher, even an untrained person often can put out a small blaze before it activates the sprinklers. An extinguisher may even slow the spread of a large fire until professionals arrive. The right extinguisher in the right place at the right time can save lives, lost work time, valuable equipment, and money needed for other purposes. The technology of fire fighting is complicated, however, requiring that the safety supervisor develop considerable expertise about extinguishers before buying, placing, and maintaining them.

Types of Fire Extinguishers. Extinguishers come in a wide variety of types, each of which is designed for certain kinds of fires. Because no extinguisher is suitable for every fire, it is essential that each piece be clearly identified and properly labeled to avoid misplacement and misuse.

Class A extinguishers are used on common fires: wood, paper, rubber, and many plastics. They contain water, loaded stream, foam, or a combination of dry chemicals. Maximum travel distance to one should not exceed 75 feet, and maximum coverage should average 3,000 square feet.

Class B extinguishers are suitable for fires of flammable liquids, gases, and greases. They hold loaded stream, foam, compressed gas (bromotrifluoromethane and carbon dioxide), dry chemicals, multipurpose dry chemicals, and vaporizing liquids. The maximum travel distance to this extinguisher should be 50 feet.

Class C extinguishers are designed primarily for fires originating from or surrounding electrical equipment. Spraying water on this kind of blaze could electrocute the firefighter. An extinguisher with non-conducting flame suppressants is required for such fires.

Class D extinguishers work effectively on fires of combustible metals such as magnesium, titanium, zirconium, sodium, and potassium. The nameplate for each piece should explain its relative effectiveness for each kind of metal fire.

For more detailed information regarding fire extinguishers, see Exhibit 8-1 in the appendix to this chapter. For additional information the safety supervisor should consult local authorities and write to such agencies as:

The National Fire Protection Association
470 Atlantic Avenue
Boston, Massachusetts 02110

National Safety Council
425 North Michigan Avenue
Chicago, Illinois 60611

Maintaining Fire Extinguishers The safety office cannot simply install an extinguisher and forget it. As time passes, both parts and materials may decay enough to render it inoperable. Someone, therefore, must periodically examine the device, and repair, recharge, or replace it if necessary. That person could be the safety officer, one of his subordinates, or possibly a private contractor. Because this maintenance can be frequent and repetitious, many recreation systems find it simplest to hire a commercial firm to handle it.

The major maintenance chore is an annual examination of each piece of equipment. At that time, the maintenance man thoroughly checks the mechanical parts for breakage and corrosion, examining the contents for deterioration and leakage. He repairs what is broken, replaces what is missing, and records his work on a dated tag affixed to the extinguisher. Whoever performs this work will need all the technical data pertinent to each type extinguisher.

A monthly inspection is also necessary to see that each extinguisher is in its designated place, that it is visible, accessible, undamaged, and free from defects. On this tour, the inspector also verifies that the maintenance tag is up to date.

The Occupational Safety and Health Act

With the enactment by Congress in 1970 of the Occupational Safety and Health Act, and subsequent administration of the act by various states, basic safety procedures that were previously practiced by a few park and recreation systems have become mandatory for many. Under provisions of the act, the U.S. Department of Labor establishes standards to be met and provides for their enforcement. As individual states establish standards at least as effective as that of the federal government, and have their plans approved by the Secretary of Labor, they assume the authority to enforce the program. Assuming that the park/recreation organization comes under the federal or state OSHA jurisdiction, the following compliance procedure is suggested.

Initial Planning   1. Establish a formal framework. The purpose of this framework is to coordinate all OSHA-related activities within the system. To coordinate all compliance activities, one individual should be designated resident expert on OSHA regulations. He would most likely be the person appointed to head or coordinate the total safety program for the recreation/park system.

2. Draw up short-term and long-term plans for compliance with OSHA. As soon as the local OSHA expert has familiarized himself with the regulations, he can begin to study the recreation system to identify areas of potential danger and noncompliance. With this information, he should formulate the sequence and timing of remedial actions that will allow the recreation organization to meet OSHA standards.

3. Allocate funds. If the long-range plan is to be effectively implemented, money must be allocated for major expenses such as: (1) equipment and reconstruction necessary to rectify hazards discovered in facilities and working procedures; (2) administrative combination; (3) potential fines for failures to comply with OSHA regulations.

Records

OSHA requires that written records be kept and made available upon request of the Secretaries of Labor and of Health, Education, and Welfare. In addition, most states require records for Workmen's Compensation Insurance. To eliminate duplicate record keeping, OSHA allows many state forms with certain modifications to be substituted for the specified federal records. (See "Employee Safety" Chapter 3.)

Inspections

The resident OSHA expert should periodically inspect the recreation/park premises and buildings to check whether or not the system continues to comply with all OSHA regulations. A checklist is provided in the appendix to this chapter, but it is intended for general guidance only and cannot take the place of systematic analysis of the regulations and their applications to a particular system.

Corrective Actions

The first step should be to eliminate the relatively simple problems that require little time and money. For the more complicated problems, the safety officer should prepare realistic estimates of the time and money required and should establish deadlines. If an OSHA inspection is probable before remedies can be completed, the safety officer should apply for the appropriate variance through prescribed channels; otherwise, the system may incur severe financial penalties.

Aspects of Public Liability and
Recreation Maintenance Practice

From World War II until the recent recession, recreation as an industry has experienced unparalleled growth. This trend in the recreation industry has sharply reversed in the recent past due to a galloping rate of inflation and a severe financial recession. The recession and inflation have resulted in unemployment and reduced government revenues necessitating reductions in the numbers of public recreation workers employed and decreases in leisure expenditures by both the government and the public. Such circumstances emphasize the need to eliminate, or at least minimize, unnecessary expenditures within the recreation industry.

The relationship between non-economical operation and poor recreation maintenance practice is best illustrated by the fact that almost all lawsuits involving park organizations, their officers, or employees are concerned with maintenance practice. It is also factual that the payment of just one moderately large legal award to an injured party might bankrupt a recreation enterprise.

Operations within the recreation industry are administered by any one of a variety of sponsors including public, nonprofit, charitable, and profit-making, commercial organizations or a combination of these. The legal responsibilities and legal duties associated with the operation of a business within any industry also apply to recreation. Consequently, persons responsible for the operation of a recreation enterprise should be aware of those aspects of their operation which subject themselves and their personnel to liability, responsibility, and duty considerations.

Constant vigilance through careful systematic inspection and preventive maintenance will go far toward the discovery of hazardous equipment, structures, areas, and facilities that might injure the user. However, oversights occur and accidents do happen. When injury does result due to the use of a recreation facility, the parties involved are subject to the same legal rules that determine fault and responsibility for injury in non-recreational cases. Legal liability infers a responsibility, which the courts recognize and enforce, between parties.

Because we are specifically concerned with legal responsibility attached to park and recreation maintenance practices, the following discussion will be concerned with tort liability only. A tort is a legal wrong and includes a large variety of acts that are deemed to have unreasonably interfered with the interest of others. In cases where a tort is proven, compensation is made to the individual who is injured in person, property, or reputation. Most legal action, in connection with tort law, is brought on the basis of *negligent* conduct. Fewer actions are brought on the basis of *nuisance*—a condition that leads to injury. The general legal principles or doctrines that relate to liability are derived from common law. If we are to understand the basis for liability, it is necessary to develop familiarity with some of these legal principles.

A generally accepted definition of negligence is *failure to act as a reasonable and prudent person would have acted under the circumstances.* A more precise and legal definition which appears in Corpus Juris[6] states that "negligence is an unintentional breach of legal duty, causing damage reasonably foreseeable without which breach damage would have not occurred." The standard used to determine negligence in the case of a park or recreation professional would exceed the standard of behavior that would be regarded as reasonable for a non-professional person. A jury, of course, makes this determination and decides whether or not the defendant's behavior conforms to the standard.

Negligence

Elements Essential to Prove Negligence In order to successfully bring a liability suit based upon negligent conduct, the following four elements must be proven to recover from the wrongdoer. These include—

1. a duty or obligation (recognized by law) to conform to a standard of behavior to protect others from unreasonable risks;
2. a breach of duty caused by failure to meet the standard required under the circumstances;
3. a close causal connection between the conduct and the resulting injury;
4. an actual injury or loss suffered by the plaintiff.

The duty of a recreation operator to protect a visitor from injury changes markedly according to the legal status of the visitor at the time of injury. There are three legal status classifications of persons who enter the premises of another. These are *trespasser, licensee,* or *invitee.*

Care Owed to Visitors

The Trespasser   A trespasser is one who enters the property of another without permission and not for the benefit of the property owner. In general, the only duty owed a trespasser is to use due care to avoid injury to the trespasser if his presence is known. If the recreation operator does this, he is in little danger of having successful legal action brought against him, if an accident befalls the trespasser. The only obligation of the operator is to protect the trespasser from intentional injury, such as shooting at him or setting traps that might injure him. Should the trespasser be discovered, care should be taken to make him aware of dangers such as a mining operation, blasting, or other similar dangerous activity. If forceful eviction is required to remove the trespasser from the premises, this should be done by a law enforcement agent.

The Licensee   A licensee is one who enters onto the property with the operator's permission but not for any economic benefit to the operator. The visitor who asks permission to hunt, ride, or ski an area and is given permission to do so becomes a licensee. Should the hunter fall into an open pit or should the skier injure himself by running into a stump hidden by snow, or should the rider's horse break a leg by stepping into an unseen hole, the licensee cannot claim damages for himself, his equipment, or his horse.

The landowner is under no obligation to inspect the premises for dangers unknown to himself, nor is he obliged to make the premises safe for the licensee. However, a hidden hazard known to the operator, such as a concealed mine shaft, a dynamiting operation, or an ill-tempered animal, requires that the operator exercise reasonable care to see that the licensee is aware of the danger. If the danger has been made known to the licensee or is by its nature obvious, then the risk is assumed by the licensee, and the owner has no further duty to the licensee.

The Invitee   This classification of visitor includes all of those who frequent public parks, public playgrounds, and other public recreation areas to use them for the purposes for which these facilities were developed and to participate in programs provided thereon. In addition, an invitee is a business visitor invited or permitted to enter the private property of another for purposes which benefit the land-owner or for the mutual advantage of the landowner and the invitee. Guests who pay fees for the use of recreation facilities are, therefore, classified as invitees. Legally, invitees are owed the highest level of care to prevent injury to them. The private landowner or the public recreation operator is obliged to be aware of any dangers; he must search out dangers and warn the invitee of them. The implication of common law toward the invitee by recreation operators is evident. The safety of patrons depends upon the condition of the premises and the facilities provided for public use. The prudent operator must not only warn or instruct the patron about existing dangers, but must also make periodic and thorough inspections of the premises and facilities, promptly making necessary repairs or safety provisions. The operator who fails to exercise such ordinary care and further fails to keep a written and dated record of inspection and repair will not have a good defense against any legal action arising from injury sustained while using a recreation area.

The obligation of the owner or recreation operator to render the area's facilities safe, however, pertains only to that part of the premises to which the invitation is extended. Once invitees go beyond the area to which they are invited, they lose their status as invitees and become licensees or trespassers. Therefore, the recreation area operator or the private landowner need not protect the visitor from absolute danger except as indicated for a licensee or trespasser. Two classical examples of plaintiffs who failed in their efforts to recover from recreation operators for injuries are to be found in a 1940 Connecticut case[7] and a 1944 Iowa case.[8] The Connecticut case centered around two inexperienced skiers who went beyond the area open for skiing and were injured when they skiied over a hidden ledge and fell. The Iowa case considered a situation wherein a young man and a female companion were injured when they left a dance held at the municipal golf course clubhouse and proceeded to the back of the building to find a dark location whereupon they fell into an open basement and were injured. In both cases the courts held that the injured plaintiffs had lost their status as invitees and became licensees when they went beyond the location to which they were invited and, therefore, took the premises as they found them.

The Doctrine of Attractive Place or Nuisance

An old legal concept holds that the landowner or operator owes no duty or care to trespassers. Obviously, under these circumstances any and all kinds of hazards could be allowed to exist on any premises regardless of the area's proximity to the school or other location frequented by children. The old rule of no duty to trespassers was later modified to exempt trespassers who were children. Therefore, landowners and operators are required to keep their premises free from hazardous conditions that might be harmful to child trespassers.

In order to qualify for legal recovery under this doctrine, it is essential to establish three conditions: first, that the child was, in fact, a trespasser; second, that the owner or the operator of the land should have known that children would be attracted to the property because of something on the property; and third, that the dangerous condition that attracted the child onto the premises be a man made condition rather than a natural one.

Numerous attempts at recovery on behalf of injured children have failed (when the injury occurred on a public park or playground) because the child is almost always an invitee and rarely a trespasser when on public park lands or in a public playground.

The Doctrine of Governmental Immunity

Our law is a product of English Common Law. The premise of governmental immunity first emerged from the eighteenth century case of law, Russell versus the Men of Devon. In this classic case, Russell brought suit against all the men of Devon County, England for damages to his wagon occurring from the collapse of a bridge which was the county's duty to maintain. Despite this, the court ruled against Russell instituting the following rationale: To rule for the plaintiff would lead to an infinity of actions; there was no precedent for such a suit; liability of this kind should be imposed only by the legislature; there are no county funds out of which to satisfy the claim. The court concluded that it is better that an individual sustain an injury than that the public should suffer an inconvenience. This reasoning still provides the nucleus for pro-governmental immunity arguments.

At present, marked differences in governmental liability exist from state to state. Betty Van der Smissen,[9] in her 1967 original study of the fifty states relative to governmental immunity to tort liability and her 1975 update of that study[10] found that since 1960, there has been considerable judicial and legislative activity toward abrogating the doctrine of governmental immunity. Many states have enacted legislation authorizing liability insurance. The trend is to provide a remedy for the injured, yet protect the tax funds of the municipality through insurance authorization and prohibit the dragging along of suits filed many years after the cause of action, by procedural statutes of notice and statutes of limitations. In most instances, it has not been a matter of changing the doctrine of governmental immunity per se, but providing that it may not be used as defense by the insurance company to the extent of the insurance carried.

Another trend that seems to be emerging relates to the basis of liability. Rather than applying the governmental-proprietary test to the function, recent statutory enactments and court decisions seem to be turning to the nature of the act being performed; that is, whether or not the act is a discretionary one of policy formulation and planning (no liability) being performed or a ministerial duty of policy execution or operational decision-making (potential liability). The governmental-proprietary function distinction is not in direct parallel contrast to the new discretionary-ministerial distinction because both types of duties are performed for proprietary functions and for governmental functions. It is also important to note that the doctrine of governmental immunity protected the corporate entity alone, while an individual now may be protected when he performs a discretionary (immune) duty within the "discretionary-ministerial" distinction. There also appears to be greater support for the liability for dangerous and defective conditions; several of the recent laws have specific provisions relating to inspections.

James J. Bonifas, Deputy Corporation Counsel for the Milwaukee County Park Commission, recently indicated that in his home state of Wisconsin there has been total abolition of governmental, eleemosynary, and religious immunity to tort liability.[11] Bonifas further stated that the fault system, which to varying degrees involves assessment of negligence, is under sharp attack and that the humanitarian social conscience today is much more concerned with the victims of society's progress and the shifting of financial losses than with the legal distinctions of immunity to suit that were formulated in the Victorian era. The attempt to socialize all loss is evident and simply involves transferring the financial burden from individuals to society. In short, for a recreation or park organization to depend upon the doctrine of governmental immunity as a guarantee against responsibility and liability is to invite a sad and abrupt awakening.

Assumption of Risk

One who participates in an activity is expected to understand the hazards and potential injury risks involved and to assume such risks. Risks or hazards due to defective equipment or dangerous areas are not assumed by an individual unless such hazards are completely obvious and the individual uses the defective equipment or dangerous area in spite of it and knowing fully what he or she is doing. The courts denied the allegation of assumption of risk as a defense when a party was injured by stepping on a broken bottle in a dressing room,[12] when a ring holding a swing broke resulting in injury to a nine-year-old girl,[13] and when a pedestrian walking through a park fell into a hole covered by snow and was injured.[14]

On the other hand, the defense of assumption of risk was upheld by the court when it was shown that the injured knew of the hazard. This occurred in connection with cases involving: the playing of softball on an area formerly used for tennis with an old post bracket still remaining on the field,[15] a basketball player colliding with a brick wall two feet behind a basketball goal,[16] and also in connection with injury to a ball player when he tripped on a curb around a ball diamond which was used to retain water for ice skating in the winter.[17]

Assumption of risk is based upon the legal theory that no harm is done to one who consents. Of course, the injured's own knowledge and the ability of the injured individual to understand the risks involved are important. In this connection, a child is not expected to have the same capability of accepting a given risk as is an adult. This is reflected in the fact that most cases where assumption of risk is used as a defense against negligence involve individuals in their teens or older. Van der Smissen believes that the courts are placing a stronger emphasis upon communication of the risk involved and the appreciation of the risk by the participant than in the past.

Contributory Negligence

Contributory negligence is different from negligence only insofar as there is no duty owed to another. However, the other tests of negligence apply. The plaintiff must conduct himself as a reasonable and prudent person in behalf of his own protection from injury. The standard, of course, is different for children and for adults. A child must exercise a degree of care for his or her own safety commensurate with capacity, age, experience, and intelligence. Some courts have held that a very young child, such as the five-year-old boy who was killed playing in a park on some corrugated metal pipes which rolled down and crushed his head was not capable of contributory negligence because he did not realize or understand the hazard and danger involved.[18] Generally speaking, children below the age of eight are regarded by the courts as being incapable of exercising understanding and reason, while children between the ages of eight and twelve are regarded as being capable of some understanding though not full understanding of the care required for their safety. Situations wherein contributory negligence has been used as a defense include a softball player who carelessly and dangerously slid into a permanent post being used as a base,[19] a small boy who had his feet crossed under a teeter totter which resulted in injury when the board came down,[20] a girl who was bitten in the process of attempting to feed a bear which was chained to a tree.[21] Contributory negligence was also alleged in court cases involving an individual proceeding on stairs or hallways in darkness,[22] exceeding a proper speed,[23] doing something after being warned or forbidden to do so,[24] walking on steps known to be insecure,[25] failure to be cautious when a reasonable person might anticipate a dangerous condition such as entering a shower room[26] or diving into water.[27]

The Statute of Limitations

Many states have a statute of limitations for tort actions stating that any suits must be filed before a given period of time following the accident or situation which gave rise to the suit. The usual length is two years. The state of Vermont has enacted a short statute of limitation of one year for skiing accidents. In North Carolina, there is a three-year statute of limitations; however, it is important to note that in connection with all such limitations the one-, two-, or three-year period does not begin for children until after they have reached legal majority at age eighteen.

Insurance

In the operation of commercial or private recreation enterprise, insurance can transfer the risk of the financial settlement from an individual to a professional risk bearer who is able to shoulder an economic loss. In essence, insurance substitutes a known loss for an unknown loss. Budgeting a recreation enterprise is important; this can be done with insurance because the insurance premium is a fixed cost that can be included in planning a budget.

To avoid the risk of staggering losses, liability insurance is indispensable to the private and commercial recreation operator. The shock of the large financial judgement may completely destroy the financial foundation of a recreation agency. Even small damage claims can seriously affect the financial stability of an enterprise. The most prudent and careful recreation operator should not assume that he will not be sued; a court decides whether the case is justified. Even though the defendant may not be proven negligent and liable, he may be faced with high defense and legal fees. Liability insurance can provide protection against such legal costs. The insurance company can also represent the defendant in a lawsuit so that the defendant does not have to appear in court. A private operator may wish to consider incorporation of his enterprise. His liability may be limited to the value of the property and all other assets that are part of the corporation. Liability insurance costs may also be less, but a lawyer should be consulted about other considerations and limitations before deciding to incorporate.

Presently, more than one-half of the states have authorized, through legislative enactment, park and recreation agencies to carry some kind of liability insurance. Such statutes usually fall into one of three categories: (1) authorization of insurance with governmental immunity maintained, but immunity may be waived as a defense; (2) general insurance authorization; and (3) authorization to carry insurance in behalf of employees, administrators, board members, personal companies, or professional service organizations related to recreation and parks.

North Carolina state law, like a number of other states, authorizes municipalities to carry liability insurance. However, the courts hold that through the act of securing liability insurance, governmental immunity is waived to the extent of the insurance for torts of agents or employees when acting within the scope of their authority. It should be noted that this situation is viewed with considerable apprehension on the part of many recreation and park administrators because they believe that the purchase of liability insurance to cover employees only invites liability suits. Therefore, park and recreation officials tend to recommend the private purchase of individual liability insurance by employees rather than blanket liability insurance coverage for employees from a policy paid for by the public jurisdiction.

Types of Liability Insurance

Special liability coverage must be obtained for the operation of most commercial recreation enterprises.[28] Comprehensive personal liability and general farm liability policies do not usually cover liabilities when a fee is charged for the use of recreation facilities. The two types of insurance policies used for the protection of recreation enterprises are the owner, landlord, and tenant policy and the comprehensive general liability policy.

The owner, landlord, and tenant policy provides coverage for liability hazards arising from the ownership, maintenance, and use of property. This is a schedule type policy commonly issued to provide protection for such operations as theaters, hotels, and stores. It may likewise be applied to recreation enterprises.

Operators of refreshment stands, snack bars, or stores should be aware of their liability for damages resulting from goods sold to guests. Products liability coverage protects against accidents occurring away from the premises as a result of purchasing a product.

The comprehensive general liability policy is designed to provide business with protection for all its exposures, including products liability, unless specifically excluded. Generally, the comprehensive general liability policy is regarded as providing more complete protection than the owner, landlord, and tenant policy because there is less chance that an unknown hazard will not be covered.

The major advantage of the comprehensive policy is that it automatically covers any hazards, such as facilities added during the year without notifying the insurance company. At the inception of the insurance contract, a survey of all existing hazards is made by the insurance company. At this time, an estimated premium will be determined, frequently on the basis of estimated income. At the close of the policy period, an audit is made which reveals the addition of any other sources of liability that were not present at the inception of the contract. At this time, the insured will be required to pay an additional premium for facilities that were added during the policy term.

Nuisance

A nuisance is whatever is injurious to health, indecent or offensive to the senses, or an obstruction to the free use of property, so as to essentially interfere with the comfortable enjoyment of life and property. Distinguished from negligence, nuisance is considered a continuing danger or permanent condition that might inflict injury, while negligence rests upon an act or failure to act as an individual. A civil action by ordinary court proceedings may be brought to stop or abate a nuisance and to recover damages sustained because of the nuisance.

Only 15 percent of the cases relating to parks and recreation allege nuisance as the basis for liability, and the recovery experience for injured plaintiffs in nuisance cases is only one out of four.[29] Until, 1967, at least 18 states had direct indications that nuisance is a basis for liability suits; however, only 10 of these states have cases where the judgement actually held for the injured plaintiff. In the past five years, six states (Georgia, Kentucky, Kansas, New Hampshire, Tennessee, Wyoming) held, either through court decisions alone or in relation to statutes, that nuisance was actionable regardless of governmental immunity.[30]

Regardless of the liability or immunity of a governmental agency for negligence, generally, it has been held by the courts that a governing body has no right to maintain a nuisance, and where such is created and maintained, liability will ensue. For this reason, many attempts have been made to allege nuisance rather than negligence in order to recover for injury. However, such allegations have not been highly successful because most courts decided that nuisance is a condition and not an act or the failure to act. In other words, most accidents and injuries to persons occur as a result of negligent conduct—failing to inspect and repair. Most courts, viewing faulty playground equipment, reason that although the faulty equipment is a condition, it is, nevertheless, the failure to inspect and repair (which is in fact negligence) that has caused the injury. Nuisance cases seem to distribute themselves into several categories relating to maintenance practice and operation. These are (1) water areas, (2) playground apparatus, and (3) other nuisance cases in various situations.

Water Areas

There are, on record, a number of court cases wherein the depth of water was regarded as being too shallow for diving thereby constituting a nuisance.[31] Faulty construction and layout was the basis of alleged nuisance in other cases involving water areas. However, as stated by the court in Stein vs. West Chicago Park Commissioners (1928), ponds and lagoons in parks have become too well recognized as means of decoration and recreation to be considered a public nuisance.

Playground Apparatus

With only two exceptions, involving a slide[32] and a swing[33], defective playground apparatus has not been regarded by the courts as constituting a nuisance. Unblocked metal pipes[34] and a hole at the end of a park slide[35] were both held to be nuisances.

A merry-go-round pivot post which caused an injury to a sixteen-year-old boy who ran into it while playing football was declared not to be a nuisance.[36] The court contended that injury was the result of contributory negligence on the part of the boy who did not care for his personal safety.

Other Nuisance Cases

A great variety of situations and conditions are found in court cases wherein nuisance is alleged as the cause of injury. For example, dry unslaked lime used to line a football field burned the face of a player but was held not to constitute a nuisance.[37] Neither a truck left unattended and running on a park trail,[38] nor the negligent operation of a power lawn mower in a park[39] was held to constitute nuisances. On the other hand, the court held that a small grass sprinkler pipe rising out of the ground, which caused injury to a person who tripped and fell, constituted an actionable nuisance.[40]

Legal Actions Directly Related to Maintenance Practices

That the courts will look for precedents or previous legal decisions, in related or similar situations, and use these as guides before making a legal judgement with respect to a particular case is important to note. Many legal actions involving park and recreation activities have been a direct result of situations created by maintenance practices in connection with equipment, areas and facilities, and recreation structures.

Inadequate maintenance of swings, teeter totters, slides, etc., makes up the great bulk of legal actions brought for the purpose of recovery for injury. Suits have been brought for injury resulting from defective chains,[41] defective supports, deteriorated footings and worn out fittings that have resulted in injuries to users.[42] Protruding and unguarded sharp objects extending from playground equipment,[43] and dangerous defects in the surfacing beneath playground apparatus[44] have served as an important basis for legal action to recover for injury. With respect to recreation areas and facilities, nearly all such legal cases have alleged poor maintenance practice. The improper construction[45] and inspection[46] of bleachers and grandstands resulting in their collapse and injury to spectators is an area in which many lawsuits have been brought.

Most of the foregoing conditions and situations would seem to suggest that simple regular maintenance practice is all that is necessary to avoid the legal backlash that results from injury to a patron. This analysis is undoubtedly correct in the majority of situations; however, we need only to look at the great number of legal actions that have been brought regarding improper maintenance practice to realize that common sense preventive maintenance programs are simply not followed in too many situations. Preventive maintenance should include regular, systematic, thorough inspections with the replacement of worn parts and material that through decay and corrosion have lost their strength and constitute a potential hazard.

The surface condition and guardrails for walkways, paths, and trails have provided the basis for a number of suits that have been filed on behalf of injured parties.[47] For the most part, the courts hold that a defective pathway or walk surface should be maintained in a safe condition and should not present a hazard.

Slippery surfaces,[48] improperly maintained baseball backstops,[49] gates,[50] railings,[51] and fences[52] have been the subjects of attention by the courts. In addition, cases have been filed in connection with improper handling and storage of explosive substances[53] and hot coals and ashes.[54] The courts have held that there is a definite responsibility to care for trees[55] to the extent that where a defective condition is obvious, it should be taken care of to avoid injury to persons who might be struck by falling limbs. The courts have also indicated that there is a duty to remove a fallen tree that might obstruct a walkway or road,[56] and that tree stumps constitute a hazard if not cared for properly.[57]

One of the greatest legal issues recently debated involves the use of barriers in natural areas for the protection of park and recreation area visitors.[58] The argument of whether or not a barrier should be erected as a protective device, or whether or not the object is in and of itself sufficient to give warning or is in a location where it should be considered a part of the hazards of the natural environment still rages. Accidents that have resulted in the death of a number of visitors to our national parks in the past several years have rekindled the interest in this issue, and it is a topic of considerable interest and concern for Congressional investigative committees that have reviewed the situation and recommended a conservative—more barrier protection—approach. Good housekeeping practices should be followed that will result in the prompt elimination of hazardous rubbish and rubble, and all the facilities and equipment needing repair should be serviced without delay. Some would argue that regular systematic preventive maintenance programs are prohibitive from the standpoint of cost. The fact of the matter is that just one judgement against the recreation operator for injury to a patron could pay for the actual cost of many years of systematic preventive maintenance very easily. Again, it should be emphasized that almost all liability suits involving park and recreation areas are related to maintenance practice.

Preventive Maintenance and Lawsuits

Recreation officials can do much to protect the recreation agency, agency personnel, and themselves from lawsuits:

1. by acquainting maintenance personnel with the legal liability aspects of recreation,
2. by supplying each employee with a pamphlet or other literature containing essential liability material covered during an orientation period. Such orientation literature should include explanation of personal legal responsibilities in connection with each individual's position. In addition, this literature should cite court cases involving the various phases of the recreation maintenance program.

The implications of liability for personnel and their responsibilities under these conditions should be discussed with all new employees and volunteers. Hopefully, this approach might save the recreation agency or individual employees from a financially disastrous and professionally embarrassing loss.

Vandalism

Willful and often pointless destruction, defacement, or defilement of property—is it a problem? Decide for yourself. The total cost of vandalism in the United States is estimated at more than a billion dollars a year. Government authorities are spending increasing sums each year in an effort to reduce vandalism. But, they are not succeeding. Park and recreation organizations are particularly hard hit with repair and replacement costs due to vandalism. In 1973, New York City Parks and Recreation facilities suffered direct vandalism damage of $1,167,904.[59] It spent another $2 million to clean up graffiti on the subways. Los Angeles experienced an estimated loss of a quarter of a million dollars due to vandalism in 1971.[60] Detroit police recorded 5,061 cases of malicious property damage during the first four months of 1974, an increase from 4,227 for the same period the year before.[61]

Repair of vandalized facilities in national forests was estimated at well over $2 million annually and does not include manpower and time lost from other projects, nor the extent of damage to the environment.[62]

Richard Krause's 1972 study of 53 of the largest cities in the U.S. disclosed that destructive vandalism had become a major problem in more than two-thirds of the cities studied. Vandalism had "not only resulted in major financial costs to park and recreation departments," but also "poses a strong threat to the continued existence of such departments."[63] Charles Nutter, New Orleans Recreation Director, stated that 30 percent of all park maintenance is cleaning up or repairing vandalism.[64]

Vandalism can be attacked by using the same problem-solving approach that we apply to other situations. First, we must define the problem. Second, we must look for causal factors. Third, we must evaluate our present circumstances. Fourth, we must evaluate present efforts toward combating the problem—what solutions work and what solutions fail. Finally, we must develop a new plan based upon our experiences.

Combatting Vandalism

Vandalism is a type of behavior, and all behavior has causes. There are motivated reasons behind every act of vandalism despite the claims of apprehended vandals who say otherwise. The inability to analyze the motivational causes of vandalism and do something constructive about it is a problem. It may be somewhat helpful, in an attempt to understand the motive of the vandal, to review his or her *modus operandi* and, rather arbitrarily, categorize the acts according to the seriousness of their results and also according to our estimate of the extent of premeditation. Such a classification might be—(1) petty or impromptu vandalism, (2) aggravated or minor planned vandalism, and (3) grossly destructive or premeditated vandalism.

Categories of Vandalism

Petty or Impromptu Vandalism Petty vandalism includes such acts as conscious street littering; tearing down banners, flags, and ropes from flagpoles; breaking small windows in storage and shelter buildings; tire slashing; and defacing walls, memorials, billboards, etc. Petty vandalism is relatively unpremeditated, low in unit cost for correction, and much more of a nuisance and eyesore than a severe damage. It does represent an enormous annual task of repetitive cleaning, and is, ultimately, quite expensive. Far worse is the aesthetic befoulment and the discouraging effect it has upon recreation personnel and the general public. The appearance of any city is badly blemished when its public areas and parks display the results of petty vandalism.

Aggravated or Minor Planned Vandalism   Under this heading is included destruction of toilet facilities, the mass breakage of windows in public buildings, theft or damage to park and recreation vehicles, grass fires, and the deliberate crashing of automobiles into baseball backstops, chain-link fences, decorative iron fences, and expensive park bench arrangements. This type of vandalism represents a degree of planned premeditation, spurred on by alcohol or drugs perhaps, and an attitude of avenging oneself on the establishment. Such vandalism usually involves three to five males, most likely between the ages of 10 and 16 years of age. The individuals involved generally have records of previous similar behavior in school or in connection with recreation programs. Damage is often considerable, and frequently is sufficient to incapacitate vehicles, playgrounds, swimming pools, or other public facilities. Patterns of vandalism are discernible because once successful vandalism attacks are committed, they usually are repeated at the same location or nearby.

Grossly Destructive or Premeditated Vandalism   Under this heading are included the severe cases of vandalism that appear to have been carefully planned. Theft is usually not involved, but rather a destructive act is committed that will damage or destroy a location or a facility permanently or for a long time. Such acts include pouring gasoline into a large recreation center and igniting it, resulting in the total destruction of the building; smashing a vehicle into or setting fire to school buses or recreation/park department vehicles, causing damages of $100,000 or more. A third illustration might be the deliberate reversal of swimming pool machinery or the turning off of safety valves causing the system to destroy itself, and thus put out of operation a swimming pool, an ice rink, or a complete lighting system for months or years. These grossly destructive acts are the workings of disturbed minds. Unlike aggravated vandalism, grossly destructive premeditated vandalism is not particularly patterned and seems to occur when individuals or groups are under severe mental or social stress. Racial unrest or street gang warfare could trigger such acts. It might be due to consumption of liquor or drugs, or a psychopathic state of mind. The act frequently includes wanton destruction, suggesting that such a person would be physically violent or dangerous if confronted. Damage is major and occasionally is such that the building or facility cannot be restored at reasonable cost.

The psychology of vandalism has been studied carefully at many universities and in many urban settings. The petty, impromptu vandalism seems due to carelessness or prankishness, while aggravated vandalism represents some antipathy toward the authority that operates, or is represented by the facility. Grossly destructive, premeditated vandalism indicates severe mental disturbance or a most passionate antagonism or hatred toward some organization or government agency.

The Psychology of Vandalism

When the psychology of vandalism is discussed, one must not exclude the attitudes of the staff who normally operate the facility that has been vandalized. When park attendants or custodians arrive on the scene of vandalism and make disparaging remarks, the attitude is perceived by the community. When this attitude is reinforced through many personalities, and when small vandalized conditions are not corrected quickly due to a fear of repetition, antiestablishment feeling grows.

The park and recreation maintenance manager must strive to install positive attitudes in the minds of co-workers. Custodians, park attendants, tradesmen, and supervisory staff must take the position that the first act of vandalism must be met by a series of corrective steps and, at the same time, a positive point of view must be put forth in the community. Every effort to enlist the sympathy and active assistance of those who use the facility must be taken. Surly and arrogant behavior on the part of the park/recreation staff may cause people to sympathize with vandals. If the reaction of the recreation official is one of unbridled anger and arrogance, community support may be lost from the start.

Because the use of drugs is so widespread and the price of drugs so high, it is no surprise that some vandalism is related to drug use and procurement. Drugs are a factor, but they are not the major cause of the high incidence of vandalism in our parks and recreation centers.

Drugs and Vandalism

Preventing Vandalism

Long research and many interviews with park and recreation officials and operators in all parts of the country brings out a series of steps which will reduce, though not completely eliminate, vandalism.

Construction

There are many ways that new facilities can be constructed to reduce the possibilities of vandalism, for example, fewer and smaller windows placed higher in the walls, one-piece roofs without shingles or tiles, doors with flush-mounted locks that cannot be forced, high window sills that prevent fluids like gasoline from being poured in across them, high roofs which are not easily scaled by small boys, drinking fountains recessed into solid walls so that large instruments cannot be brought down to smash them, and so on. These and a number of other preventive measures should be included in the designs of all buildings.

Lighting and Policing

Every new facility, regardless of its susceptibility to vandalism, should be planned so that it is well lighted throughout the night. Floodlighting a building from all sides constitutes a 50 percent, or better, chance of it escaping major vandalism. Police action is equally important and should be instituted from the opening of a new facility. With all facilities, this requires a meeting to stimulate police interest in what was formerly a stereotype vandalism target. The point to be emphasized is that when police become accustomed to a facility or a building being vandalized, they tend to ignore it. Thus, small acts of vandalism can grow and grow until the unit or facility is reduced to a total shambles.

Staff Education

Much effort is needed to enlighten the staff, particularly middle-age and older members. Positive attitudes toward the visiting public, and understanding of the causes of vandalism are important. When staff members believe that vandalism can be curbed and that the public can appreciate good facilities, the administrator has come a long way toward improving the situation.

A continuous community- and city-wide program is required if the public (remember that the public changes with each new generation) is to be enlisted in an active anti-vandalism program. Finger waving or chastising is not the answer. The public must be reminded constantly that they paid for and own park and recreation facilities, and that use will be curtailed if vandalism continues. Furthermore, they must be urged to bring about the apprehension and conviction of people who commit acts of vandalism on public facilities.

Community Education

In any facility, the employment of spirited, dedicated, reliable recreation and maintenance workers is a major deterrent to crime and vandalism. If the leadership is active, it will involve young, middle-aged, and elderly people, and it will help the community to identify with a happy feeling on the playground. Maintenance personnel who go out of their way to keep the facility particularly attractive are an asset since they give the public reason to be protective and proud of the facility.

Program and Leadership

Without a doubt, the most important anti-vandalism ingredient is people in, around, and using the facility. The crowded beach, the busy picnic area, the recreation center jumping with traffic stand a better chance of avoiding vandalism than the remote, isolated, or little used facility. Active participants are the best "policemen," and the recreation administrator must see that his facilities are used as much as possible to reduce the incidence of vandalism. Acts of vandalism reflect a low ebb in man's behavior; yet there is no justification for a negative, defeatist attitude. However, our relative affluence and our reliance upon technological devices tend to make us less sensitive to vandalism and destruction. As recreation and park managers, we must work constantly to keep vandalism in check. This is done through education, through positive programming, and through repeated demonstrations that the department is serious about reducing vandalism.

Participants and Visitors

Review Questions

1. Distinguish between public relations and public relations management.

2. Explain the idea that a recreation maintenance division must be responsive to its publics (plural) rather than public (singular).

3. Explain how local park/recreation employees are protected by the federal Occupational Safety and Health Act (OSHA) of 1970, even though the original act specifically exempts public employees.

4. Describe the three major types of fire protection equipment for buildings.

5. Discuss the incidence of liability lawsuits and recreation maintenance practice.

6. In order to successfully bring a legal liability suit based upon negligent conduct, what elements must be proved to recover damages from the wrongdoer?

7. Discuss the current trend relative to governmental immunity.

8. Define vandalism. How much of a problem is vandalism?

9. What suggested corrective steps should be taken to control vandalism?

Notes to Chapter 8

1. Lawrence A. Appley, *Management in Action* (New York: American Management Association, 1956), p. 53.

2. Oka T. Hester, "Let's Take a Look," *Public Relations Manual*, Greensboro, N. C.: Greensboro Park and Recreation Department, 1974.

3. Gerald J. Driessen *et al.*, "Safety and Risk Management in Selected Areas of the National Park System" (Chicago: The National Safety Council, 1972).

4. American National Standards Institute, "Method of Measuring and Recording Patron and Non-Employee Injury Statistics" (ANSI Standard Z 108.1), 1430 Broadway, New York, N. Y. 10018.

5. American National Standards Institute, "Specifications for Making Buildings and Facilities Accessible to and Usable by the Physically Handicapped," (A 117.1), 1430 Broadway, New York, N. Y. 10018.

6. 45 Corpus Juris 631.

7. Balaas *vs.* Hartford, 126 Connecticut 510, 12 A(2nd) 765 (1940).

8. Cox *vs.* Des Moines, 235 Iowa 178, 16 NW(2nd) 234 (1944).

9. Betty Van der Smissen, *Legal Liability of Cities and Schools for Injuries in Recreation and Parks* (Cincinnati, Ohio: W. H. Anderson, 1968), pp. 42-43.

10. Betty Van der Smissen, *1975 Supplement to Legal Liability of Cities and Schools for Injuries in Recreation and Parks* (Cincinnati, Ohio: W. H. Anderson Company, 1975), pp. 2-8.

11. James J. Bonifas, "See You in Court," An address delivered at the Southern District Recreation and Park Conference, Atlanta, Georgia, April 5, 1971.

12. Orrison *vs.* Rapid City, 76 SD 145, 74NW (2nd) 489 (1956).

13. Kelley *vs.* School District, 102 Wash 343, 173 Pac 333 (1918).

14. Stolpe *vs.* Duquesne, 337 Pa 215, 9 A(2nd) 427 (1939).

15. Bennett *vs.* Scranton, 54 Lack Jur 81 (CP 1953).

16. Maltz *vs.* Board of Education, 114 NYS (3nd) 856 (Sup Ct 1952).

17. Scala *vs.* New York City, 200 Misc. 475, 102 NYS(2nd) 790 (Sup Ct — 1951).

18. Gottesman *vs.* Cleveland, 142 Ohio St 410, 27 Ohio Op 353, 52 N.E.2nd 644 (1944).

19. Bennett *vs.* Scranton, 54 Lack Jur 81 (Pa CP 1953).

20. Brueen *vs.* North Yakima School District, 101 Wash 374, 172 Pac 569 (1918).

21. Byrnes *vs.* Jackson, 140 Miss 656, 105 So 861 (1925).

22. Cheyney *vs.* Los Angeles, 119 Cal App(2nd) 75, 258 P (2nd) 1099 (1953).

23. Nelson *vs.* Duluth, 172 Minn 76, 214 NW 774 (1927).

24. Turner *vs.* Moverly, 224 MoApp 683, 26 SW(2nd) 997 (1930).

25. Woodard *vs.* Des Moines, 182 Iowa 1102, 165 NW 313 (1917).

26. Orrison *vs.* Rapid City, 76 SD 145, 74 NW(2nd) 489 (1956).

27. Cardinali *vs.* New York, 1 App Div(2nd) 1018, 151 NYS(2nd) 514 (1956).

28. "Liability and Insurance Protection in Rural Recreation Enterprises," Extension Bulletin 580 Cooperative Extension Service, Michigan State University, 1967.

29. Van der Smissen, *Legal Liability,* 1968 p. 103.

30. Van der Smissen, *1975 Supplement to Legal Liability,* 1975 p. 6.

31. Cabbiness *vs.* North Little Rock, 228 Ar 356, 307 W.W.(2nd) 529 (1957); Selden *vs.* Cuyahuga Falls, 132 Ohio St 223, 7 Ohio Op 511, 6 NE(2nd) 976 (1937); Walker *vs.* Forest Preserve Dist. of Cook County, 27 Ill(2nd) 538, 190 NE(2nd) 296 (1963); Cummings *vs.* Nazareth, 430 PA 255, 242 A(2nd) 460 (1968).

32. Lubbock *vs.* Greene, 201 F(2nd) 146 (5th Cir 1953).

33. Emmons *vs.* Virginia, 152 Minn 295, 188 NW 561 (1922).

34. Gottesman *vs.* Cleveland, 142 Ohio St 410, 27 Ohio Op 353, 52 NE(2nd) 644 (1944).

35. Schmidt *vs.* Cheviot, 31 Ohio NP 12 (CP 1933).

36. Iacono *vs.* Fitzpatrick, 61 RI 28, 199 Atl 689 (1938).

37. Mokovich *vs.* Independent School District, 177 Minn 446, 225 N.W. 292 (1929).

38. Husband *vs.* Salt Lake City, 92 Utah 449, 69 P(2nd) 491 (1937).

39. Ballanger *vs.* Dayton, 66 Ohio L. Abs 388, 117 NE(2nd) 469 (1952).

40. Johnson *vs.* Tennessean Newspaper, Inc., 192 Tenn 287, 241 SW (2nd) 399 (1951).

41. White *vs.* Charlotte, 211 NC 186, 189 SE 492 (1937).

42. Thrasher *vs.* Cincinnati, 28 Ohio Op 97, 13 Ohio Supp 143 (1944). Foyston *vs.* Charlotte, 278 Michigan 255, 270 NW 288 (1936); Rich *vs.* City of Goldsboro, 192 SE(2nd) 824 NC (1972).

43. Fort Collins *vs.* Roten, 72 Colo 182, 210 Pac 326 (1922); Kingsport *vs.* Lane, 35 Tenn App 183, 243 SW(2nd) 289 (1952); Fetters *vs.* Des Moines, 260 Iowa 490, 149 NW(2nd) 815 (1967); Pichette *vs.* Manistique Public Schools, 50 Mich App 770, 213 NW(2nd) 784 (1973).

44. Paraska *vs.* Scranton, 122 Pa Super 1, 184 Atl 276 (1936); McCullough *vs.* Philadelphia, 32 Pa Super 109 (1906); Schmidt *vs.* Cheviot, 31 Ohio NP 12 (1933); Hall *vs.* Columbus Board of Education, 32 Ohio App(2nd) 297, 61 00(2nd) 396, 290 NE (2nd) 580 (1922).

45. Adams *vs.* Schneidar, 71 Ind App 249, 124 NE 718 (1919); Canner *vs.* Meuer, 232 Wisc. 565, 288 NW 272 (1939); Boyer *vs.* Iowa High School Athletic Assn. 127 NW(2nd) 606 (Iowa 1964).

46. Guymon *vs.* Finicum, 265 P(2nd) 706 (Okla. 1953); Harllee *vs.* Gulfport, 120 F(2nd) 41 (5th Cir 1941); Novak *vs.* Delavan, 31 Wis(2nd) 200, 143 NW(3nd) 6 (1966).

47. Florey *vs.* Burlington, 247 Iowa 316, 73 NW(2nd) 770 (1955); Bagby *vs.* Kansas City, 338 Mo 771, 92 SW(2nd) 142 (1936); Miller *vs.* Philadelphia, 345 Pa 1, 25 A(2nd) 185 (1942).

48. Harvey *vs.* Savannah, 59 Ga 12, 199 SE 653 (1938); Cambereri *vs.* Board of Education, 246 App Div 127, 284 NY Supp. 902; Tulsa *vs.* Going, 437 P(2nd) 257 (1967); Campbell *vs.* Peru 48 Ill App(2nd) 267, 198 NE(2nd) 719 (1964); Cumberland College *vs.* Gaines 432 SW (2nd) 650 (Ky 1968).

49. Snowden *vs.* Kittitas County School Dist. 38 Wash(2nd) 691, 231 P(2nd) 621 (1951).

50. Luan *vs.* Needles Elementary School Dist., 154 Cal App(2nd) 803, 316 P(2nd) 773 (1957).

51. Levine *vs.* New York City, 2 NYC(2nd) 246, 140 NE(2nd) 275 (1957).

52. Shields *vs.* School Dist., 408 Pa 388, 184 A(2nd) 240 (1962); Caltavuturo *vs.* Passaic, 124 NJ Super 361, 301 A(2nd) 114 (1973).

53. Carradine *vs.* New York City, 16 App Div(2nd) 928, 229 NYS (2nd) 328 (1962).

54. Ackeret *vs.* Minneapolis, 129 Minn 190, 151 NW 976 (1915); Bingham *vs.* Board of Education, 118 Utah 582, 223

P(2nd) 432 (1950); State *vs.* San Mateo Co. 69 Cal Rptr. 683, 263 Cal App(2nd) 396 (1968); Peterson *vs.* Honolulu 496 P(2nd) 5 (Hawaii 1972).

55. Kilbourn *vs.* Seattle, 43 Wash(2nd) 373, 261 Pa(2nd) 407 (1953); Pietz *vs.* Oskaloosa, 250 Iowa 374, 92 NW(2nd) 577 (1958). Smith *vs.* United States, 117 F Supp 525 (SO Cal 1953).

56. Rockett *vs.* Philadelphia, 256 Pa 347, 100 Atl 826 (1917).

57. Sapula *vs.* Young, 147 Okla 179, 296 Pac 418 (1931).

58. Houston *vs.* George, 479 SW(2nd) 257 Tex Supp (1972). Mahoney *vs.* Elmhurst Park Dist., 47 Ill(2nd) 367; 265 NE(2nd) 654 (1971).

59. Joseph P. Davidson, "The Vandals Were Here." A brochure. New York Parks, Recreation and Cultural Affairs Administration. The Arsenal, 830 5th Ave., New York, N. Y. 10021.

60. Los Angeles City Dept. of Recreation and Parks, "Open Forum on Vandalism" *Proceedings,* (Los Angeles CA, October 4, 1971, AM Session), p. 1.

61. "Vandalism—A Billion Dollars a Year and Getting Worse," *U.S. News & World Report,* (June 24, 1975), p. 39.

62. U.S.D.A., "Vandalism Depletes Forest Recreation Funds," U.S. Department of Agriculture, Office of Communication, XXXII, no. 8 (April 18, 1973. Washington, D. C. 20750).

63. Richard Kraus, *"Urban Parks & Recreation: Challenge of the 1970's,"* a Research Study by the Community Council of Greater New York, February 1972.

64. "Vandalism—A Billion Dollars a Year," p. 39.

65. Joseph Curtis, "Vandalism," a monograph prepared for the Park and Recreation Maintenance Management School, North Carolina State University, Raleigh, 1973.

Bibliography

Public Relations Management

Appley, Lawrence A. *Management in Action.* New York: American Management Association, 1956.

Public Safety

Cook, Walter L. *Manual and Survey for Public Safety, Management Aid Bulletin #20.* Wheeling West Virginia: American Institute of Park Executives, 1962.

National Safety Council. *Public Employee Safety Guide—Parks and Recreation.* Chicago: National Safety Council, 1974.

Public Liability Aspects of Recreation Maintenance Practice

Van der Smissen, Betty, *Legal Liability of Cities and Schools for Injuries in Recreation and Parks.* Cincinnati: The W. H. Anderson Company, 1968.

———. *1975 Supplement to Legal Liability of Cities and Schools for Injuries in Recreational Parks.* Cincinnati: The W. H. Anderson Company, 1968.

Vandalism

"Vandalism—A Billion Dollars a Year and Getting Worse." *U.S. News and World Report.* June 24, 1974: 39–41.

Curtis, Joseph E. "Vandalism." A monograph prepared for the Park and Recreation Maintenance Management School, North Carolina State University, Raleigh, 1973.

Bachman, Donald G. "Vandalism." A monograph prepared for the Park and Recreation Maintenance School, North Carolina State University, Raleigh, 1975.

Appendix

NATIONAL ASSOCIATION OF FIRE EQUIPMENT DISTRIBUTORS

PORTABLE FIRE EXTINGUISHER SELECTION CHART SHOWING UNDERWRITERS' LABORATORIES CLASSIFICATIONS, CHARACTERISTICS AND NFPA MAINTENANCE REQUIREMENTS

FIRE EQUIPMENT MANUFACTURERS ASSOCIATION (FEMA)

Type of Extinguisher	Sizes Commonly in Use (Nominal Capacity)	Class A	Class B	Class C	Class D	Extinguishing Agent	Approx. Horizontal Range	Approx. Discharge Time	Hydrostatic Test Interval	Protection Required Below 40° F
Water — Stored Pressure	2½ Gal.*	Yes	No	No	No	Water	30-40 ft.	1 Minute	5 Yrs.	Yes
Water — Pump Tank	2½ and 5 Gal.	Yes	No	No	No	Water	30-40 ft.	1 to 2 Minutes	5 Yrs.	Yes
Loaded Stream — Stored Pressure	2½ Gal.*	Yes	Yes	No	No	Alkali-Metal Salt Solution	30-40 ft.	1 Minute*	5 Yrs.	No
Carbon Dioxide	2½ to 20 lbs.*	No	Yes	Yes	No	Carbon Dioxide	3 to 8 ft.	8 to 30 Sec.*	5 Yrs.	No
Regular or Ordinary Dry — Stored Pressure	2 to 30 lbs.*	No	Yes	Yes	No	Sodium-Bicarbonate Base	5 to 20 ft.*	8 to 25 Sec.*	12 Years on Aluminum, Brazed-Brass or Mild-Steel Shells. (See Para. 1330 on reverse.) 5 Years on Stainless Steel, or Soldered-Brass Shells.	No
Regular or Ordinary Dry — Cartridge Operated	4 to 30 lbs.*	No	Yes	Yes	No	Sodium-Bicarbonate Base	5 to 20 ft.*	8 to 25 Sec.*		No
Potassium Bicarbonate "Purple K" — Stored Pressure	2 to 30 lbs.*	No	Yes	Yes	No	Potassium Bicarbonate Base	5 to 20 ft.*	8 to 25 Sec.*		No
Potassium Bicarbonate "Purple K" — Cartridge Operated	4 to 30 lbs.*	No	Yes	Yes	No	Potassium Bicarbonate Base	5 to 20 ft.*	8 to 25 Sec.*		No
Potassium Chloride KCL — Stored Pressure	2 to 30 lbs.*	No	Yes	Yes	No	Potassium Chloride Base	5 to 20 ft.*	8 to 25 Sec.*		No
Potassium Chloride KCL — Cartridge Operated	4 to 30 lbs.*	No	Yes	Yes	No	Potassium Chloride Base	5 to 20 ft.*	8 to 25 Sec.*		No
Multi-Purpose "ABC" — Stored Pressure	2 to 30 lbs.*	Yes	Yes	Yes	No	Ammonium Phosphate Base	5 to 20 ft.*	8 to 25 Sec.*		No
Multi-Purpose "ABC" — Cartridge Operated	4 to 30 lbs.*	Yes	Yes	Yes	No	Ammonium Phosphate Base	5 to 20 ft.*	8 to 25 Sec.*		No
Potassium Bicarbonate Urea — Stored Pressure	11 to 23 lbs.*	No	Yes	Yes	No	Potassium Bicarbonate/Urea Base	5 to 30 ft.*	20 to 31 Sec.*		No
Potassium Bicarbonate Urea — Cartridge Operated	11 to 23 lbs.*	No	Yes	Yes	No	Potassium Bicarbonate/Urea Base	5 to 30 ft.*	20 to 31 Sec.*		No
Halogenated Agents	2½ to 5 lbs.	No	Yes	Yes	No	Halon 1301 & 1211	4 to 8 ft.	8 to 10 Sec.	12 Yrs.	No
Dry Powder Special Compound — Cartridge Operated	30 lbs.*	No	No	No	Yes for specific metals only	Sodium Chloride Base	5 to 20 ft.*	25 to 30 Sec.*	12 Yrs.	No

MINIMUM INSPECTION & MAINTENANCE: MONTHLY: Inspection — SEMI-ANNUALLY: Complete maintenance which may include recharging. In certain locations more frequent inspection may be required.

Special Note: CARTRIDGE OPERATED (Inverting Type) WATER, WATER SODA ACID, LOADED STREAM, FOAM — NO LONGER MANUFACTURED

CLASS A fires are fires in ordinary combustible materials, such as wood, cloth, paper, rubber, and many plastics.

CLASS B fires are fires in flammable liquids, gases, and greases.

CLASS C fires are fires which involve energized electrical equipment where the electrical nonconductivity of the extinguishing media is of importance.

CLASS D fires are fires in combustible metals, such as magnesium, titanium, zirconium, sodium, and potassium.

NOTE: CAPACITY OF AGENT IN DISPOSABLE UNITS MAY BE LESS THAN SHOWN UNDER NOMINAL CAPACITY.

NOTE: DISPOSABLE UNITS MUST BE THROWN AWAY AFTER ANY USE.

NOTE: ADDITIONAL AGENT CAPACITY, HORIZONTAL RANGE AND DISCHARGE TIME MAY BE AVAILABLE IN WHEELED UNITS.

Additional copies available at a nominal cost from FEMA, 1901 ... and NAFED, 111 E. Wacker Dr., Chicago, Illinois 60601

Exhibit 8-1 Portable Fire Extinguisher Selection Chart

Checklist of OSHA Violations

The following checklist should demonstrate the general emphasis of the OSHA program, and perhaps identify general areas of hazard related to facilities and programs. It illustrates many of the health and safety points a compliance officer would look for in conducting an on-site inspection. The checklist was prepared in early 1972 by the Middle Atlantic Region of the Occupational Safety and Health Administration as a tool for guidance in workshops and seminars. It should be used for general guidance alone, and should not serve as a replacement for the systematic analysis of OSHA standards as they relate to specific recreation system environments. A satisfactory "score" on the checklist should not forestall the process of becoming completely familiar with OSHA regulations, standards and record keeping requirements.

Walking-Working Surfaces

1.	All factory walkways properly marked and cleared.	Yes	No
2.	All office area walkways cleared.	Yes	No
3.	All exterior walkways cleared and in good repair.	Yes	No
4.	All floor holes, floor openings, wall openings and skylights are properly guarded.	Yes	No

Yes   No   5. Non-slip mats, gratings, false floors and other like materials are in use in wet and other hazardous areas.

Yes   No   6. All mats, gratings, etc., are in good repair.

Yes   No   7. Floor openings, hatchways, manholes are properly guarded with covers meeting specifications.

Yes   No   8. All open sided floors, platforms and runways four ft. or more above ground or floor level are properly guarded with toe boards installed.

Yes   No   9. All railings and toeboards meet specifications and are in good repair.

Yes   No   10. All elevated load-bearing floors and roofs are conspicuously posted reflecting safe load limits.

Yes   No   11. All other load-bearing surfaces (roofs of ovens, crane cab roofs, duck boards, etc.) are properly installed, in good repair, with load capacity clearly marked.

Stairs and Stairways

Yes   No   1. All stairways (other than fire exits) and elevator and escalator shafts are clear, handrails and/or guardrails provided, treads and risers in good repair with non-slip surfaces and adequate illumination.

Ladders and Scaffolds

Yes   No   1. All ladders (except fixed and tressel ladders) equipped with safety feet.

Yes   No   2. All ladders in good condition; wooden ladders maintained un-painted.

Yes   No   3. Precautions are taken to prevent the use of metal ladders where there is possibility of electrical shock.

Ventilation

Yes   No   1. All work areas appear to be properly ventilated; no accumulation of smoke, dust, etc., was noted.

Yes   No   2. Temperature, humidity and air movement in work areas apparently within comfort limits.

Life Safety

1. Location and easy accessibility of at least two fire emergency exits (minimum requirement) for each work area confirmed with special attention to high hazard area.   **Yes   No**

2. Each fire emergency exit is properly marked and illuminated.   **Yes   No**

3. Is the route to safety clear and unobstructed from the fire doors?   **Yes   No**

4. All fire emergency doors swing in the direction of exit travel.   **Yes   No**

5. Fire emergency doors cannot be locked from inside; each is equipped with panic or other simple type of releasing device.   **Yes   No**

6. In checking fire alarm system, all post indicator valves examined and opened and sealed; all gravity tanks full.   **Yes   No**

Fire Suppression Equipment

1. Does this facility have a volunteer fire brigade?   **Yes   No**

2. Are there regular training sessions being conducted?   **Yes   No**

3. All portable fire extinguishers are readily accessible, properly located, and show servicing is up-to-date; maximum travel distance for all units not in excess of 75 feet, or 50 feet in hazardous areas.   **Yes   No**

4. Each extinguisher has been checked for its adaptability to the hazard presented in the immediate area.   **Yes   No**

5. Clearance of 36 in. maintained between sprinkler deflectors and top of stored material.   **Yes   No**

6. All fire hoses in proper position and appear to be in good condition.   **Yes   No**

7. Where manual fire alarm boxes are used, each is accessible from maximum travel distance of 200 ft., the travel path unencumbered.   **Yes   No**

8. Where fire control systems are used which are a hazard in themselves, appropriate warnings of such hazard are posted.   **Yes   No**

9. All potential sources of fire and/or explosion from gases, vapors, fumes, dusts, and mists inspected for correctable hazards.   **Yes   No**

Electrical Wiring, Apparatus and Equipment

1. Clearly illustrated instructions for resuscitation of persons suffering from electrical shock are posted in all electrical   **Yes   No**

stations, switchboards and transformers; entrance restricted to unauthorized persons.

Yes No 2. Procedures for de-energizing electrical circuits reviewed for effectiveness.

Yes No 3. Examine extension cords and other temporary wiring for breaks, fraying, or other defects.

Yes No 4. All interior wiring systems have grounded conductors continuously indentified throughout the plant's electrical system.

Yes No 5. Electrical equipment operating between 50 and 600 volts are protected against accidental contact by an approved cabinet or other enclosure.

Yes No 6. Insulation mats and protective gear are provided in all areas where more than 150 volts to ground are necessarily exposed within eight ft. from the floor.

Yes No 7. Sufficient access and working space is provided and maintained about all electrical equipment for ready and safe operation.

Yes No 8. Each electrical outlet box is provided with a cover which effectively protects the hazard from accidental contact.

Yes No 9. Inspection reveals instructions for disconnection are attached to each electrical motor and appliance.

Yes No 10. All portable electrical tools are equipped with hand-operated switches which are manually held in the closed position; all electrical cables in good condition.

Yes No 11. In locations where dust collects on electrical motors causing potential ventilation deficiency, suitable type of enclosed motor is used.

Yes No 12. In battery rooms, provision has been made for diffusion of gases to prevent the accumulation of an explosive mixture.

Industrial Sanitation

1. Toilet facilities meet the following standards:

Yes No a) Separate facilities are provided for each sex.

Yes No b) All are within 200 ft. of the work area where practicable.

Yes No c) The number of facilities for each conforms to standard.

Yes No d) Toilet rooms are clean, adequately lighted and ventilated.

Yes No 2. Dressing rooms, where required, are clean, adequately lighted and equipped with individual clothes facilities.

Yes No 3. Lavatories are provided in appropriate numbers with hot and cold water, individual hand towels, and are maintained in good repair; lavatory area is clean and well lighted.

4. Drinking fountains are installed within 200 ft. of all work areas; they are clean and maintained in good working condition.   **Yes** **No**

5. Outlets for non-potable water are clearly marked to indicate that the water is not for human use and/or consumption.   **Yes** **No**

6. There are no cross-connections, open or potential, between a potable and non-potable water supply.   **Yes** **No**

7. Receptacles for waste are adequate in design and number; they are leak-proof, well-maintained and serviced regularly.   **Yes** **No**

8. Adequate control over insects, rodents and vermin.   **Yes** **No**

9. The lunch room is adequate in size, clean, well-maintained and physically separated from areas offering the hazard of exposure to toxic materials.   **Yes** **No**

10. All food is properly stored, refrigerated where appropriate, and handled under acceptable sanitary practices.   **Yes** **No**

11. Vending machine areas are maintained in a good sanitary condition.   **Yes** **No**

Material Handling

1. All fiber rope and fiber rope slings used in material handling are in good condition; no evidence of excessive wear or visible defects.   **Yes** **No**

2. All wire rope and wire rope slings are in good condition; no evidence of mechanical damage, bumps, broken strands, or other visible defects.   **Yes** **No**

3. All chain slings, including end fastenings, are in good condition; no evidence of excessive wear or mechanical damage; all are properly stored.   **Yes** **No**

4. Each chain bears a current inspection tag.   **Yes** **No**

5. Repairs to chains are made only under qualified supervision; all are proof tested for load under the prescribed standards.   **Yes** **No**

6. All hooks and rings are being tested before being put into service with records of dates and results of such tests.   **Yes** **No**

7. Inspection of all hooks reveals all in good operation; no visible defects.   **Yes** **No**

8. Shackles are in good repair; no visible defects.   **Yes** **No**

9. Cranes and hoists are in good operating condition; regular schedule for servicing maintained; no visible defects; inspection records properly maintained; proper operating procedures are followed.   **Yes** **No**

10. All industrial trucks are equipped with warning devices; all are equipped with overhead guards.   **Yes** **No**

Yes   No   11.   All industrial trucks, other than electrical-powered are re-fueled only in fire-safe areas specifically designated for that purpose.

Yes   No   12.   All L-P gas-powered industrial trucks are properly stored away from underground entrances or elevator shafts to avoid the hazard of exlosion.

Yes   No   13.   In refueling operations, all engines are stopped; smoking is prohibited.

Yes   No   14.   Where electric batteries are recharged, facilities are provided for flushing and neutralizing spilled electrolite, for fire protection, and adequate ventilation is provided for dispersal of gas emanating from batteries.

Yes   No   15.   The load capacity is indicated on each truck and strictly observed.

Yes   No   16.   All conveyor systems in good operating order; no visible defects; adequate clearance from aisles and walkways; stopping devices adequate in number and location.

Hand and Portable Powered Tools

Yes   No   1.   All hand and portable power tools are in good operating condition; no defects in wiring; equipped with ground wires.

Yes   No   2.   All portable equipment is equipped with necessary guarding devices.

Yes   No   3.   All compressed air equipment used for cleaning operations is regulated at 30 p.s.i. or less; chip guarding and personal protective equipment is provided.

Machine Guarding and Mechanical Safety

1.   Every production machine has been inspected as to the following items, all found to be in satisfactory operating conditions:

Yes   No   a)   Cleanliness of machine and area

Yes   No   b)   Securely attached to floor

Yes   No   c)   Operations guarded

Yes   No   d)   Illumination

Yes   No   e)   Effective cut-off devices

Yes   No   f)   Noise level

Yes   No   g)   Adjustment

Yes   No   i)   Material flow

Material Hazards

1. All hazardous gases, liquids and other materials are properly labeled and stored. **Yes No**
2. Areas where hazardous materials are in use are fire-safe and restriced to authorized employees. **Yes No**
3. Where x-ray is used, the area is properly shielded and dosimeters are used and processed for all authorized employees. **Yes No**
4. Protective clothing is worn by employees when oxidizing agents are being used. **Yes No**
5. All hazard areas are posted with NO SMOKING signs. **Yes No**
6. All areas where caustics or corrosives are used have been provided adequately with eye fountains and deluge showers. **Yes No**

Material Storage

1. All material is stored so as not to create either a fire hazard or a safety hazard to personnel. **Yes No**
2. All commodities shall be stored, handled and piled with due regard for their fire characteristics. **Yes No**
3. Outside storage of material is maintained at least 15 ft. from an exterior wall. **Yes No**
4. Outside storage areas are in good condition; weeds and grass under control. **Yes No**

Surface Preparation, Finishing and Preservation

1. All spray and dip painting areas are properly shielded, adequately ventilated and well-maintained; equipped with non-explosive electrical equipment. **Yes No**
2. All dip operations are provided with an automatic fire extinguishing system; adequate first aid supplies and equipment are in immediate area. **Yes No**
3. All spray booths are of adequate construction with a three-ft. clearance area surrounding each. **Yes No**
4. Face shields and other protective equipment are provided in steam cleaning operations. **Yes No**
5. All abrasive blasting areas properly shielded; no evidence of leakage of shot; operators have adequate protective equipment. **Yes No**
6. All drying equipment is properly controlled, vented and maintained. **Yes No**

Personal Protective Equipment

Yes   No   1. Adequate protective clothing and equipment is required for all hazardous operations.

Yes   No   2. All protective clothing and equipment is properly stored for ready use.

Welding, Cutting, Heating and Brazing

Yes   No   1. All compressed gases are stored and used according to standards.

Yes   No   2. Welding operations are properly screened.

Yes   No   3. Fire watchers are designated where required.

Medical Facilities and Records

Yes   No   1. The dispensary is equipped, the availability of professional or trained personnel, and the maintenance of records conform to corporate minimum standards and are in compliance with OSHA Standards.

Most Commonly Cited Violations

The following list of OSHA standards most often cited for violations was transmitted in a Department of Labor News Release. The Department makes such lists public periodically, and the following material represents an update of listings released in October, 1972. Sections of the Occupational Safety and Health Act cited as the basis of alleged violations are listed in descending order. Part 1910 of the Act covers general industry and Part 1926 covers construction standards.

General Industry		Construction	
Section Cited	Subject of Section	Section Cited	Subject of Section
1910.309	National Electrical Code	1926.500	Guardrails, handrails, and covers
.219	Mechanical power transmission apparatus	.451	Scaffolding
.157	Portable fire extinguishers	.450	Ladders
.212	General requirements for all machines	.350	Gas welding & cutting
.213	Woodworking machinery	.401	Grounding and bonding
.23	Guarding floor and wall openings and holes	.550	Cranes & derricks
.22	General requirements — walking and working surfaces	.25	Housekeeping
.252	Welding, cutting, & brazing	.152	Flammable & combustible liquids
.215	Abrasive wheel machinery	.400	General electrical
.178	Powered industrial trucks	.402	Electrical equipment installation & maintenance
.265	Sawmills	.150	Fire Protection
.37	Means of egress, general	.652	Trenching
.106	Flammable & combustible liquids	.601	Motor vehicles
.141	Sanitation	.100	Head protection
.107	Spray finishing using flammable or combustible liquids	.552	Materials hoists & personnel hoists & elevators
.242	Hand and portable power tools and equipment — general	.50	Medical services & first aid
.176	Handling materials — general	.501	Stairways
.36	General requirements, means of egress	.300	General requirements, hand and power tools
.179	Overhead & gantry cranes	.651	Excavation
.25	Portable wood ladders	.51	Sanitation
.95	Noise exposure	.28	Personal protective equipment
.151	Medical services & first aid	.102	Eye & face protection
.132	Personal protective equipment — general	.302	Power operated hand tools
.133	Eye & face protection	.351	Arc welding & cutting
.27	Fixed ladders	.105	Safety nets

Index